GENDER REVERSALS AND GENDER CULTURES

The theme of gender reversals has occurred in all societies since the beginning of recorded history. This volume explores some of the vast historical and cultural range of experience of the phenomenon: from the gender crossing of early Christian martyrs to Hindu and Buddhist beliefs in salvation through gender modification; from the mutating gender of actors in Chinese theatre to sacred genders in Siberia; from gender variance in North American Indian cultures to the androgynous beings of the cultural imagination of the Bimin-Kuskusmin of Papua New Guinea.

These original essays are written from a broad mix of perspectives. Their common focus is the complex relation of gender reversals to taboo, and what this tells us about particular cultures.

Sabrina Petra Ramet is Professor of International Studies at the University of Washington. She is the author of several books, including *Nationalism and Federalism in Yugoslavia 1962–1991* (1992) and *Social Currents in Eastern Europe* (1995).

i

GENDER REVERSALS AND GENDER CULTURES

Anthropological and historical perspectives

Edited by
Sabrina Petra Ramet

London and New York

First published 1996
by Routledge
11 New Fetter Lane, London EC4P 4EE

Simultaneously published in the USA and Canada
by Routledge
29 West 35th Street, New York, NY 10001

© 1996 Selection and editorial matter, Sabrina Petra Ramet;
individual chapters, © 1996 the contributors

Typeset in Garamond by
Ponting–Green Publishing Services, Chesham, Bucks
Printed and bound in Great Britain by
Clays Ltd, St. Ives PLC

British Library Cataloguing in Publication Data
A catalogue record for this book is available from the
British Library

Library of Congress Cataloguing in Publication Data
Gender reversals and gender cultures: anthropological and historical
perspectives / edited by Sabrina Petra Ramet.
Includes bibliographical references and index.
1. Sex role.   2. Gender identity.   3. Transvestism.
4. Transsexualism.   5. Taboo.   6. Androgyny (Psychology)
GN484.35.G46 1996   95–26198
305.3–dc20   CIP

ISBN 0–415–11482–9 (hbk)
ISBN 0–415–11483–7 (pbk)

To all who question
society's rules,
To all who place Natural Law
above all else,
To all who accept Rosa Luxemburg's principle:
Freedom means nothing unless it is
the freedom to think differently.

And to Chris,
who has always had the courage
to think differently.

CONTENTS

vii

CONTENTS

NOTES ON CONTRIBUTORS

Marjorie Mandelstam Balzer (Ph.D., 1979) teaches in the Sociology and Russian Area Studies departments of Georgetown University. She is editor of the journal *Anthropology and Archeology of Eurasia*, and of the books *Shamanism: Soviet Studies of Traditional Religion in Siberia and Central Asia* (1990); *Russian Traditional Culture* (1992); and *Culture Incarnate: Native Anthropology from Russia* (1995). Using data from several years of fieldwork focused on Siberia, she has written on gender, religion, and nationalism for *American Anthropologist, Slavic Review, Arctic Anthropology, Shaman*, and other journals. She is currently finishing the following books: *The Tenacity of Ethnicity* and *Siberian Women's Lives: Autobiographies from the Sakha Republic (Yakutia)*.

Anne Bolin received her Ph.D. in cultural anthropology from the University of Colorado. She is an Associate Professor of Anthropology at Elon College. Her book, *In Search of Eve: Transsexual Rites of Passage* (1988), received a *Choice* Magazine Award for an Outstanding Academic Book for 1988–9. She has co-authored a textbook on the anthropology of human sexuality, *Biocultural Perspectives in Human Sexuality* (1996, in press). She is co-editor of *Athletic Intruders: Women, Culture, and Exercise* (1996, forthcoming). Her current ethnographic research is with competitive women bodybuilders for a book entitled *Elegant Ironworkers: Beauties and Beasts in Bodybuilding*. She is an active competitor in amateur women's bodybuilding and continues her research with the transgender community.

Israel Burshatin is a Professor of Spanish at Haverford College. He has published numerous studies on the discourse of Orientalism in early modern Spain, including "The Moor in the Text: Metaphor, Emblem and Silence," in Henry Louis Gates, Jr. (ed.), *"Race," Writing and Difference* (1986), "Power, Discourse and Metaphor in the *Abencerraje*," in *MLN* (1984); and "Playing the Moor: Parody and Performance in Lope de Vega's *El primer Fajardo*," in *PMLA* (May 1992). He is currently working on a book-length study of the trial of Eleno de Cespedes.

Cynthia Ann Humes is an Associate Professor of Religious Studies at Claremont McKenna College. Her publications concern contemporary use of Sanskrit literature, modern ritual in North Indian goddess worship, political and economic dimensions in Hinduism, and issues of gender in world religions. She is the author of *Goddess of Blood, Goddess of Love: Divinity and Power in the Devi Mahatmya and Vindhyachal Temple* (forthcoming from SUNY Press). She is also co-editor of *Living Banaras: Hindu Religion in Cultural Context* (SUNY Press, 1993).

László Kürti is a cultural anthropologist who has been conducting research on Hungarian culture for the past fifteen years. His publications have appeared in professional journals including *Anthropology Today, East European Quarterly, East European Politics and Societies,* and *Anthropological Quarterly*. He is currently a visiting professor in the Department of Ethnography and Folklore at the Eotvos Lorand University in Budapest.

Sabine Lang was born in Frankfurt, Germany, in 1958, and studied social anthropology, European prehistory (Vor- and Frühgeschichte), and ancient Mesoamerican cultures and languages (Altamerikanistik) at the Universities of Tübingen (1978–0) and Hamburg (1980–0). She obtained her M.A. degree in 1984 and her Ph.D. in 1990, writing a Ph.D. dissertation entitled "Männer als Frauen – Frauen als Männer" [Men as Women, Women as Men], which deals with multiple genders in Native American cultures. Lang has done fieldwork in Mexico (1982) and in urban and rural Native American communities in the United States (1992–3), her recent fieldwork centering around gender variance and homosexual identities. She works as an independent scholar, living in Hamburg, Germany.

Judith Ochshorn was a Professor of Women's Studies at the University of South Florida, co-founded the department twenty-four years ago, and headed it for nine years. Working in the areas of women's history, feminist spirituality, and feminist theory-building, she was the author of *The Female Experience and the Nature of the Divine*, co-edited (in 1995) *Women's Spirituality, Women's Lives,* and published a number of essays on goddess traditions and rituals in antiquity, gender roles in the ancient Near East, mother–daughter relationships in ancient Near Eastern and biblical literature, and the witch hunts in early modern Europe. Professor Ochshorn passed away during the production of this book.

Fitz John Porter Poole is an Associate Professor in the Department of Anthropology at the University of California, San Diego. He has previously taught in Anthropology and Religious Studies at the University of Rochester. He received his M.A. and Ph.D. in Anthropology and Social Psychology from Cornell University. On the basis of field research among the Bimin-Kuskusmin of Papua New Guinea, he has published numerous articles on ethnopsychology, gender, myth and ritual, selfhood and personhood, socialization and enculturation, and aspects of the cultural contours of imagination.

He is completing a monograph on *The Rites and Passages of Childhood among the Bimin-Kuskusmin*.

Sabrina Petra Ramet is a Professor of International Studies at the University of Washington in Seattle. Born in London, England, she received her Ph.D. from UCLA in 1981. She is the author of five books, three of which have been published in expanded second editions. These are: *Nationalism and Federalism in Yugoslavia, 1962–1991*, 2nd edn (Indiana University Press, 1992); *Social Currents in Eastern Europe: The Sources and Consequences of the Great Transformation*, 2nd edn (Duke University Press, 1995); and *Balkan Babel: The Disintegration of Yugoslavia from the Death of Tito to Ethnic War*, 2nd edn (Westview Press, 1996). She is also the editor or co-editor of ten previous books.

Winfried Schleiner, Professor of English at the University of California, Davis, has published three books: *Medical Ethics in the Renaissance* (Georgetown University Press, 1995), *Melancholy, Genius, and Utopia in the Renaissance* (Otto Harrassowitz, 1991), and *The Imagery of John Donne's Sermons* (Brown University Press, 1970), as well as articles on English and Comparative Literature, gender relations, and the history of medicine.

Karen Jo Torjesen holds the Margo L. Goldsmith Chair of Women's Studies in Religion at the Claremont Graduate School. She has taught Patristic Theology at the Georg August University in Göttingen, Germany, the History of Christianity at Mary Washington College in Fredericksburg, Virginia, and now teaches Women's Studies and Early Christianity at Claremont Graduate School in Claremont, California. She has published extensively on women's roles in the formation of Christianity. Her most recent book is: *When Women Were Priests: The Role of Women in the Early Church and the Scandal of Their Subordination in the Rise of Christianity* (Harper-SanFrancisco, 1995).

Sophie Volpp is an Assistant Professor of East Asian Languages and Literature at Smith College. Her publications include: "The Discourse on Male Marriage: Li Yu's 'A Male Mencius's Mother',", in *positions: east asia cultures critiques* (Summer 1994), translations and critical biographies of twelfth- and thirteenth-century poets in *An Anthology of Chinese Women Poets from Ancient Times to 1911*, edited by Kang-I Sun Zhang; and "Secondhand Emotions: Thought and Feeling in Zhou Bangyan's Song Lyrics," in *Papers on Chinese Literature* (Spring 1993). She is currently engaged in research on seventeenth-century Chinese theater.

J. L. Welch, a freelance writer and horticulturist who lives and works in Seattle, Washington, is co-author of *Religious America* (McGraw-Hill, 1974), which was nominated for a National Book Award.

PREFACE

The theme of gender reversals has occurred in all societies since the beginning of recorded history. Many societies in the past institutionalized procedures for permanent or temporary gender reversal or gender change; other societies, such as the Aztec system and sections of modern Protestant America have endeavored to enforce a rigid gender system in which nothing may ever change and in which no boundaries may be crossed. The fixation on maintaining fixed boundaries and on suppressing gender change is as much a clue as the prevalence of such change across history to the centrality of this theme in human culture.

Why gender reversal? Gender lies at the core of an individual's self-definition. We establish our identities through work and friends, through nationality and religious affiliation, but underlying all of these, as a kind of foundation upon which any individual builds, is gender. One might say (with apologies to Descartes), "I am a woman [or a man]; therefore, I am." Human existence without gender identity is inconceivable. One can live without a sense of nationality, without a religion, without a job or career, even (although with much more difficulty) without friends; but without a concept of one's gender identity, existence itself is thrown into question. It is for this reason that changing gender is associated with intense energy, with magic, with miracle, even (as amply demonstrated in ancient religious rituals of gender transformation, explored in Judith Ochshorn's chapter) with the supernatural. Inevitably, the theme of gender reversals has occupied a salient position in religion, in literature, in drama, and in folk traditions.

Gender reversals also appear in another guise, viz., as a route to individual career advancement (examples provided in chapters 1 and 7) and as a mechanism through which a community assures stability and harmony (as suggested in the chapters by Sabine Lang and Fitz John Porter Poole in this collection).

There is a growing literature dealing with gender reversals. A pioneering book by Will Roscoe investigated gender traditions among American Indian tribes and was, for many, the first time that the theme of gender reversal occupied center stage. Previous books by Marjorie Garber, Lesley Ferris, and

Vern and Bonnie Bullough have focused primarily on transvestism, although each of these books also included some discussion that moved beyond this sphere. Kim Elizabeth Stuart and Anne Bolin have separately produced important studies of transsexualism that have enabled non-specialist audiences to obtain a basic grasp of the issues. And a recent collection edited by Julia Epstein and Kristina Straub, while highly variable in quality, brought together some fine historical studies, including magnificent studies by Elizabeth Castelli and Gary Kates. This volume most closely resembles Gilbert Herdt's 1994 collection, *Third Sex, Third Gender: Beyond Sexual Dimorphism in Culture and History*. Like Herdt's book, the present study brings together works of anthropology and history. Where I hope that this book makes a unique contribution is in the range of its coverage, the attention paid to non-Western societies, and the blend of ancient, medieval, early modern, and contemporary subjects.

I am grateful to Gary Kates and Kristina Straub for their most helpful comments on the original manuscript, and to Claire L'Enfant, my publisher at Routledge, for her wise counsel and hard work in moving this manuscript along. I am also most grateful to my spouse Chris Hassenstab, for her unflagging interest in my work and for her detailed comments on earlier drafts of my introduction.

Sabrina Petra Ramet
Seattle, Washington

1

GENDER REVERSALS AND GENDER CULTURES

An introduction

Sabrina Petra Ramet

The ancient Greeks told of a certain Teiresias, a legendary blind seer, born a man, who was miraculously transformed into a woman, returning to his male form only after having lived eight years as a woman. Later, according to the story, the divine royal couple, Zeus and Hera, turned to Teiresias to help them settle an argument. Each of them, it seemed, claimed that the other derived more pleasure from sex. Since Teiresias had the benefit of experience in both sexes, they asked him his opinion. Without a moment's hesitation, Teiresias answered that the woman obtained far more pleasure from sexual relations than did the man. Hera was angered at this disclosure and punished Teiresias by blinding him; but Zeus compensated Teiresias by imparting the power of prophecy and by granting Teiresias a life lasting seven generations.[1] For the Greeks, Teiresias' sex change was, quite apart from Zeus' intervention, the clue to his miraculous gifts and in time, he came to be described as "the greatest of the mythical seers."[2]

The story of Teiresias is not an isolated example, however.[3] On the contrary, the theme of gender reversal frequently occurs in ancient religion and mythology, as well as in ancient rituals, and has recurred in diverse societies in every era. But the significance attached to gender reversal varies greatly, depending on the context, the specific form of the reversal, and the given gender culture.

The concept of *gender culture* is crucial to an understanding of the phenomenon of gender reversal, because the latter arises within the parameters set by a gender culture and because it is a society's culture that informs its members as to the meanings of specific forms of individual and collective behavior. This concept of "gender culture" is derived from the growing literature on the social construction of gender. In brief, this literature is concerned with how societies generate and enforce standards for expected gender-linked behavior, and socialize their members to abide by those standards.[4] This literature is thus concerned also with issues of social control. Gordene MacKenzie probably speaks for most adherents of this approach when she writes that

1

Gender is ... one of the most effective means of social control. From birth we are enculturated into a dual gender system, reinforced by all the major institutions.[5]

MacKenzie uses the terms "gender code" and "gender ideology" to refer to the relevant standards of behavior, warning that they are enforced by institutions which act as "gender police."[6] Martine Rothblatt uses the expression "gender dictates" to refer to the same standards, thus implying that they are dictatorial in character.[7] Social constructionists are, accordingly, interested in the socialization processes which assure gender conformity, but there is no inherent requirement that a social constructionist deny the existence of innate psychological differences between the sexes (although some writers do so).

For the purposes of this book, I have elected to use the expression *gender culture* rather than one of the alternatives identified above. The advantages of this term are that it is nonjudgmental and that it links the concerns of this book with anthropological studies of culture and socialization, as well as with political culture theories, to which it is related, both by analogy and by parallel logic. For the sake of definitional clarity, let us take it that by *gender culture* is meant a society's understanding of what is possible, proper, and perverse in gender-linked behavior, and more specifically, that set of values, mores, and assumptions which establishes which behaviors are to be seen as gender-linked, with which gender or genders they are to be seen as linked, what is the society's understanding of gender in the first place, and, consequently, how many genders there are. Thus, among certain Indian nations of the Pacific Northwest, for example, there were (until the latter part of the nineteenth century) four or more genders; the possibility of having more than two genders was opened up by divorcing gender from sexual morphology and by associating gender rather, indeed primarily, with social role and labor tasks.[8] *Gender reversal* may be understood to be any change, whether "total" or partial, in social behavior, work, clothing, mannerisms, speech, self-designation, or ideology,[9] which brings a person closer to the other (or, in polygender systems, *an*other) gender. Gender reversal need not involve an effort to blot out any memory of the person's pretransformative past; indeed, except for twentieth-century transsexuals, many of whom create fictitious histories in the hope of concealing their gender transformation, most male-to-female gender reversals have been open and explicit. (Since women historically often tried to pass as men in order to breach career barriers, the opaqueness of their disguise was of the essence.) Among the Plains tribes in the nineteenth century, not only was cross-gender status explicit, but it was also most often partial. In fact, among the aforementioned nations, cross-gender status did not necessarily involve cross-dressing, and some cross-gender females continued to wear female clothes even though they were engaged exclusively in male tasks and took wives to take care of household tasks associated with females.[10] Sexual behavior, however, is not considered directly relevant to the subject of gender reversal. Not only is same-sex sexuality a separate topic not to be confused with gender reversal, but in two-gender systems, in particular, it becomes semantically treacherous to speak of "same-sex" and "hetero-sexual" liaisons on the part of a cross-gendered individual. The confusion which can arise from these terms can be discerned in the disagreement among those therapists attempting to describe male-to-female transsexuals who are attracted to women; for some therapists, such transsexuals are "hetero-sexual," for others, "homosexual." When antonyms can be understood to mean the same thing, it is time to look for alternative vocabulary.

Gender cultures also define the limits of social tolerance and, in this regard, may be seen within the scope of the overarching cultural system as a whole. Cross-dressing, thus, while nowadays narrowly construed to refer but to dressing across gender lines, was at one time a much broader concept, referring to any breach across the rigid regulations governing attire. These regulations, found in all ancient societies including the Aztec and Inca, as well as in European society as late as the seventeenth century,[11] were designed to keep people in their assigned places, and included often precise prescriptions relating to class, trade, and lineage, as well as gender. Often specific colors were off limits to certain groups: in the Ottoman Empire, for example, only Muslims were permitted to wear green, while in Tudor England purple cloth was reserved for persons of noble extraction.

But the scope of such regulations has been steadily narrowed, so that there are only three sectors in which attire is still strictly regulated: gender; certain occupations (such as clergy, nurses, policemen); and certain religious groups (for example, the specific clothing regulations of the Amish and, affecting also the level of gender, the requirement in some Muslim societies that women wear a veil). Violations of regulations of attire in these spheres are sensitive matters, and no one is surprised that the offense of impersonating a police officer is vigorously punished or that religious groups take seriously de-viations from codes regulating attire. But the vast, all-encompassing regu-lation of all attire in society is largely a thing of the past. And as the purview of such regulations has narrowed, the meaning attributed to the act of donning the attire of the opposite sex has necessarily changed. Perhaps the single most important development which affected the way in which such cross-dressing has been understood was the decay of the old polytheist religions and the spread of new moral codes, as advanced first by the Orphics and later by the Christians.

Much as gender cultures vary over space and change over time, so too do the functions played by gender reversals. And it is this theme of the functions of gender reversals which will occupy my attention for the remainder of this introduction.

3

THE FUNCTIONS OF GENDER REVERSALS IN RELIGIOUS MYTHOLOGY AND RITUAL

The theme of gender reversal occupies a prominent place in the ancient cult of Inanna, in the Olympian religion of the ancient Greeks (most specifically in the cult of Dionysos), in Mahayana Buddhism, in Hinduism, and even in medieval Christianity. In its earliest incarnations, the capacity of the deities to change their gender at will and to project both female and male avatars was a natural corollary of the belief of the ancients in their deities' capacity to adopt any form at will. Among the Aztecs, for instance, Quetzalcoatl, the sky god, was sometimes represented as a dragon, covered with feathers, over a serpent-like body; at other times, he was portrayed as a bicephalic amphibean.[12] The Aztec god Xolotl, himself an avatar of Quetzalcoatl, had his own subsidiary avatars, including any of a number of animal forms, that of a dog being his most usual choice.[13] Again, in Hindu mythology, Krishna, an avatar of the god Vishnu, transforms himself into a beautiful woman in order to destroy the demon Araka.[14] Zeus, the supreme god of the Greek pantheon, is said to have assumed the form of a bull on at least one occasion, while Artemis was sometimes called the "bear-goddess".[15] And, of course, the ancient Greek deities had the power to cast spells changing humans into any of a number of animals or plants. In other words, gender reversals in certain polytheist religions are situated within the context of a wide array of transformations of form and presentation, none of which, however, imply a change of essence.

It was quite consistent with this notion that the adherents of certain cults would emulate their deities by donning animal masks and skins, or by cross-dressing. The ancient Sumerian goddess Inanna (also called Ishtar) is a good example of both gender ambiguity and gender reversal. She was described variously as the goddess of love and of war, and was said to live the life of a young man, engaging in warfare and avariciously seeking ever more lovers.[16] In the ritual surrounding Inanna, she was said to turn men into women, and women into men, and at cultic celebrations of her glory each sex donned the garb of the other sex.[17] In the Dionysian rites of ancient Greece, which endured as late as the seventeenth century CE, women dressed as men and men as women in celebration of a male deity renowned for his effeminacy. Philostratus, a third century writer, justified the practices, noting, "In the revel it is permitted women to dress like men and men to put on a woman's dress and walk like a woman."[18] In these religions, cross-dressing assumes the role of emulation and celebration of the cross-gendered deity, and perhaps of lifting the participant out of his or her normal persona, by creating a special altered state for the religious rite.

In some religious traditions, gender reversal seems to hint at an earlier matriarchal system. In traditional Japan, for example, Amatarasu-no-Omikami, the sun goddess, is still the most important deity in the Shinto pantheon. And when a new emperor is enthroned, he must take part in the *daijosai* enthronement ceremony, in which he is ritually dressed as a female, as a symbolic incarnation of the goddess, Amatarasu.[19]

Cross-dressing may also be associated with purification and with elevation to a higher state. In some Tantric sects of Hinduism, for example, ". . . male transvestism is used as a way of transcending one's own sex, a prerequisite to achieving salvation."[20] Mahayana Buddhism shows evidence of similar thinking. As Cynthia Humes relates, in her chapter for this book, the theme of gender reversal emerges in Mahayana Buddhism in the belief that ". . . it is not only one's female physical appearance that must change, but also one's 'women's thoughts', that is, her woman's nature and mental attitude."

The same motif appeared in Christianity at an early stage. The apocryphal *Gospel of Thomas* closed with the admonition:

Simon Peter said to them [the other disciples], "Let Mary leave us, because women are not worthy of life." Jesus said, "Behold, I myself shall lead her so as to make her male, that she too may become a living spirit like you males. For every woman who makes herself male will enter the kingdom of heaven.[21]

From the start, Christian women viewed their bodies as encumbrances to salvation, and inevitably, in the course of the medieval period, holy women cast off their female garb and assumed male attire. These were the so-called "transvestite saints", among whom were Pelagia (also known as Pelagius), Marina (later known as Marinus), Athanasia (Athanasius), Wilgefortis (also Uncumber), Hildegard of Bingen, Catherine of Siena, and Margery Kempe, to mention just a few of the better known.[22] Ironically, while young girls were raised on stories of female transvestite saints and taught to believe that the route to God ran through somehow "becoming male," the very symbology of gender in the Western tradition, as Caroline Bynum has pointed out,

. . . suggested that men – powerful, clerical, authoritative, rational, "divine" men – needed to become weak and human, yet spiritual, "women" in order to proceed toward God.[23]

Gender is perhaps the most fundamental level of individual identity, the touchstone of one's personhood. In identifying a person, it is natural that among those signifiers we mention first is some clue as to the person's sex. Yet many religions aspire to that level of centrality and primacy – for can God be satisfied with being secondary in importance to bodily form? Thus, it is not surprising that religious systems have often seen the transformation of gender as linked with the process of coming closer to the Godhead, however it is construed.

THE FUNCTIONS OF GENDER
REVERSALS IN DRAMA

Theatrical cross-dressing was known to the ancient Greeks – indeed, Plato condemned the practice of men playing the role of women, lest they become feminized.[24] Later, in Christian Europe, the Church's ban on women performing in public had the inevitable effect of promoting young boys to act women's parts on stage and of encouraging the castration of young boys so that they could sing the soprano parts in choral and solo vocal performances. As Lesley Ferris records, they were often greeted, at their performances, with shouts of "Long live the knife!"[25] Later, in seventeenth-century England, women started to break into theater and eventually were not only acting the parts of women but increasingly taking men's roles. At one level, as Kristina Straub observes, "the obvious reason for dressing actresses in men's clothes at the end of the seventeenth century is virtually the same as one of the reasons for putting women on the stage at all: conventionally attractive female bodies sell tickets."[26] But something more was involved, something of a psychological or even ideological nature: if women were "supposed" to be meek and subservient to men but were allowed to play the roles of men on stage, then the stage could become the arena for fundamental challenges to the sex/gender system.

Indeed, it was understood as such, and already in the polemics surrounding cross-dressing in England in the years 1580–1633, preachers and pamphleteers inveighed against cross-dressing. The ensuing controversy came to a head in 1620, when, under pressure from conservative forces, King James I ordered the clergy to devote themselves to condemning the practice of women wearing men's clothes in public. Indeed, women were repeatedly donning men's clothes as a prelude to participating in food riots, demonstrations against enclosures, and other lower-class protests.[27] Thus, the association of female cross-dressing, whether on the stage or in the streets, with threats to the gender and class system and even with social upheaval, was clear enough. But Puritans also worried about cross-dressing among males. Some Puritan moralists[28] thus expressed concern that men and boys wearing female garb on-stage might take to wearing female garb off-stage – a practice which the Puritans considered especially heinous.

Beginning in the latter part of the eighteenth century, a reversal occurred within Shakespearean theater. Where boys had once been used to play women's roles in Shakespeare's plays, now women were being cast to play Hamlet or even Romeo. Erika Munk has dismissed the Hamlet role as not particularly liberating since, in her view, Prince Hamlet could be characterized as "a waffling neurotic prone to violent fits"[29] – a characterization that accords all too well with some stereotypes of women. But in 1990, two separate productions of *King Lear* cast a woman in the title role; one of these, staged in Atlanta, made some adjustments, placing the action in 1950s

Georgia, with Lear depicted as "a southern matriarchal figure with three sons."[30] Ruth Maleczech, who played Lear in the New York City production that same year, highlighted the same theme that had troubled English preachers in the early seventeenth century: "When a man has power, we take it for granted. But when a woman has power, we're forced to look at the nature of power itself."[31] Casting a woman in the role of King Lear or Hamlet tantalizes the audience with veiled allusions to female gender culture, and prompts questions about the gender ambiguity of behavior. We are enabled to ask, would a woman in fact behave in this way, speak in this way, or are our assumptions of differences often largely arbitrary conventions? Sally Potter, the English writer who directed the 1993 film *Orlando*, which cast Quentin Crisp as Queen Elizabeth I and Tilda Swinton as Orlando, tried to explain the double gender reversal of the film in these words:

> One of the things we're saying here is that men and women have far more in common than we've imagined, that the differences between us have been grossly exaggerated and made the basis for huge pain, grief and misery. Women have difficult lives, but men have difficult lives too.[32]

But there is more to it than that, of course. The steady flow of films which include elements of cross-dressing is clue enough. These films have included the cult classic *The Rocky Horror Picture Show*; the haunting tale of neo-pagan rituals, *Wickerman*; Roman Polanski's *The Apartment*; Julie Andrews' *Victor/Victoria* (itself based on a German film of 1933, *Viktor/Viktoria*); the Gore Vidal character *Myra Breckinridge*; Dustin Hoffman's *Tootsie*; Robin Williams' *Mrs. Doubtfire; Paris is Burning*; and two films of 1994 – *Priscilla, Queen of the Desert* and *Just Like a Woman* – as well as *The Birdcage* (1996). One may also think of certain recent television shows which have offered sympathetic portrayals of cross-dressing, such as *Twin Peaks* and *Picket Fences*, as well as *Bosom Buddies*, which offers a neutral view of cross-dressing, making use of the unlikely vehicle of two men cross-dressing in order to obtain low-cost women-only housing. Going back a little in time, one might also recall Marlene Dietrich's famous performance in the cabaret scene in *Morocco* (1930), in which she wore a top hat and tails and flirted with a woman in the cabaret audience, and, for that matter, the 1934 British production, *Girls Will be Boys*, which cast Dolly Haas in "male drag" to sing to piano accompaniment.[33] Few people go to these films in search of philosophical enlightenment, any more than audiences attending drag shows expect mind-broadening experiences. RuPaul, the alias of Andre Charles, who soared to fame after 1991 with drag-queen rock videos and a self-presentation that exults in sheer camp, has been described by one of his oldest friends as "a six-foot-seven monster-model-woman thing."[34] RuPaul highlights the feeling of magic associated with drag. Watching beautiful women sing and dance is a delightful experience, but watching beautiful women who are really men sing and dance necessarily evokes additional feelings. In RuPaul's words: "A drag queen is like a priest or a spirit familiar. We represent the myths, the duality of the universe. We're like little microcosms of the world."[35] Part of the magic is the realization that

> Beneath the volutes and tendrils of his many platinum-blond hairpieces, he is an ageless ... and unquestionable beauty. Out of drag, RuPaul is just a pleasant-looking freckled bald man with an earnest smile.[36]

THE FUNCTIONS OF GENDER REVERSALS IN SOCIAL ORDER AND SOCIAL MOBILITY

Gender reversal has also figured in maintaining social order and as a subtheme of social mobility. Taking up social order first: in traditional societies (especially rural ones), it is often a matter of great consequence that there be male offspring, whether to carry on the name or to assume responsibility for carrying out tasks associated with males. In contemporary China, where families have been limited in the number of children they might raise, adults have addressed these concerns by drowning female babies. The Balkan people, like many Indian nations of North America, found "adaptive" alternatives. In the Balkans, the practice of raising biological females as males became accepted among Serbs, Montenegrins, and Ghegs, in families which were unable to give birth to a biological male. Known as *muškobanje* (the plural of *muškobanja*), these cross-gendered individuals assumed a male social identity and performed work associated with men. They were not allowed to take either sex for a spouse, but were sworn to virginity. They were often highly respected in their communities, and at least one such *muškobanja* (in late nineteenth-century Montenegro) was allowed to vote in parliamentary elections, even though female suffrage had not yet been introduced.[37] This practice was the subject of Srdjan Karanović's 1991 film, *Virgina*.[38]

Among various Indian nations of North America, similar practices survived until the latter part of the nineteenth century. By contrast with the Balkan peoples, the Indians allowed their cross-gendered persons to marry, although they were expected to marry persons whose gender was in some sense "opposite" to their own. In practice, this meant that a cross-gender "female," insofar as he was recognized as a social male, was expected to marry a traditional female, while a cross-gender "male" was expected to marry a traditional male. At issue was the preservation of a clear, gender-based division of labor within the household – something that would have broken down if social females (or males) had married each other. While some cross-gendered persons were self-selected (their dreams often serving a legitimating function in this regard),

> among the Kaska, a family that had all female children and desired a son to hunt for them would select a daughter (probably the one who

showed the most inclination) to be "like a man". When she was five, the parents tied the dried ovaries of a bear to her belt to wear for life as protection against conception. Though in different tribes the socializing processes varied, girls achieved the cross-gender role in each instance through accepted cultural channels.[39]

Both Balkan peoples and the Indians thus created an institutionalized cross-gender role which would permit persons of one gender to live as members of the other. Among the Balkan peoples, only the female-to-male transformation was without shame. But among the Indians, transformations in both directions were possible, and such persons were often highly respected within their nations. Such transformations served to assure that gender-associated tasks were performed without violating the gender system, and thus served to preserve and protect the gender division of labor prescribed by their culture. It thus further served to preserve social stability and social order by containing at least some potential pressures for social change.[40]

Social mobility, the second subtheme of this section, pertains largely, if not exclusively, to women seeking careers reserved for men. One such case is recounted by Israel Burshatin in his chapter for this book, concerning the case of Eleno/Elena. The most notorious cases of cross-dressing may well be those involving pirates, since, as it turned out, a number of eighteenth-century women who fancied a life of adventure as a swashbuckling buccaneer coped with sexual prejudice by donning false beards and moustaches and passing themselves off as men. In one such case, riddled with irony, a certain pirate, whose real name was Anne Bonny, cross-dressed as a male and fell in love with a handsome, bearded pirate, only to find out that this pirate was herself a cross-dressed female by the name of Mary Read.[41]

The "golden age" of female cross-dressing in Europe, according to Dutch social historians Rudolf Dekker and Lotte van de Pol, was the period running from the late sixteenth century until sometime in the nineteenth century.[42] In a comprehensive study of this period, they documented and researched one hundred and nineteen cases of female transvestism in the Netherlands alone, but found evidence of female cross-dressers across Europe, with an especially large concentration in northwestern Europe, but with cases also in Spain and Italy as well. Some of these women adopted male disguise in order to enlist in the army, such as Catalina de Erauso (b. 1592), the so-called "nun-ensign," who ran away from a convent in northern Spain in order to join the Spanish army. She served for several years before being discovered. She was subsequently granted a license by Philip IV of Spain, which authorized her to wear men's clothes.[43] Christian Davis, alias Christopher Welsh, an Irish woman (b. 1667), took to a life of soldiery for what were, at first, romantic reasons: her husband had enlisted in the English army (which was at the time fighting the French in Flanders) and since she had not heard from him, she took a male disguise in order to gain entry into that same army. Eventually she became convinced that her husband had died in battle, but she reenlisted in the dragoons. When her true sex was finally discovered, her commander summoned Welsh, who had long been known as the "pretty dragoon," discharged her, but ordered the continuance of her pay.[44] Others came to less fortunate ends. There is the example of Catherine Rosenbrock, who served as a Dutch sailor and soldier for twelve years, only to be imprisoned at age forty-two, by her own mother, for the "negation of her feminine sex," or the case of Maria van Antwerpen (b. in Breda in 1719) who succeeded in passing for thirteen years only to end with a nervous breakdown.[45]

Of course, not all women who cross-dressed wanted to be soldiers or pirates. Some wanted to sign on board a ship bound for the Dutch East Indies, and make their fortune there; others cross-dressed in order to engage in a life of crime, or alternatively, in order to elude the police, who might be searching for a *female* offender.[46]

Some of these female transvestites even took wives, at least some of whom claimed to have been fooled, at least for a time. One example here is Catharina Lincken, a German woman, who was brought to trial in 1721. According to the court records, she had succeeded in passing as a man

> ... even in her married life, as she made use of "a leather-covered horn through which she urinated and [which she kept] fastened against her nude body."[47]

Inevitably, such stories became the subject of popular songs, such as the case of Barbara Adriaens and Hilletje Jans, whose marriage inspired a song in 1632:

> For when the bride made free
> To feel if there might be
> Cock and balls, said she,
> "T'is most rare
> I perceive them not, yea, nothing there,"
> How may I then assay
> My heat with thee to allay
> In the nuptial bed where we two lay?[48]

Perhaps the most famous female cross-dressers of all time are Joan of Arc (1412–31), the legendary military leader who led a French army against the English and won a remarkable battle at Orléans, and Georges Sand (1804–76), the French novelist, who shocked and tantalized Europe with her love affairs with composer Frederic Chopin, poet Alfred de Musset, and many others.[49]

THE FUNCTIONS OF GENDER REVERSALS IN FANTASY PLAY

Cross-dressing is a common feature in sexual fantasy play, or, more specifically, sado-masochism, and bondage and discipline. These forms are often confused and some clarification may be of help. Sado-masochism, strictly speaking, is a consensual activity in which one person inflicts physical pain on another for the purpose of giving the recipient pleasure. Bondage and discipline is a consensual activity involving physical restraint, light physical punishment purely for purposes of humiliation (such as spanking), verbal abuse, scolding, training, and humiliation. In such fantasy play, there is always a "top," the person who takes charge and administers punishments, and a "bottom," who is required to follow orders and who is the recipient of the punishments. Cross-dressing commonly figures in these forms of play, especially in the case of male "bottoms." Females rarely adopt male personae in such play. Although either sex may be the "top," and either the "bottom," in heterosexual fantasy play, it is far more common for females to take the role of "top" and for males to assume the role of the subservient "bottom". The term "dominatrix" reflects this division of "labor;" there is no equivalent word which refers exclusively to a male top in the scene. The rarity of male domination in fantasy play is readily explained. The whole point of such play is to create a world of fantasy through which one might escape the realities of one's life; in a patriarchal society, men are already on "top," and replicating that in sexual play would constitute neither fantasy nor escape. As Angela Carter puts it, "[the submissive's] pain is in the nature of a holiday from his life."[50]

The *Urvater* of sado-masochism were the Marquis Donatien-Alphonse-François de Sade (1740–1814), a Parisian novelist, and Leopold von Sacher-Masoch (1835–95), a Professor of History in Lemberg (Lvov). De Sade, who advanced an argument for female equality in his *La Philosophie dans le boudoir*, "... denounced the existing sexual order as one based upon a monopolistic conception of property [in persons]."[51] While conceiving all sexuality in terms of domination, de Sade nonetheless sketched a "true republic," in which sexual liaisons would be "... but temporary contractual engagements for pleasure, without loyalty or moral involvement beyond the moment of enjoyment."[52] And he went further, and defended the validity of the sheer "diversity of individual psychic needs."[53] In this way, de Sade laid the basis for consensual fantasy play that dispenses with considerations of what is "normal" or "proper" and orients itself only to what is "pleasurable" and what is "therapeutic."[54]

While de Sade seems content with fleeting episodes of intense play, Sacher-Masoch conjures up a world of prolonged submission, with formal contracts and fixed roles. In his classic semi-autobiographical novel, *Venus in Furs*, he describes quite explicitly the fascination that submission holds for him:

> "Yes, you have brought my dearest fantasies
> to life", I exclaimed. "They have lain dormant
> too long."
> "And what are they?" She put her hand on the
> nape of my neck.

11

> A sweet dizziness came over me on feeling the
> warmth of her little hand, and on meeting the
> tender, searching gaze that she let fall on me
> through half-closed eyes.
> "To be the slave of a woman, a beautiful
> woman whom I love and worship."
> "And who in return ill-treats you!" laughed
> Wanda.
> "Yes, who fetters me, whips me and kicks
> me . . ."[55]

The focus is on the abnegation of one's own power and the surrender of one's will to another – a retreat from responsibility and rationality to a world of, despite occasional spankings, *complete safety and predictability*. Anne Rice's novel, *Beauty's Punishment*, makes the same point:

> If I was saying something silent it was, "You are my Mistress. You own me. And I will not look away until you tell me to. I will look into what you are and what you do." And she seemed to hear this and to be fascinated.[56]

In the early 1970s, Martha Stein conducted a study of more than 1,200 men who visited call girls. Setting up camp behind see-through mirrors, she observed their behavior and analyzed trends. Of her sample, one hundred and fifty-six were submissives ("slaves," in her terminology). Of this number, twenty-four liked to be "forced" to dress in female clothing, whether as "punishment" or to serve their Mistress as her maids.[57] At first sight, this would appear to be profoundly paradoxical. After all, insofar as the session presumes and celebrates an ideology of female superiority, female clothing ought to be a badge of superiority, not a source of humiliation and degradation. But the role of cross-dressing in sexual fantasy is, in fact, *independent* of this ideology of female superiority, and reflects instead an exploitation of the taboo of men wearing women's clothing (which is to say, that this fetish is culture-bound). Anyone who has seen heterosexual men accompanying their wives to shop for lingerie cannot but have noticed how embarrassed such men typically are, as if they were frightened for dear life lest anyone think they had any interest in the merchandise. This fear, itself a product of the omnipotent taboo, becomes the source of sweet humiliation in domination scenes involving cross-dressing. But for a transvestite, this taboo exerts its influence at best as a memory of what is "forbidden" and, in his case, it is not so much the act of wearing female clothing that is humiliating; it is the fact of being *compelled* to do so. Or, in fantasy play, it is the *illusion* of being so compelled.[58]

Cross-dressing may, thus, serve as a key to unleash a flood of intense psychological pleasure, but the pleasure depends on the dominant's striking the right balance between mock humiliation and supportive reinforcement.

12

Reflecting on this dynamic, one professional dominatrix commented, "The Superior helps the [submissive] transvestite realize how reasonable his fantasy is, how tame and commonplace compared to others."[59] And in this way, the submissive finds reassurance.[60]

One final note about the functions of female domination and cross-dressing in fantasy play: many authors depict such games as if they were merely the reverse of what they seemed, thus as if femaleness were still devalued. But, as Terence Sellers has pointed out, the reality is much more complex and while some so-called submissives are really dominants who want to " top from the bottom," for most of the submissives involved in cross-dressing scenes, ". . . the Mistress helps the [submissive] transvestite build up a good positive image of himself as a woman, . . . [and] make[s] a strong effort to treat the transsexual and transvestite in all respects as a woman – and to impress upon her that to be female is good."[61]

Social scientists have largely shied away from any serious analysis of domination/submission, as if the phenomenon had no conceivable connection with the rest of culture, or, to put it differently, as if it did not reflect, in distortion, the values and behavioral norms of society. On the contrary, the behavioral norms embedded in the gender culture of a given society underlie every aspect of fantasy play – but with this difference: in domination/submission, the rules of that gender culture are reversed, exaggerated, or mimicked in the spirit of play. In the scripts of fantasy play are revealed the stresses of "normal" life. Infantilism, for example, tends to attract judges, corporate executives, and other men in positions of responsibility and authority; their desire to return to the cradle in fantasy play provides a clue as to the psychological overload they experience in their careers.

The inclusion of cross-dressing in fantasy play figures on several levels. First, gender reversal is an efficient way, arguably the most total way, in which a person may shed his or her identity and assume a new persona; moreover, by assuming a new persona, the cross-dresser creates a buffer that can absorb any psychological pain that might otherwise be associated with the attendant humiliations. This, in turn, provides an interesting commentary on the prevailing gender culture, under which individuals are expected to maintain the same gender identity and the same persona at all times (a notion recently called into question by Martine Rothblatt, as we shall see in the next section).

Second, the energizing character of cross-dressing as a violation of the great taboo alerts one simultaneously to the intensity of the widespread fear that men have of being viewed as "sissies" and to the intense pleasure that may lie at the very core of that fear and in the very act of violating the taboo.

And third, male cross-dressing behavior in fantasy play reflects the strains associated with "achieving" maleness. As Nancy Chodorow points out,

In some sense "feminine identity" is more easily and surely attainable than "masculine identity". Margaret Mead claims that from the time of birth, girls can begin to take on feminine identity through identification with their mothers, while for little boys, masculine identification comes through a process of differentiation, because what would be his "natural" identification – identification with the person he is closest to and most dependent upon – is according to cultural values "unnatural", [and] this works against his attainment of stable masculine identity.[62]

Male cross-dressing in fantasy play, in short, is a clue to the greater difficulties created by Western gender culture for the achievement of "manliness", by comparison with "womanliness".

TRANSGENDERISM

In the course of the 1980s, a grass-roots movement emerged in the United States and Western Europe. Identifying itself as "transgenderist", this movement has been characterized by a consensus that the existing gender culture, or, if one prefers, gender system, is oppressive. As Rothblatt puts it, "the guiding principle of this movement is [the notion] that people should be free to change, either temporarily or permanently, the sex type to which they were assigned since infancy."[63] Self-designated transgenderists share the conviction that the existing dyadic gender culture constitutes "an apartheid of sex" into which people are "brainwashed."[64] Rothblatt claims that the entire notion of identifiable male and female "natures" amounts to pure mythology, and offers, in place of the existing two-gender system, the proposition that "there are five billion people in the world and five billion unique sexual identities."[65] MacKenzie takes up the same theme, in consequence characterizing transsexualism as ". . . a symptom of the cultural illness brought on by a rigid bipolar gender system, whose cure may only be effected by the radical transformation of the current gender system."[66] MacKenzie concludes her book with an exhortation ". . . to dismantle the current one-nation-under-gender-divided-and-unequal and recognize the transgender nation. Only when this becomes a possibility, can there occur a true Gender Revolution."[67]

Kate Bornstein, born in 1948 with male anatomy, is one of the most articulate advocates of transgenderism. Describing herself, she put it this way in her 1994 book, *Gender Outlaw*:

Gender identity is assumed by many to be "natural"; that is someone can feel "like a man", or "like a woman". When I first started giving talks about gender, this was the one question that would keep coming up: "Do you feel like a woman now?" "Did you ever feel like a man?" "How did you know what a woman would feel like?"

I've no idea what "a woman" feels like. I never did feel like a girl or a woman; rather, it was my unshakable conviction that I was not a boy or a man. It was the absence of a feeling, rather than its presence, that convinced me to change my gender.[68]

Bornstein's choice, thus, was not to opt for mindless conformity to the gender prescriptions of the dominant social ideology, but rather to switch from "variations on a theme of male" to "variations on a theme of female." Her book serves, hence, as a reminder that we are all (or almost all of us) doing "variations" on one of these themes, or, as one wit once put it, we are all "passing".

And this furnishes, in turn, a more than adequate rejoinder to those transophobic critics such as Judith Shapiro and Thomas Kando who attack transsexuals for gender conformism (!) and lack of originality (!).[69] One wonders why *originality* (and in the eyes of the beholder, at that) should be seen by some as the precondition of authenticity, and whether, for that matter, they see themselves as "original" in gender terms. Quite apart from the fact that the enormous variety that one finds among members of the species is fully replicated among members of the transsexual population, rendering any generalizations about the allegedly "conformist" predilections of transsexuals as utterly simplistic, transophobes who find male-to-female transsexuals too feminine for their tastes might ask themselves if what they really want is to force the objects of their gaze to remain male, thus conforming to the Western static-binary gender system.[70] Far from being the conformists that some writers (such as Shapiro and Kando) would make of them, transsexuals and transgenderists overthrow the rigid gender system which occupies such a central position in lands touched by Protestantism, not only by rejecting the right wing's favored doctrine of the unchangeability of sex but also, in enough cases to be significant, by blending the clothing of each sex and often by taking on a mixture of household tasks, blending some of the stereotypical "female" tasks with some of the stereotypical "male" tasks. For right-wingers, all of this strikes at the very heart of the system of rigid conformity that they wish to impose on society. Far from being conformists or "Uncle Toms," as Thomas Kando put it in a strangely acerbic attack, transsexuals could, with justice, be described as the most authentic *dissidents* in liberal society.

CONCLUSION

Gender reversals, cross-dressing, and gender innovations have been found in all historical epochs. Cross-dressers have included Hatshepsut (an Egyptian ruler of the fifteenth century BCE), Roman Emperor Elagabalus, Rudolf Valentino, J. Edgar Hoover, and British pop star Boy George.[71] The sixteenth-century King of France Henri III habitually wore female attire and even asked of his courtiers that they refer to him as "Her Majesty."[72] Similarly, in eighteenth-century Russia, Empress Elizabeth regularly wore men's clothing when riding on her steed, and in 1744 started holding regular "meta-morphosis" balls in which all the guests were expected to cross-dress.

Elizabeth herself liked to come to these events dressed variously as a cossack, as a French carpenter, or as a Dutch sailor with the twice-dubious name Mikhailova.[73] In this century, film-maker Ed Wood was a heterosexual transvestite and, according to legend, wore women's silk underwear beneath his combat fatigues when he landed in the South Pacific during World War Two.[74]

Transsexual cases have been documented not only in the US and Britain, contrary to what transophobes sometimes claim, but also in many other countries from Russia[75] and Poland,[76] to Spain,[77] Germany,[78] Japan,[79] Egypt, Brazil,[80] and Mexico. In most states of the European Community, transsexuals are able to obtain at least partial refunds for relevant surgery and, in 1989, the European Parliament issued a call for an end to discrimination against transsexuals whether at the workplace or elsewhere.[81] Where Asia is concerned, transsexualism is likewise gaining increased public acceptance, and, in autumn 1994, New Delhi played host to an international transsexual congress.[82] Transsexualism and other forms of cross-gender behavior are worldwide phenomena.

This book is an endeavor to record some of the diversity surrounding this theme, and to contribute both toward an appreciation of the universality of gender reversals across cultures and history and toward an understanding of the contexts and functions of gender reversals.

NOTES

1 P.M.C. Forbes Irving, *Metamorphosis in Greek Myths*, Oxford: Clarendon Press, 1990, pp. 162–3.
2 Ibid., p. 168.
3 Even among the Greeks, there were other such stories, including the tale of Kaineus, transformed from female to male, and Atalanta, a female reincarnated as a male athlete. See Ibid., pp. 155–62.
4 See Betty Yorburg, *Sexual Identity: Sex Roles and Social Change*, New York: John Wiley & Sons, 1974, pp. 1–2; Gerda Siann, *Gender, Sex and Sexuality: Contemporary Psychological Perspectives*, London: Taylor & Francis, 1994, pp. 3, 125; Herbert Barry III, Margaret K. Bacon, and Irvin L. Child, "A Cross-Cultural Survey of Some Sex Differences in Socialization", in *Journal of Abnormal and Social Psychology*, vol. 55, No. 3 (November 1957); Nancy Chodorow, "Being and Doing: A Cross-Cultural Examination of the Socialization of Males and Females", in Vivian Gornick and Barbara K. Moran (eds), *Woman in Sexist Society: Studies in Power and Powerlessness*, New York: Mentor Books, 1971; Heidi Dahles, "Performing Manliness: On the Meaning of Poaching in Dutch Society", in *Ethnologia Europaea: Journal of European Ethnology* (Copenhagen), vol. 21 (1991), No. 1; Andrea G. Hunter and James Earl Davis, "Constructing Gender: An Exploration of Afro-American Men's Conceptualization of Manhood", in *Gender & Society*, vol. 6, No. 3 (September 1992); and James A. Geschwender, "Ethnicity and the Social Construction of Gender in the Chinese Diaspora", in *Gender & Society*, vol. 6, No. 3 (September 1992). Margaret Mead and Michel Foucault have also contributed to developing theories of the social construction of gender.

5 Gordene Olga MacKenzie, *Transgender Nation*, Bowling Green, Ohio: Bowling Green State University Popular Press, 1994, p. 1.

6 Ibid., pp. 13–14, 62, 95.

7 Martine Rothblatt, *The Apartheid of Sex: A Manifesto on the Freedom of Gender*, New York: Crown Publishers, 1995, p. 43.

8 Evelyn Blackwood, "Sexuality and Gender in Certain Native American Tribes: The Case of Cross-Gender Female", in *Signs*, vol. 10, No. 11 (Autumn 1984), pp. 28, 31, 35–6.

9 I am thinking here of the way in which many male-to-female transsexuals who, while they may have been strongly sympathetic to feminism even prior to crossing over, become fiercely feminist, occasionally even being attracted by lesbian separatism.

10 Blackwood, "Sexuality and Gender", p. 37.

11 Jean E. Howard, "Cross-dressing, the Theater, and Gender Struggle in Early Modern England", in Lesley Ferris (ed.), *Crossing the Stage: Controversies on Cross-Dressing*, London and New York: Routledge, 1993, pp. 22–3.

12 Burr Cartwright Brundage, *The Phoenix of the Western World: Quetzalcoatl and the Sky Religion*, Norman, Okla.: University of Oklahoma Press, 1982, pp. 20, 25.

13 Ibid., p. 197.

14 Serena Nanda, "Hijras: An Alternative Sex and Gender Role in India", in Gilbert Herdt (ed.), *Third Sex, Third Gender: Beyond Sexual Dimorphism in Culture and History*, New York: Zone Books, 1994, p. 376.

15 Irving, *Metamorphosis in Greek Myth*, pp. 45, 66.

16 Tikva Frymer-Kensky, *In the Wake of the Goddesses: Women, Culture, and the Biblical Transformation of Pagan Myth*, New York: Free Press, 1992, pp. 25, 27.

17 Ibid., p. 29.

18 Quoted in Arthur Evans, *The God of Ecstasy: Sex Roles and the Madness of Dionysos*, New York: St. Martin's Press, 1988, p. 20.

19 Nicholas Bornoff, *Pink Samurai: Love, Marriage, & Sex in Contemporary Japan*, New York: Pocket Books, 1991, p. 436.

20 Nanda, "Hijras: An Alternative Sex", p. 376.

21 Quoted in Elizabeth Castelli, "'I Will Make Mary Male': Pieties of the Body and Gender Transformation of Christian Women in Late Antiquity", in Julia Epstein and Kristina Straub (eds), *Body Guards: The Cultural Politics of Gender Ambiguity*, New York and London: Routledge, 1991, p. 30. Cf. (for Islam) Farid al-Din 'Attar: "A woman on the path of God becomes a man, she cannot be called a woman." Quoted in Richard Gordon, "Mithraism and Roman Society: Social Factors in the Explanation of Religious Change in the Roman Empire", in Sabrina Petra Ramet and Donald W. Treadgold (eds), *Render unto Caesar: The Religious Sphere in World Politics*, Washington D.C.: American University Press, 1995, p. 121n.

22 Vern L. Bullough and Bonnie Bullough, *Cross Dressing, Sex, and Gender*, Philadelphia: University of Pennsylvania Press, 1993, pp. 51–5; and Caroline Walker Bynum, *Holy Feast and Holy Fast: The Religious Significance of Food to Medieval Women*, Berkeley and Los Angeles: University of California Press, 1987, p. 291.

23 Bynum, *Holy Feast and Holy Fast*, p. 287.

24 Lesley Ferris, "Introduction: Current Crossings", in Ferris (ed.), *Crossing the Stage*, p. 9.

25 Ibid., p. 15.

26 Kristina Straub, "The Guilty Pleasures of Female Theatrical Cross-Dressing and

the Autobiography of Charlotte Charke", in Epstein and Straub (eds), *Body Guards*, p. 143.

27 Howard, "Cross-dressing, the Theater", p. 29.

28 E.g. William Prynne, *Histrio-Mastix: The Players Scourge*, London, 1633, as cited in B. R. Burg, "Ho Hum, Another Work of the Devil: Buggery and Sodomy in Early Stuart England", in Salvatore J. Licata and Robert P. Petersen (eds), *Historical Perspectives on Homosexuality*, New York: Howarth Press and Stein & Day, 1981, p. 76.

29 Quoted in Ferris, "Introduction", p. 2.

30 Ibid., p. 3.

31 Quoted in Ibid., p. 3.

32 Quoted in *New York Times* (15 February 1993), p. B1.

33 Andrea Weiss, *Vampires and Violets: Lesbians in Film*, New York: Penguin Books, 1992, pp. 33, 44–5.

34 Quoted in Guy Trebay, "Cross-Dresser Dreams", in *New Yorker* (22 March 1993), p. 49.

35 Quoted in Ibid., p. 50.

36 Ibid., p. 51.

37 René Gremaux, "Woman Becomes Man in the Balkans", in Herdt (ed.), *Third Sex, Third Gender*, p. 250.

38 Reviewed in *New York Times* (27 March 1993), p. 12.

39 Blackwood, "Sexuality and Gender", p. 30.

40 A similar phenomenon is found in Omani society, where the *xanith*, a biological male, is permitted a socially defined role which is intermediate between female and male, mixing elements of each. For details and discussion, see Marjorie Garber, *Vested Interests: Cross-Dressing and Cultural Anxiety*, New York and London: Routledge, 1992, pp. 348–52. For further discussion of cross-gender roles in Indian society, see Will Roscoe, "We'wha and Klah: The American Indian Berdache as Artist and Priest", in *American Indian Quarterly*, vol. 12, No. 2 (Spring 1988); and Will Roscoe, *The Zuni Man–Woman*, Albuquerque: University of New Mexico Press, 1991.

41 Tony Horwitz, "Scholars Plunder Myths About Pirates, and It's Such a Drag", in *Wall Street Journal* (23 April 1992), p. A10. For a brief review of a book on this subject by Julie Wheelwright, see *The Sunday Times* (London), 1 April 1990.

42 Rudolf M. Dekker and Lotte C. van de Pol, *The Tradition of Female Transvestism in Early Modern Europe*, trans. from Dutch by Judy Marcure and Lotte van de Pol, London: Macmillan, 1989, p. 2.

43 Mary Elizabeth Perry, *Gender and Disorder in Early Modern Seville*, Princeton, N.J.: Princeton University Press, 1990, pp. 127–8.

44 Bullough and Bullough, *Cross Dressing*, pp. 101–3.

45 Dekker and van de Pol, *Female Transvestism*, pp. 3, 19, 23–4.

46 Ibid., pp. 32, 34–6.

47 Ibid., p. 16.

48 Quoted in Bullough and Bullough, *Cross Dressing*, p. 100.

49 Her given name was Amantine-Aurore-Lucile Dupin. For an especially fine treatment of Sand, see Paul G. Blount, *Georges Sand and the Victorian World*, Athens, Ga.: University of Georgia Press, 1979.

50 Angela Carter, *The Sadeian Woman and the Ideology of Pornography*, New York: Pantheon Books, 1978, p. 21.

51 Frank E. Manuel and Fritzie P. Manuel, *Utopian Thought in the Western World*, Cambridge, Mass.: The Belknap Press of Harvard University Press, 1979, p. 545.

52 Ibid., p. 546.

53 Ibid., p. 547.

54 As Martha L. Stein concludes, in her study of 156 submissive men, "the Slave scenes ... appeared to function therapeutically by allowing clients to enjoy various sexual practices without guilt, to relieve anxieties by a symbolic retreat into childhood, to compensate for [assertive] or domineering behavior in other areas of their life, to act out self-destructive impulses in a controlled context that channeled the impulses toward a pleasurable end. The sessions certainly enabled the men to relieve sexual tensions by acting out fairly strong desires they would otherwise have [had] to suppress." – Martha L. Stein, *Lovers, Friends, Slaves ...*, New York: Berkley Medallion, 1974, p. 302.

55 Leopold von Sacher-Masoch, *Venus in Furs* (1870), in *Masochism: Coldness and Cruelty: Venus in Furs*, New York: Zone Books, 1991, p. 180.

56 Anne Rice, writing as A. N. Roquelaure, *Beauty's Punishment*, New York: Plume, 1984, p. 154.

57 Stein, *Lovers, Friends, Slaves*, pp. 279, 286.

58 On this point, see Anne McClintock, "Confessions of a Psycho-Mistress: An Interview with Mistress Vena", in *Social Text*, no. 37 (Winter 1993), pp. 65–6.

59 Terence Sellers, *The Correct Sadist: The Memoirs of Angel Stern*, Brighton: Temple Press, 1992, p. 99.

60 See also Robert J. Stoller, *Pain & Passion: A Psychoanalyst Explores the World of S&M*, New York: Plenum Press, 1991, pp. 80–1, 85, and *passim*.

61 Sellers, *The Correct Sadist*, p. 98.

62 Chodorow, "Being and Doing," p. 271.

63 Rothblatt, *Apartheid of Sex*, p. 16.

64 Ibid., p. 19.

65 Ibid., p. xiii.

66 MacKenzie, *Transgender Nation*, p. 114.

67 Ibid., p. 172.

68 Kate Bornstein, *Gender Outlaw: On Men, Women, and the Rest of Us*, New York and London: Routledge, 1994, p. 24.

69 Shapiro writes: "While transsexuals may be deviants in terms of cultural norms about how one arrives at being a man or a woman, they are, for the most part, highly conformist about what to do once you get there." See Judith Shapiro, "Transsexualism: Reflections on the Persistence of Gender and the Mutability of Sex," in Epstein and Straub (eds), *Body Guards*, p. 253. Kando condemns transsexuals even more explicitly: "Unlike various liberated groups, transsexuals are reactionary, moving back toward the core-culture rather than away from it. They are the Uncle Toms of the sexual revolution. With these individuals, the dialectic of social change comes full circle and the position of greatest deviance becomes that of the greatest conformity." – Thomas Kando, *Sex Change: The Achievement of Gender Identity among Feminized Transsexuals*, Springfield, Ill.: Charles C. Thomas Publ., 1973, p. 145, as quoted in Shapiro, "Transsexualism: Reflections," p. 255. This sweeping generalization about an entire group smacks of the most simple-minded thinking, bordering on schizoid paranoia. If someone were to write that all heterosexuals were conformists or that all Scotsmen were fanatics, it would be readily apparent that the writer of such generalizations had lost hold of his senses. Such sweeping generalizations about transsexuals have precisely the same order of validity.

Some transophobes literally foam at the mouth when discussing sex change. Take, for example, Julie Burchill who, in a column for *The Times* of London, equates transsexuals with "third sex" transgenderists, as if there were no difference between the aspiration to be a woman or a man and the aspiration to fashion some original gender, and blasts both groups as "extremely reactionary ... because they really do seem to believe ... that gender is actually more important than anything else." I, for one, have never met a transsexual or transvestite who believed that gender was "more important than anything else." Indeed, this hateful endeavor to portray transsexuals as monomaniacs void of any sense of the importance of love, family, career, art, truth, justice, and loyalty reveals the fundamental bigotry intrinsic not only to Julie Burchill's transsophobia but to all politicized transsophobia. Interestingly enough, Burchill's remonstration against transsexuals' alleged reactionary conformism was run under the aggressively conformist headline "Two sexes are plenty thank you." (*The Times*, 11 June 1995), on *Nexis*.

Regrettably, the charge of "conformism" recurs throughout the literature, especially in sources based on minimal or nonexistent fieldwork. Even Anne Bolin, an otherwise quite sophisticated observer, offers the following generalization about *all* male-to-female transsexuals: "Transsexuals consciously and deliberately alter the way they walk, taking smaller steps and keeping the arms close to the body ... They consciously use weaker expletives choosing to be generally more polite than males." Anne Bolin, *In Search of Eve: Transsexual Rites of Passage*, Westport, Conn.: Bergin & Garvey, 1988, p. 134. In my own contacts, I have seen sufficient variety – vast variety in fact – to convince me that such generalizations are, at best, total obfuscations, myths. For example, in my own case, in making the transition from male to female, I became convinced that it was imperative to avoid giving any signal that would suggest weakness to simple minds. I have therefore avoided frilly or delicate clothing, have avoided making any adjustment whatsoever in my gait, have made a point of being firm in statements where firmness seems to me appropriate, and have gone out of my way to spread myself out (physically) at meetings with colleagues, thus using body language to communicate power. Why anyone should think that people change sex in order to conform to specifically the most demeaning stereotypes is quite beyond me. Why anyone would presume to generalize about "all transsexuals" as if we were some sort of disciplined military unit is, again, beyond me.

70 The best works on the subject of transsexualism are: Bolin, *In Search of Eve* (despite occasional lapses); and Kim Elizabeth Stuart, *The Uninvited Dilemma*, Portland, Oregon: Metamorphous Press, 1981. Also interesting is: Robert J. Stoller, *Presentations of Gender*, New Haven, Conn.: Yale University Press, 1985, especially chapters 2–4.

71 Bullough and Bullough, *Cross Dressing*, pp. 23–4, 39; and Garber, *Vested Interests*, p. 360.

72 MacKenzie, *Transgender Nation*, p. 31.

73 Tamara Talbot Rice, *Elizabeth – Empress of Russia*, London: Weidenfeld and Nicolson, 1970, pp. 33, 90, 136.

74 *Irish Times* (Dublin), 6 May 1995, p. 5.

75 For discussion, see Lynne Attwood, *The New Soviet Man and Woman: Sex-Role Socialization in the USSR*, Bloomington, Ind.: Indiana University Press, 1990, especially ch. 5.

76 See Stanislaw Dulko, "Sexual Activity and Temperament in Polish Transsexuals", in *Archives of Sexual Behavior*, vol. 17, No. 2 (1988).

77 MacKenzie, *Transgender Nation*, p. 64. See also *Newsweek* (5 December 1988), p. 88; *The Jerusalem Post* (24 February 1989), on *Nexis*; *Evening Standard* (17 July 1992), p. 29; and *The Guardian* (10 November 1993), on *Nexis*. Male-to-female sex reassignment surgery has been performed in Spain since at least 1960. See *Daily Telegraph* (London), 9 January 1992, p. 19.

78 *Süddeutsche Zeitung* (Munich), 16 August 1994, 24 November 1994, and 11 February 1995 – all on *Nexis*.

79 *The Independent* (London), 30 July 1994, p. 48.
80 *Scotland on Sunday* (27 June 1993), on *Nexis*.
81 *Reuters* (12 September 1989), on *Nexis*.
82 *Neue Zürcher Zeitung* (28 November 1994), on *Nexis*.

2

TRAVERSING GENDER
Cultural context and gender practices

Anne Bolin

Hermaphroditic genders, two-spirit traditions (formally referred to as *Berdache*[1]), cross-gendered roles such as the North Piegan manly-hearted women, woman-marriage, boy-marriage, and rituals in which cross-dressing and/or other cross-gendered behaviors are institutionalized demonstrate five forms of gender variance found on a global scale.[2] While there are undoubtedly many other ways to classify gender variant identities and behaviors offered by the ethnographic record, this classification scheme represents a pilot endeavor to create a typology. The goal of this typology is to foster comparisons and locate commonalities among gender variant phenomenon not usually found sharing the same pages. Mildred Dickemann states this far more eloquently in the following:

> ... good science involves the movement of thought, both analytic and intuitive, back and forth between more abstract, generalizing levels of theory and hypotheses and more particular levels of description and classification. (All description is of course low level generalization.) Description and classification, in the curious mind, provoke theory, because they provoke questions about the nature of relationships.[3]

This five-form model was inspired by Gilbert Herdt's 1988 "Cross-Cultural Forms of Homosexuality and the Concept Gay."[4] In this work Herdt presented a fourfold model of homosexual practices found historically and cross-culturally.[5] My typology is an incipient effort to encourage the kind of analysis that moves beyond the classic and modern approaches to gender as transformed statuses.[6] I have tried to illustrate this in my title through the term "traversing." It was suggested to me by a collaborator from the transgendered community that my previous use of the word "transcending," in an article on transgenderism, implied moving from one social position to another.[7] This terminology did not seem to denote the experience of many in the North American transgendered community who were actively engaged in the creation of a new "genderness" – a process of gender construction.

Traversing is defined by Webster's *New Collegiate Dictionary* (1974) as "1: something that crosses or lies across." This article will investigate the cross-

22

cultural expressions of gender variance in terms of cross/alternative/additional genders; cross-gendered roles, rituals in which cross-gendered behavior occurs as well as data collected recently from members of the emergent North American transgendered community. Consequently, I hope the term "traverse" captures something of the gestalt of this article and is satisfactory to the transgendered community and academic audiences alike.[8] The working image of *traverse* implies crossing as well as interpenetrating and shifting aspects of gendered symbols.

The intent of this article is a modest one. First, I will present the five-form gender variance typology through selected examples from the ethnographic literature. These examples will illustrate each of five identified forms of gender variance: 1) hermaphroditic genders; 2) two-spirit traditions; 3) cross-gendered roles as in the manly-heart types of traditions; 4) woman-marriage; and 5) cross-gendered rituals. Each type will be discussed in terms of the contributions of the cultural constructionist orientation emphasizing the social context of the form[9] and offering comments about relevant debates. The theoretical focus will be placed on the "symbolic load" of gender variance, that is, on sets of embedded gender relations given symbolic expression.[10] While the emphasis is on gender, not sexual behavior, data on sexuality will be incorporated to illustrate that sexuality is not an essential characteristic but is socially constructed in relation to existing gender categories/social gender identities.[11]

The presentation of the five types will be followed by a discussion of the implications these diverse forms of gender variance have for deconstructing the contemporary North American gender paradigm.[12] Despite the apples and oranges of comparing institutions, statuses, roles, and ceremony, all five forms involve the cultural manipulation and reassortment of gendered attributes. These categories of gender variance represent a collage of either the conflation of and/or disassembling and realignment of physiological or bodily insignias and behavioral traits that are culturally assigned as gendered. These forms problematize our Western biocentric paradigm of gender as bipolar and biologically unequivocal. Each category will be examined in terms of its cultural context including interpretive suggestions for understanding gender as practiced.

Not only does the cross-cultural record have implications for decanting the Euro-American gender paradigm, but this knowledge has the potential to impact and infiltrate as well. I found this to be true for at least one population. The anthropological literature and constructionist/interpretivist theories have had a receptive audience among many who identify themselves as members of the transgendered community. The cross-gendered evidence from ethnology has been one factor in the cultural changes that have occurred in the emergence of a transgendered community from local transsexual and transvestite groups. This research is specific to those who have identified as male-to-female transsexuals, male cross-dressers, and transvestites.[13]

CONCEPTUAL ORIENTATION

Before continuing, it is necessary to include working definitions for terms and concepts used throughout this work. The term gender variance includes reference to gender-based Western scientific concepts of status and role. A status is defined as a position or office in a society that includes rights and duties. A role is a set of socially expected behaviors associated with a status.[14] While gender variant statuses such as two-spirit institutions are prominent in anthropological literature, it is important to note that gender variant statuses are only one kind of gender variation as represented by this five- form model.

Components of the North American/Western gender paradigm include sex and gender. Sex typically refers to biological components including ". . . chromosomes, external genitals, gonads, internal sexual apparatuses, hormonal states, secondary sexual characteristics and even the brain" according to Stoller.[15] It generally includes genitals and other physiological features ascribed to males and females.[16]

Gender is defined here as the psychological, social, and cultural domain of being male or female. Gender is a social construction and system of meanings with multiple dimensions including gender identity, both personal and social. Gender identity is interpreted as including components of both personal identity and social identity, that is to say, the self as both individual and cultural.[17] Gender identity has been defined as "[t]he sameness, unity, and persistence of one's individuality as a male or female (or ambivalent), in greater or lesser degree, especially as it is experienced in self-awareness and behavior."[18] However, given anthropological and social-historical investigation of gender variation, this definition needs revision to include the possibility of third and/or supernumerary (additional) gender identities as personal and social constructions.[19]

Gender identity incorporates the private experience of personal identity or one's self concept, while social identity refers to the sociocultural recognition or categorization of gendered identities. It includes status or position in society as a gender that is, as a woman, man, girl, boy, and role concomitants such as appearance, demeanor, and behaviors. In Western culture, this includes social concepts of femininity and masculinity.[20] Gender identity and social identity may or may not converge in the individual's life or in a particular interaction.

Because contemporary societies understand sex as signifying gender, what are regarded as the quintessential insignias of sex have little stability historically and comparatively. This has implications for understanding how gender variant identities are contextually situated within a broader system of meanings associated with femaleness and maleness cross-culturally and in North America. My theoretical moorings consist of influences from symbolic and interpretive anthropology[21] and social history[22] conjoined with postmodern discourse analysis.[23] Recognition of the importance of the individual's experience and meanings within the cultural context follows works by Herdt[24] and Nanda[25] on gender variance and the importance of polyvocality.

THE FIVE-FORM MODEL OF GENDER VARIANCE

1 Hermaphroditic Genders

Pseudohermaphroditism is of interest as this phenomenon reveals cultural classification systems of physiological variation. The prefix pseudo "was once used to denote the fact that the gonads were not hermaphroditically mixed (ovarian plus testicular tissue) as in true hermaphroditism, but were either testicular (male pseudohermaphroditism) or ovarian (female pseudohermaphroditism).[26] For brevity the term hermaphrodite is used and defined as "a congenital condition of ambiguity of the reproductive structures so that the sex of the individual is not clearly defined as exclusively male or exclusively female."[27]

The Navajo provide an example of a culture in which a hermaphrodite status is highly valued, although this is not to suggest a universal ethnographic trend as cultural responses to genital ambiguity vary.[28] For example, Edgerton's study[29] of the Pokot of Kenya investigates the *sererr*, a recognized hermaphrodite status that is demarcated as neither male nor female. Among the Pokot, the essential insignias of status as a man or a woman are prepubertal and adolescent sex play, ritual circumcision of both genders, and reproduction. But because of the *serrers'* incomplete genital development, they cannot assume the appropriate sexual and reproductive roles, nor can their undeveloped genitals be circumcised because of the nature of their development. The words of one Pokot are indicative: "A sererr cannot be a real person. To be a real Pokot, you must be very skilful at sex. You do this sex or you cannot think well of yourself and no one will think well of you either."[30] They are denied status as women or men and occupy a netherworld of genderlessness if they are not killed at birth.[31]

The Navajo recognize three physical sexes: hermaphrodites, males, and females,[32] and at least three or more gender statuses: men (boys), women (girls), and *nadle*. There are three kinds of *nadles*: real *nadle* and *nadle* pretenders who may be genital men (males) and women (females). It is not clear whether the genital male and female *nadle* pretenders are regarded as *nadle* or yet another category. The *nadle* are assigned their position on the basis of ambiguous genitals. They assume occupational tasks and behaviors associated with women but they also have special rights not shared by other Navajo.[33] *nadle* sex partners may include women or men but not other *nadle* or *nadle* pretenders. Women may therefore select as sexual partners men, *nadle*, or *nadle* pretenders, and men may choose as partners women, *nadle*, or *nadle* pretenders. Homosexuality, defined as intercourse between partners of the same gender, is not permitted. This serves to illustrate problems of interpretation cross-culturally. If the *nadle* is a third gender status, then the term homosexual is meaningless and illustrates that Western concepts of sexual orientation and behavior are linked to the polarity of that gender schema. Such partnerships cannot be classified within our Western schema based on heterosexuality, homosexuality, or bisexuality. In fact, heterosexism decomposes in the face of this evidence. The permutations become even more interesting in the case of the *nadle* pretender who is recognized as a *nadle* but whose genitals are not hermaphroditic. The paradox in the *nadle* status is that while the hermaphroditic genitals define the position, they do not prevent those who are not hermaphrodites from acquiring the status – hermaphroditic genitals define but do not limit participation as a *nadle*.

While this is not an exhaustive review, Serena Nanda's study of the *Hijras* of India warrants mention. The *Hijra* are a recognized third gender composed ideally of hermaphroditic impotent men who undergo a ritualized surgical emasculation in which the genitals are removed.[34] However, the *Hijra*'s social identity may be similar to the *nadle* in that it also provides opportunities for "pretenders." As a variant third gender, the *Hijra* community

> ... attracts different kinds of persons, most of whom join voluntarily as teenagers or adults. It appears to be a magnet for persons with a wide range of cross-gender characteristics arising from either a psychological or organic condition. The *Hijra* role accommodates different personalities, sexual needs [including either sex with males or the ideal of an ascetic sexless life], and gender identities without completely losing its cultural meaning.[35]

Sagarin's reanalysis[36] of the Imperato-McGinley[37] 1974 report of eighteen pseudohermaphroditic males, known in the study site of Santo Domingo as *guevedoce*, provides additional insight into the question of gender identity, status, and role. The *guevedoce* has been discussed from the clinical perspective of Imperato-McGinley as an example of the primacy of hormonal factors over socialization factors in determining gender identity and psychosexual orientation. The *guevedoce*, due to a recessive gene expressed through inbreeding, were at birth genitally ambiguous. They were reared as girls until puberty when radical virilization occurred, their gender identity changed, their behavior became masculine, and they chose females as their sexual objects. Imperato-McGinley attributes this change to the impact of testosterone in utero and at puberty.

In contrast, Sagarin proposed an emic or "insider" interpretation of the pseudohermaphrodites' seemingly remarkable gender reversal. He noted they were not raised as girls but as members of a special indigenous category of children with female characteristics who will become males at puberty.[38] By understanding the *guevedoce* as a folk classification, Sagarin has offered a sociocultural explanation which challenged the Imperato-McGinley view that testosterone accounted for the reversal of gender identity, role behavior, and female sexual partner choice. Thus, according to Sagarin, the *guevedoce* was not someone who had a cross-sex identity problem that needed reversing, but rather was someone who was expected to become a male at twelve. Sagarin's early sociological critique was on the cutting edge of anthropological contributions to the study of gender as a cultural construction. While the discourse on third and alternative genders was not well developed until the 1990s, Sagarin offered a rudimentary critique that began to explore the subject of gender categorization. Subsequently, numerous other critiques have followed addressing flaws in the methodology and procedures of the Imperato-McGinley research.[39]

Studies by Herdt[40] and Herdt and Davidson[41] of five alpha-reductase deficiencies among the Sambia directly bear on the Imperato-McGinley[42] biocentric empire of hormonal determinism. Herdt and Davidson note the presence of a third gender category for which nine Sambian male pseudo-hermaphrodites were identified, known as *kwolu-aatmwol*, "male thing-transforming-into-female thing" or in Neo-Melanisan Pidgin "turnim-man" emphasizing turning into a man. They were raised with the stigmatized status of *kwolu-aatmwol* males: "persons more male-like than female-like, known to be hermaphroditic."[43] They are reared as male-like because they undergo some masculinization of the genitals at puberty. Interestingly, in a situation similar to Money and Ehrhardt's matched pairs of hermaphrodites,[44] an additional five were accidentally assigned as women, only to have their status reversed subsequently as adults. Apparently, these women only reluctantly changed to the ambiguous status, contradicting the Imperato-McGinley notion of hormone-induced gender identity change.[45]

2 Two-spirit Traditions

The classic anthropological literature on two-spirit traditions is biased heavily toward examples of presumed genetic/genital males. However, women also occupied these positions.[46] Whether female two-spirit forms are similar to male forms is unclear. It may be argued convincingly that, because gender statuses are structured differently for women and men globally, gender variant statuses for women may not be expected to be mirror images of men's gender variance.[47] Two-spirit persons have been defined as embodying the following characteristics: (1) a culturally recognized position as gender transformed and/or as an additional status that includes dressing partially or completely as the other gender; (2) adopting the behaviors and demeanors associated with the other gender or a unique combination of men's and women's behaviors (that is, a blended status);[48] and (3) in some cases choosing a partner of the same physiological sex although this is debated and seems culture specific.[49] The ethnographic record argues strongly that gender identity is prior to and/or independent of sexual behavior.

Two-spirit traditions reported on ethnographically offer a diversity of characteristics enmeshed within the structure of the gender system including: recognition of the status at an early age, status occupancy in adulthood, intermittent occupancy, and shaman complexes among other expressions. Two examples from an extensive literature are offered briefly for discussion.

Two-spirits may be identified at an early age. Among the Pima, if a boy gave indication of interest in female tasks he was put through a test. A bow and a basket were placed near him in a hut. The hut was set on fire, and if he grabbed for the basket in fear, then he was *wi-kovat*, a *Berdache* (two-spirit) of marginal status.[50] This form has direct bearing on the issue of gender ascription. In this case, genitalia are not the essential insignias of a gender. Gender is literally chosen by those who demonstrate potential career interest. For some societies gender dichotomous behaviors in terms of work tasks are the core features of gender.[51] In this regard, Harriet Whitehead has asserted that:

> Two dimensions of personal identity stood out as central to North American Indians' notions of gender. On the one hand, there was one's sexual anatomy and physiology, on the other, one's participation in the sexual division of labor and – somewhat less salient – one's public appearance (dress, demeanor) ... When not reinforced by the quint-essentially manly activities of hunting and warfare, and at the same time contradicted by stereotypical feminine tasks, the male identity that emerged was that of the "part-man, part-woman" the berdache [two-spirit personage][52]

The indigenous form of the Polynesian *mahu* was a gender variant status for males in old Polynesia that included "homosexual" practices. The position seems to be a combination of a life span tradition in which the *mahu* began cross-gendered tasks and dressing at a young age[53] with an option for intermittency – one need not remain *mahu* throughout one's life.[54] Levy[55] regards the Tahitian *mahu* as an example of a role variant for men's gender rather than as a third gender, although his discussion is suggestive of an alternative gender. For Levy the *mahu* is an embodiment and visible representation of gender dichotomies in a society with low gender disparity. The essence of the *mahu* position is that it functions to highlight gender differences so that men can see how to avoid non-manly behaviors. Besnier[56] shies away from regarding the *mahu* of Polynesia as a third gender and adopts the term gender liminality in reference to the *mahu*, conceptualizing the identity as an intermediate category.

According to Levy,[57] the *mahu* tradition has continued from precontact times, although attributes of the status have changed somewhat today so that while the *mahu* still performs work activities that are considered traditionally women's work, they no longer cross-dress in Tahiti. The *mahu* are regarded as being "natural" although one does not have to occupy *mahu* status throughout one's life. In addition, there is a conception of "femininity" associated with the *mahu*. One can also be "mahuish" without being a *mahu*.

The *mahu* are not stigmatized for their status or their homosexual behavior. In Tahiti, each village could have only one *mahu*. Apparently the *mahu* engaged in fellatio with non-cross-gendered male partners. The homosexual aspects of the *mahu* were not central to the social identity, but rather it was the cross-gendered aspects of dress and behaviors that were key signifiers of the status. This is suggested by several lines of evidence according to Besnier who concludes that "[in] 'traditional' Polynesian contexts, partaking in homosexual activities is neither a necessary nor a sufficient criterion for gender-liminal status . . . [consequently] sexual relations with men are seen as an optional consequence of gender liminality, rather than its determinant, prerequisite or primary attribute (as Charles Callender and Lee M. Kochems show, this pattern is cross-culturally widespread).[58] Levy[59] argues that "a mahu is seen as a substitute female."

Kirkpatrick's report[60] of Marquesan *mahus*, in contrast to his report about the Tahitian status, notes that it is an ambiguous or disvalued status. According to Kirkpatrick, homosexual behavior is not the salient attribute for the Marquesan gender variant, but rather occupation and peer relations (as in Tahiti). The Marquesan *mahu* are not considered women, but rather men who want to act as women.[61]

The case of the mahu is suggestive in terms of how indigenous systems of gender variant forms may be reinvigorated by Western types of gender variance associated with gay culture; for example, gay transvestite traditions of theatrical performance and sex work. Chanteau and Spiegel[62] conducted serological studies of risk for LAV/HTLV-III infection among Tahitian homosexual populations who frequented hotels, bars, restaurants, and night clubs. These studies included cross-dressing ("transvestite") homosexuals. They also noted that some of this population had had plastic surgery and female hormone therapy. This argues there are a number of possible gendered identities in such a population. It is impossible to assess from their reports the nature of these identities or how cross-dressing and homosexuality figure in the genderscape. Are these *mahu* expressions influenced by Western gay cross-dressing, or it a postmodern synthesis of both patterns, or yet some other genesis or blend of multiple identities?

Two-spirit traditions may also be intermittent, that is an individual may temporarily take on two-spirit status, thereby challenging our Western notion of gender as immutable. Such individuals may adopt and shed a given gender status several times throughout their lives.

Wikan[63] has provided a powerful example of an intermittent two-spirit tradition among the Omani. Her research examined the Omani *xanith*, a third gender option. The *xanith* does not cross-dress, but belts the man's tunic like women belt their garb. This gendered status includes an economic component in terms of occupational specialization and homosexual prostitution.

According to Wikan this third gender functions as an "inexpensive sexual outlet" to preserve women's purity as well as providing economic opportunity and upward mobility for men. The status can be shed and the *xanith* can resume his position as a man, including marriage and a family. The *xanith* carries no negative stigma upon repositioning as a man. Wikan estimates that one in fifty men choose this option. The implication is that the *xanith* is a safety-net gender for men who fall upon hard times economically. The role of being an insertee in penile intercourse is a salient feature. Among the Omani recipients of penile intercourse are either women or *xanith*.

The two-spirit traditions in all their many genders demonstrate that the Western dual gender classification system is just one of many, itself a cultural system of gender. The research in the field suggests that the two-spirit tradition may well be a third gender category separate from male and female; for the two-spirited tells us that man and woman, male and female are not the only universal categories for gender.

3 Cross-gendered roles

Cross-gender roles are distinguished from various gender transformed statuses. This is a subtle distinction that may be more evident through example than explanation. However, the categories themselves are problematic since their discreetness may be a by-product of the process of Western scientific categorization. It is very likely that this distinction is an artifact and that other liminal or alternative gender forms may not disengage into status and role; after all the social scientific literature often conflates the two.[64] This pilot model invites further scrutiny. For now it represents the dilemma of moving from modernist reports into postmodern interpretations. But, for the purposes of this inquiry, I will hypothetically argue that there may indeed exist a cross-gendered role that is not a transformed or alternative gender. The gender may be unchanged but the occupant's demeanor and behavior include attributes usually associated with the other gender (in situations where there are only two). Reports of this form are limited in the literature and are relegated to female variance. Two examples of female gender role variance are illustrative: the North Piegan *manly-hearts* and the Marquesan *mako* shark woman.

The North Piegan are a high sex role disparate culture in which men are aggressive while women are submissive. The manly-hearts are "macho" women characterized by ". . . aggression, independence, boldness and sexuality, all traits associated with men's role behaviors. But to be a manly-heart also requires that one be wealthy and married."[65] The manly-hearts gender is not transformed, although they "act like men."[66] While some consider the manly-heart a blended gender status,[67] it is perhaps more reasonable to regard it as an alternative role for women, in something like the vein of the Western tomboy. Unlike tomboyism, which is age-restricted, this may become a permanent role for the manly-hearts. Nor is it a stigmatized role, in contrast to Western culture when women adopt behaviors typically associated with males.

Among the Marquesan Islanders, Kirkpatrick[68] has described the *vehine mako* or shark woman. This gender category is unlike the *mahu* in that it is not based on relational or occupational criteria, but seems from my reading more akin to the manly-heart than the *mahu*. The shark woman is characterized by an aggressive and vigorous sexuality. The defining feature of the *vehine mako* woman is that she is the sexual (heterosexual) initiator, an activity relegated to the masculine/manly domain. This form of gender variance is ripe for further analysis. It would be interesting to consider whether there may be a pattern or formula to be found that will explain why in one situation gender variant behaviors (and which ones for that matter – dress, demeanor, or action) yield role variants while in other cultural contexts fully-fledged alternative third genders are formed.[69] Lang[70] argues that the Piegan manly-hearts inscribes the privileging of masculinity for both males and females, while women's pursuits were valued in females only.

4 Woman-Marriage and Boy-Marriage

Woman-marriage is a predominantly African institution where one woman marries another. There are a number of types of woman-marriage, but debates occur over the kinds of sexual practices associated with this form of marriage and/or whether a woman-husband is a transformed status. Blackwood[71] argues that lesbian behavior cannot be ruled out while others consider woman-marriage a non-sexual institution.[72] Evans-Pritchard's[73] study notes that woman-marriage occurs among the Nuer in situations where a female is barren. The barren woman will take a wife, hence becoming a cultural man, and also arrange for a progenitor for the wife so that "she" becomes a father. This functions as a kin recruitment strategy.[74]

Among the Nandi, women-husbands engage in male work tasks of cultivating and herding.[75] Blackwood[76] maintains that woman-marriage was not a cross-gender institution, although Oboler[77] reports that the woman-husband was considered a man. The meaning of what it is to be a woman-husband in this institution is not resolved, nor is it clear whether lesbian relations occurred within it. And indeed if the woman-husband is regarded as a man, then the term lesbian is ethnocentric. Blackwood proposes that woman-marriage presents a "model of relations between women within the gender system" rather than a cross-gender role.[78]

Evans-Pritchard's study of "Sexual Inversion among the Azande"[79] focuses on "homosexual" relations among young warriors and boys, reflecting the theoretical discourse of the times. Evans-Pritchard has documented a form of temporary marriage between bachelor youths and boys (aged anywhere from twelve to twenty years old) that occurred among the Azande of the Sudan. In this institution, youthful men were organized into bachelor military-work companies. "It was the custom for members ... to take boy wives."[80] Evans-Pritchard explained this institution in terms of three interlocking variables. Polygynous practices, including large harems kept by the wealthy, resulted in a scarcity of marriageable women among the Azande. This led to delayed marriage for less wealthy young men until their mid-twenties to thirties. And

> because girls were engaged (in a legal sense married) very young, often at birth, the only way youths could obtain satisfaction from a woman was in adultery. But that was a very dangerous solution to a young man's problem, for the fine his father would have to pay was heavy.... [I]t sometimes happened that the husband was so enraged that he refused compensation and chose instead to mutilate the offender, cutting off his ears, upper lip, genitals, and hands. So, the risk being too great, it was the custom for cautious bachelors in the military companies who were living at court, if they were not content to masturbate – a practice to which no shame is attached, though a young man would not do it in public – to marry boys and satisfy their sexual needs with them.[81]

The cultural solution was boy-marriage, which followed the pattern of heterosexual marriage. The boys were regarded as "women": "*Ade nga ami*," they would say, "we are women." A boy was addressed by his lover as *diare*, "my wife," and the boy addressed him as *kumbami*, "my husband." Kinship rules and terminology were followed for these marriages. While the boy might perform many tasks usually associated with a woman's roles as a wife, he did not perform every activity. Apparently there was not complete overlap between boy-wives and women-wives, although Evans-Pritchard is sketchy on this, noting for example that they did not cook porridge for their husbands and that they carried their husbands' shields on journeys (presumably women wives did not).

> With regard to the sexual side, at night the boy slept with his lover, who had intercourse with him between his thighs (Azande expressed disgust at the suggestion of anal penetration). The boys got what pleasure they could by friction of their organs on the husband's belly or groin. However, even though there was this side to the relationship, it was clear from Zande accounts that there was also the comfort of a nightly sharing of the bed with a companion.[82]

After reaching adulthood, the boy-wives would become warriors and take their own boy-wives, while their former husbands went on to marry women.

A reinterpretation suggests that it is the young boys' position as wives to bachelor warriors that may be central to the status rather than the homosexual relations *per se*. A postmodern and constructionist lens begs for comparison with the forms of woman marriage previously described. As a temporary status, was the boy-wife a transformed gender or an alternative gender? How might this complex be differentiated from ritualized Sambian homosexuality as described by Herdt?[83] How did it fit into the gender system? Clearly reanalysis of the ethnographic record offers a wealth of material for expanding our understanding of gender and institutionalized forms of gender variant marriage patterns.

5 Cross-gender Rituals

To attempt to surround cross-gender rituals definitionally is a difficult one since rituals are generally embedded with symbols of gender and gender opposition. However, for purposes of this discussion, the focus will be on rituals and gender crossing in which one gender adopts temporarily the role concomitants of the other gender (where there are two.) I shall make no attempt to survey this vast literature but rather focus on cross-gendered rituals in terms of Victor Turner's construct of liminality.

Perhaps one of the best known and earliest modern investigations by an anthropologist of cross-gendered rituals was Bateson's analysis of the sex ethos of the Iatmul. It is now a classic study of institutionalized cross-dressing (transvestism) during ceremonial occasions.[84] Bateson's hypothesis is that when a person of one gender finds her- or himself in a unique circumstance that demands behaviors of the other gender, s/he will adopt through dress "bits" of the other gender's culture.[85] He describes the transvestite riding habit of women as an example and then relates it to the Naven ceremonials in which both women and men cross-gender ritually. However, when women cross gender boundaries, they dress and act as proud warriors, while men embody old "hags" and generally present themselves as decrepit women in a parody.[86] Bateson's analysis ties these expressions to dichotomies in the sex ethos of each gender. New Guinea societies are characterized by inequality in the system of gender relations and it is this inequality that is symbolically expressed in the transvestite components of rituals.

Bateson's analysis dovetails with Victor Turner's analysis of ritual behavior as it relates to "liminality" and "communitas." Turner has described liminal phases of rituals in which an individual occupies a symbolic space "betwixt and between" the structures of society.[87] For Turner, the reversal of the ordinary and the culturally expected temporarily transforms the structures of society into antistructure.[88] In cross-gendered rituals, the profane elements of gender would be elevated to the sacred, allowing for the articulation of schisms and conflicts embedded in gender dichotomies and hierarchies to be manifested in communitas.[89] Rituals of the type Bateson described relate to communitas in that an event may allow participants to equalize and deconstruct gender relationships momentarily. Shared aspects of identity among the genders (that is to say, our common humanity), that are culturally denied by gender role expectation and hierarchy, may be conveyed in communitas through cross-gendered rituals. The Iatmul rituals transcended mundane gender divisions. As Young has noted, such rituals of reversal may "have served as an ideological resource" by presenting "a more egalitarian model of relations between the sexes [genders]."[90]

Liminal positions are symbolically dangerous as it is possible that transformation may be an outcome of experiencing antistructure. Perhaps the evolving non-surgical options and new gender hybridization in the transgendered community may be interpreted in this light. In this regard, Turner states:

> The liminal areas of time and space ... are open to the play of thought, feeling, and will; in them are generated new models, often fantastic, some of which may have sufficient power and plausibility to replace eventually the force-backed political and jural models that control the centers of a society's ongoing life.
>
> The antistructural liminality provided in the cores of ritual and aesthetic forms represents the reflexivity of the social process wherein society becomes at once subject and direct object; it represents also its subjunctive mood, where supposition, desires, hypotheses, possibilities, and so forth, all become legitimate.[91]

In conclusion, ritualized cross-gendered behavior is fertile ground for analysis. Definitions and identifications of types of cross-gendered behaviors in rituals are necessary preliminary prerequisites. It seems that this field is ready for comparative studies, including controlled comparisons and cross-cultural correlational studies of the HRAF variety. As one possible model, Zelman's study[92] of ritual and power is instructive. Zelman reported a correlation between female pollution-avoidance rituals, male rituals associated with the female reproductive cycle (the couvade), and gender equality and inequality. While the literature in which rituals are analyzed in terms of gender is vast, the theoretical development of cross-gendered ritual behavior as a form of gender variance remains to be developed, particularly in relationship to the other forms. Where are the consistencies and where are the cleavages among these pure forms?

THE WESTERN GENDER PARADIGM: IMPLICATIONS AND INFILTRATIONS

Gender variance has interested anthropologists from the early days of the discipline. Research on the subject was published as early as 1906 in the ethnological work of Edward Westermarck.[93] Scholars of anthropology have described and theorized these five forms of gender variance in diverse ways as discussed. Two-spirit and manly-heart (North Piegan) types of traditions have been investigated in terms of culturally instituted identities/statuses and roles.[94] Cross-cultural cases of hermaphroditism as socially recognized alternative categories of gender have been framed in terms of essentialism and cultural constructionism.[95] African woman-marriage has been discussed in relation to kinship[96] and debated as to the issue of lesbian activity.[97] Cross-gendered rituals have been investigated by two of anthropology's most notable theorists: Gregory Bateson[98] and Victor Turner[99] among others.[100]

The cross-cultural data on gender variance offer field cases in which gender identity as a social construction and representation is problematic. In addition, two-spirit careers offer evidence that gender identities may be acquired and shed, while the hermaphrodite data presently indicate that identities are not clearly or directly tied to a detectable biological baseline/ hormonal environment but are interpreted through the cultural lens. Such evidence intimates that further studies of this kind of phenomena are in order in the analytic genre that includes liminal positions as well – those that are not only at the bottom or outside but between the gender order as well.[101]

The phenomenon of gender variance has cross-culturally challenged scholars and scientists to reexamine our own scientific understandings that span the spectrum from the essentialistic to the constructionist. It includes the appropriation of behavior from a biocentric perspective as in some of the sociobiologically oriented work that assigns chromosomes, endocrinological functioning, and reproductive strategies as antecedents of gender dimorphic behavior and even cultural practices.[102]

The constructionist position in the study of gender has conflated sex and gender, while scholars of gender variance have segregated sex and gender, thereby challenging Euro-American heterosexism. Some researchers have re-entangled sex and gender but in complex synthetic paradigms that are historically and culturally contextualized. The studies of the *mahu*, *xanith*, and *hijra* include homosexual components but are social identities that are not derivative of sexual orientation/practice. The ethnographic record has indeed revealed a fluidity and flexibility in sexual behaviors and choice of sexual partners.

Modern Western genetic and endocrinological testing methods to identify an individual's sex are irrelevant for the emic or indigenous construction of gender variance. Paradoxically, the more scientific the methods to assess the biological sex of an individual, the less clear and the more cloudy the assessment actually becomes, as witnessed by the Olympic games discourses on evaluating the "true" sex of an athlete.[103] Nonetheless, Western gender variation is framed within a syndrome model that argues for a "basic biological mandate" for the expression of gender oppositions and has been extended to imply universals in gender "anomalies."[104]

The contemporary Euro-American folk gender paradigm, essentially a nature theory of gender, is reproduced in the scientific literature. Thus, not only is gender identity regarded as unfolding according to a biological map but variation in obviously cultural behaviors such as dress casts aspersions upon the "nature" of the individual's identity. Gender identity is regarded as something that comes to fruition, given a biological time clock, by approximately five years old and once acquired is not changed unless there has been a major biological input error. It is not regarded as a temporary way of expressing a gendered personhood as in the case of the Omani *xanith*. In short, gender is an ascribed, not an achieved characteristic in the Western gender schema.[105]

A deconstruction of the Western gender paradigm reveals that ". . . gender is a social construct that mediates another social construct of biology."[106] In fact, ". . . gender can become a metaphor for biology, just as biology can become a metaphor for gender."[107] Girl/woman and boy/man as genders are attributed on the basis of role presentations and read as femininity/ masculinity in daily encounters, and then retroactively reduced to a metatext of sex and genitalia. The metatext is the dominant and prevalent Western gender schema which takes as its "incorrigible propositions" the centrality of sex and biology as natural determinants of masculinity and femininity.[108] Masculinity and femininity are the embodiments of biological differences.[109]

From the meanings we assign to insignias that cover everything from adornments to muscles are transcribed gender and *de facto* sex. That capitalism and patriarchy narrowly circumscribe these into a gender schema is true. It is just as true that broad changes in the social, the economic, and the political have been textualized on the male and female body to create pluralism in the expressions of masculinity and femininity. These meanings, in turn, influence perceptions of gender, gender variance, and ideologies reactively, proactively, and recursively. Gender begins with the visible inspection of the genitalia when an assignment is made, unless there is an anomaly present such as hermaphroditism. The genitals, and in adulthood, other secondary characteristics are the icons of gender revealing the rules by which gender is culturally produced. These premises underlay the North American gender paradigm and are regarded by society as natural: that there are only two sexes, that these are inviolable and are determined by genitalia.[110]

Western society spawns its own forms of gender variance. Western transsexualism, for example, both reproduces and rebels against gender dualism and biocentrism. As a social identity, transsexualism posits the analytic independence of four gender markers that are embedded in the Western gender schema as "incorrigible propositions."[111] These are presented in a number of scientific discourses as well as among the public as "naturally" linked: sex, gender identity, gender role, or social identity (including behaviors and appearance), and, in some cases, sexual orientation. Herdt has referred to this as the "principle of dimorphism" . . . "an invention of modernism."[112]

A deconstruction of the transsexual social identity suggests that these primary categories of classification revolve around a binary and oppositional gender paradigm that is regarded as immutable. These oppositions reverberate with an ideological underpinning of patriarchal heterosexism.[113]

The power of a natural system and the meaning that it has for individuals as actors must be explored as a symbolic layer in the scientific paradigm for gender variation. How do actors construct their own variance *vis-á-vis* a powerful biological gender theory when their own experience, such as in the case of the male-to-female transsexual, may reproduce yet refute it? It is undeniable that transsexual surgery supports the essential genital-gender paradigm on one hand, yet contests its basis in terms of evolutionary reproduction (*à la* Darwin) and heterosexism.[114]

People who identify themselves as preoperative, post-operative, and nonsurgical male-to-female transsexuals as well as male cross-dressers collectively form a transgender community which is in the process of creating not just a third gender, but the possibility of numerous genders and multiple social identities. As such they impugn the dominant American gender paradigm with its emphasis on reproduction and the biological sexual body as the *raison d'être* of gender identity and role. Without a naturist system that regards biology generally and genitals specifically as the *sine qua non* of gender, it may be questioned whether the phenomenon we label transsexualism would exist at all.

TRANSGENDERED COMMUNITY[115]

Elsewhere, I have described the emergence of the transgendered community.[116] It is argued here that the theoretical development of cultural constructionist approaches to the study of gender variance cross-culturally has been (along with other factors) one impetus for the transgendered community to encompass diversity. Before proceeding, a caution issued by anthropologist Jason Cromwell is in order:

> Unlike many male transgendered people (male transvestites or cross dressers and male-to-female transsexuals), very few female-to-male transsexuals identify with the concept of Native American berdache [two-spirits]. Nor do they identify with its linguistic cousins: female berdache [two-spirit], amazons, cross-gender females, manlike women, female "man-woman," or dykes .... Furthermore ... such terminology is inappropriate and, as such berdache [two-spirits] does not have any symbolic meaning or significant relevance for contemporary US female gender variant individuals.[117]

Transgendered and non-surgical options for social identities were not available sixteen years ago when I first studied North American male-to-female transsexualism in the Berdache Society.[118] At that time, among the population I worked with, there were only two social identities options available: surgically oriented male-to-female transsexuals and male transvestites who were not self-identified as gay.[119]

Male-to-female transsexuals defined themselves by a bottom-line criterion of desire for hormonal reassignment and surgery.... If one was not absolutely committed to having the surgery, then one was *de facto* a transvestite. Transvestites were delineated as heterosexual men (men attracted to women) who had the urge to cross-dress but were not "really" women. If these individuals had a feminine identity, the reasoning went, they would be pursuing surgery – with no apologies.[120]

In 1992, I initiated a study of social identity with transgendered individuals and found that the polarization of male-to-female transsexuals and male transvestites had been challenged from within and replaced by a concept of continuity and multiplicity of social identities.[121]

Through recent research, it has become apparent that there has been a movement in which people of various gender-transposed identities have come to organize themselves as part of a greater community, a larger in-group, facing similar concerns of stigmatization, acceptance, treatment and so on. This recognition of similarity fostered by growing political awareness of gender organizations has facilitated the burgeoning of new gender options, such as the "transgenderist." Transgenderist is a community term denoting kinship among those with gender-variant identities. It supplants the dichotomy of transsexual and transvestite with a concept of continuity ... This sense of collective interests is important for understanding cultural-historical change in gender identities and in clarifying the relationship of individual experience to the social construction of gender variance.[122]

Holly Boswell, in an article ("The Transgender Alternative") that is rapidly becoming a political classic in the transgendered community, defines transgenderism as a "middle ground," "a viable option between cross-dresser and transsexual person, which also happens to have a firm foundation in the ancient tradition of androgyny."[123] According to Dallas Denny, transgenderists may be:

described as persons who change gender roles, but do not plan to have reassignment surgery. They have alternatively been defined as persons who steer a middle course, living with the physical traits of both genders. Transgenderists may alter their anatomy with hormones or surgery, but they may purposefully retain many of the characteristics of the gender to which they were originally assigned. Many lead part-time lives in both genders; most cultivate an androgynous appearance.[124]

and Denny continues elsewhere:

Even many of those who have chosen to alter their bodies with hormones and surgery, like myself, maintain a proud transgender identity rather than attempting to assimilate into the mainstream culture. In fact, we have a term for those who do so – "wood-workers."[125]

While there are other sociocultural influences giving impetus to the cultivation of transgenderism, the grass-roots organizational adoption of a political agenda is an important one.[126]

The dominant Euro-American gender system of biological reductionism does much to shape the construction of social and hence personal identities. Consequently, in my early research gender identities across a broad spectrum were shuffled into two categories: male-to-female transsexual and male transvestite. A cultural awakening to gender pluralism among transgendered people has challenged the dominant paradigm that a social woman is a genital one. This pantheon of personal identities was the raw material for the infusion of a political agenda for gender diversity and cross-cultural studies provided the fuel. For the purposes of this analysis, the issue of whether the examples of gender variant traditions can be framed in Western terms such as homosexuality or transsexualism (which I doubt) is not relevant. What is important is the use made of this knowledge by the diverse constituencies in the transgender community.[127]

Although I am not arguing that schism and divisions do not persist, the national organizations have made significant progress in creating unity within diversity. In this regard, one post-operative male-to-female transsexual reports:

I think that over the past few years one of the biggest changes I have seen in the transgender community is you no longer have to fit in a box. You do not have to be TS or TV. It is ok to be transgendered. You can now lie anywhere on the spectrum from non-gendered to full trans-sexual. You do not have to have SRS [sex reassignment surgery] just because you are transgendered.

The organizational gatekeepers of the gender community, which include at least five very prominent national organizations with large memberships along with other smaller national, local and regional groups, have embraced the ethnographic record, anthropology's relativism and theoretical cultural constructionism.[128] This is evidenced in a number of ways as reference to the "berdache" and two-spirited persons is incorporated into the transgendered self-discourse. In a recent letter to the editor of *SOLGAN* (The Society of Lesbian and Gay Anthropologists Newsletter), Dallas Denny, Executive Director of the American Educational Gender Information Service, Inc., states:

Being transgendered myself, I was especially pleased to learn that the AAA [American Anthropological Association] Commission on Lesbian and Gay Issues in Anthropology has included language about transgendered anthropologists in its mission statement. Contrary to stereotypes perpetuated by the media . . ., many transgendered persons indeed identify as "two spirited" and rebel against binary gender roles.[129]

At regional and national gender community conferences I have attended over the years, symposia including historical and cross-cultural aspects of cross-dressing are a mainstay. Anthropologists are invited experts to address the subject, although community members themselves are well read on the anthropological literature and some are speakers and writers of the subject themselves. Over the past three years I have presented papers annually on cross-cultural gender variance at one of the national conferences. On a personal note, my sense of the audience is that I feel as if I were interacting with anthropologists who were specialists on gender variance. The transgendered audience is familiar with the writings of Nanda, Roscoe, Herdt, Cromwell, Williams, and others.

Two themes related to ethnography and gender dominate the concerns of the audience and program planners: societies in which two-spirit/ hermaphrodite and gender role variance are positively regarded; and the topic of the cultural explanations of third and/or alternative genders. These themes are an important discourse to the transgender community, as is demonstrated among the publications and educational/community support documents available through organizations. Several examples from my research at the annual meetings are illustrative.

Holly Boswell has written an article entitled "Reviving the Tradition of Alternative Genders" in which she states:

> While contemporary societies still seem determined to polarize gender along strictly anatomical lines, the vast majority of cultures throughout history and around the globe understood that anatomical sex does not dictate gender identification any more than it does sexual orientation . . . Ancient Goddess religions and other natural spiritual world views respected men and women as equals, regarded Nature as divine, [and] revered diversity . . .
>
> Since the replacement of Mother Nature with God the Father (about 5,000 years ago), the constructs of gender have been defined more narrowly and rigidly to suit the purposes of those in control of each particular society . . . .[130]

Another document, entitled "Historical Facts of Interest to the Gender Community," written by Wendy Parker,[131] contains two full pages of citations representing:

1 Societies, events and individuals where crossdressing was accepted and tolerated, for example:

30,000 BC – Siberian tribes cross over ice "link" to N. America bringing third gender "berdache" traditions from Asia. Existence of berdaches has been documented in at least one hundred and thirty North American tribes. 1702 – Royal Governor of Colonial New York, the Viscount, lives openly as a woman conducting much government business crossdressed . . .

2 Events and explanations of why crossdressing was discriminated against. 1200's – The beginning of church/state campaign against gender and sexual variations begin during Medieval period of Crusades. Brought in from Persia, sexual relations with young feminized boys was considered an accepted Islamic practice and therefore considered "heresy" as it was a "pagan" ritual.

3 Information concerning important transgendered figures in the history of crossdressing, including the "invention" of various clinical terminologies. 1930 – Very first experimental "sex change" surgery in Germany. First known post op TS Hans Eighner becomes "Lillie Elbe." 1960's Harry Benjamin . . . first popularizes the term "transsexual." . . .

4 And important events in the organization of crossdressing.
1960 – First issue of *Transvestia* published by Virginia Prince.
1975 – Ariadne Kane founds the Outreach Institute and begins the first Fantasia Fair. This major crossdressers' convention has been given yearly uninterrupted to today.

The historical and anthropological record is integrated into a developing gender system by the transgendered community. Anthropological studies of gender variance are valued by the transgendered community as a vehicle for identity enhancement and destigmatization for individuals and the community at large. As a consequence of identifying culture as an important component in the construction of gender ideologies, identities and status, the common enemy of transgenderism has emerged as society and its institutions. Demonstrating time and spatial dimensions allows individuals, regardless of their self-identity, to employ this information as . . . a "neutralization technique" or disclaimer. Because relativism is a ". . . reflection on the process of interpretation itself,"[132] it becomes for transgendered people an avenue for recreating and reinventing themselves.[133] The common adversary of societal oppression has fostered a recognition of unity and community within diversity as a form of cultural creativity.

The transgendered identity is not a docile one in Foucauldian terms.[134] Non-surgical solutions, gender mixing, and hybridization, client desires for hormones without surgery and the like, challenge medical orthodoxy and treatment agendas prescribed for transsexuals and transvestites. The new transgendered option creates rebellious bodies – hybrid and hermaphroditic ones that create disarray and threaten to overthrow the "biopower" of the medical profession who have the capability of "controlling the very sex of the human body."[135] It can be argued that the "knowledge" of cross-cultural

gender variance is constitutive of the empowerment of an evolving transgenderism and the birth of new identities.

There is a serendipity between the transgendered community and the gay
community in relationship to two-spirit traditions. According to Midnight
Sun "cross-cultural material is often used to support claims about contemporary western homosexuality."[136] In *Living the Spirit: A Gay American
Indian Anthology*,[137] gay Native Americans claim their antecedents in two-
spirit traditions of transgendered people. By being "other" and seeking roots
with "otherness," transgendered people and gay men and women can
transform their status collectively. Evidence of variant traditions cross-
culturally is a vehicle through which the transgender community and the
lesbian and gay community(ies) have become active participants in reshaping
their identities.[138] This may result in inter-community solidarity among
transgendered, gay and lesbian peoples; or conversely knowledge of alternative genders may also lead to the birth of new gender forms and the
consolidation and revision of existing social identities crossing both groups.
For example, transgendered empowerment has followed from the active
process of self-definition and in locating their own history and traditions. In
this light, Denny writes:

> The current interest in alternate genders and alternate sexes is en-
> couraging, but I would caution gay and lesbian anthropologists to be
> careful not to appropriate transgender history.... There is an un-
> fortunate tendency for transgender lives to be rewritten as gay and
> lesbian lives, when it is convenient to do so. Transgendered persons are
> not a subset of the gay community, although the obverse may be true:
> gay men and lesbians, after all, transgress gender roles by their selection
> of same sex partners.[139]

As anthropology turns to issues of multiculturalism both globally and in
North America, new understandings of "ethnic diversity as a source of
strength and resilience, rather than as a maladaptive process ..." are being
addressed.[140] This is a complex process of revision, or to use Roscoe's
concept "cultur-ing."[141] The transgender community is crafting new forms
of identities and seeing new relationships in social forms as identities. As
one transgendered consultant explained to me, "We have pride in ourselves
and in our own history. We are the first generation who can assimilate or
choose not to."

CONCLUSION

Although the "male-to-female transsexual identity" as a socially recognized
phenomenon is recent, a trend toward blurring of the extant variant gender
identities for genital males such as transsexual, non-surgical transsexual,
transvestite, and cross-dressers has gained momentum over the last decade.

The components of the Western gender schema including biological attributes, gender identity, role concomitants, and gender of erotic interest are rearranged and recombined in new ways by those in the gender divergent community. This reshuffling both reflects and infiltrates the Western gender paradigm as gender change is felt in wider society and experienced personally and through cultural symbols.

NOTES

1 Sue-Ellen Jacobs, "Native American Two-Spirits," in *Anthropology Newsletter*, vol. 35, No. 8 (November, 1994), p. 7.
2 Sue-Ellen Jacobs states in "Native American Two-Spirits:"

> The term *"berdache"* [*sic*] as used by anthropologists is outdated, anachronistic and does not reflect contemporary Native American conversations about gender diversity and sexualities. To use this term is to participate in and perpetuate colonial discourse, labeling Native American people by a term that has its origins in Western thought and languages.
> The preferred term of Native Americans who are involved in refining understanding about gender diversity and sexualities among Native American peoples is "two spirit" . . . or terms specific to tribes.

I have adopted this usage where it seems appropriate to refer to gender transformed/alternative genders throughout the nonwestern ethnographic record.
3 Mildred Dickemann, "Wilson's Panchreston: The Inclusive Fitness Hypothesis of Sociobiology Re-Examined," in *Journal of Homosexuality*, vol. 28, No. 2 (1995), pp. 147–83.
4 Gilbert Herdt, "Cross-Cultural Forms of Homosexuality and the Concept Gay," in *Psychiatric Annals*, vol. 18, No. 1 (Spring, 1988), pp. 37–9.
5 Herdt, "Cross-Cultural," pp. 37–9.
6 This research will bring in evidence of gender variance that includes a wider scope than that generally undertaken in studies in efforts to move beyond the limits set by our own Western constructs, and to challenge scholars to reassess the applicability of the concepts "status" and "role" cross-culturally.
7 Anthropology's new reflexive mood includes a view that regards people among whom we research as collaborators, rather than informants or subjects. Some samples of this approach can be found in the following examples: George E. Marcus and Michael M. J. Fischer, *Anthropology as Cultural Critique: An Experimental Moment in the Human Sciences*, Chicago: University of Chicago Press, 1986; Anne Bolin, "Transcending and Transgendering: Male-to-Female Transsexuals, Dichotomy and Diversity," in Gilbert Herdt (ed.), *Third Sex, Third Gender: Beyond Sexual Dimorphism in Culture and History*, New York: Zone Books, 1994, pp. 447–85, 589–96.
8 Bolin, "Transcending and Transgendering," pp. 447–8, 589–96.
9 Nancy Bonvillain, *Women and Men: Cultural Constructs of Gender*, Englewood Cliffs, New Jersey: Prentice-Hall, 1995; Judith Lorber, *Paradoxes of Gender*, New Haven, Conn.: Yale University Press, 1994; Sherry B. Ortner and Harriet Whitehead (eds), *Sexual Meanings: The Cultural Construction of Gender and Sexuality*, New York: Cambridge University Press, 1981.
10 Mary Douglas, *Purity and Danger: An Analysis of the Concepts of Pollution and Taboo*, London: Routledge, 1966, p. 100; Erving Goffman, *Stigma: Notes on the*

Management of a Spoiled Identity, Englewood Cliffs, New Jersey: Prentice-Hall, 1963; Erving Goffman, *Interaction Ritual*, Garden City, New York: Doubleday, 1967.

11 See Gilbert Herdt, 'The Sambia 'Turnim-Man:' Sociocultural and Clinical Aspects of Gender Formation in Male Psuedohermaphrodites and 5-Alpha-Reductase Deficiency in Papua, New Guinea," in *Archives of Sexual Behavior*, vol. 17, No. 1 (February, 1988), pp. 37–9; cf. R. W. Connell, "The Big Picture: Masculinities in Recent World History," in *Theory and Society*, vol. 22, No. 5 (October, 1993), p. 602.

12 E.g. Suzanne J. Kessler and Wendy McKenna, *Gender: An Ethnomethodological Approach*, New York: John Wiley, 1978; Holly Devor, *Gender Blending: Confronting the Limits of Duality*, Bloomington, Indiana: Indiana University Press, 1989.

13 My research has been limited to self-identified male-to-female transsexual, cross-dressing/transvestite and transgendered people. People who were assigned as females and girls at birth but who identify as "f-to-m" (argot) or transgendered are also part of the newly emergent transgendered community. There is very little research with this population with the exception of anthropologist Jason Cromwell's ethnographic work. Vern L. and Bonnie Bullough, in *Cross Dressing, Sex and Gender*, Philadelphia: University of Pennsylvania Press, 1993, pp. 94–112, argue that cross-dressing among women has great historical significance while cross-dressing among men is a recent phenomenon. Although I refer to collectivities of such groups as male-to-female transsexuals, male transvestites, and transgenderists as a literary convenience, I am by no means suggesting scientific representativeness. My findings were based on a limited population using a convenience sampling technique and ethnographic methods.

14 Eugene N. Cohen and Edwin Eames, *Cultural Anthropology*, Boston, Massachusetts: Little, Brown and Company, 1982, pp. 418–9.

15 Robert J. Stoller, *Presentations of Gender*, New Haven, Conn.: Yale University Press, 1985, p. 6. See also, Kessler and McKenna, *Gender*, p. 7.

16 Harold Garfinkel, *Studies in Ethnomethodology*, Englewood Cliffs, New Jersey: Prentice-Hall, 1967, p. 77; Harold Garfinkel and Robert J. Stoller, "Passing and the Managed Achievement of Sex Status in an 'Intersexed' Person," Harold Garfinkel (ed.), *Studies in Ethnomethodology*, Englewood Cliffs, New Jersey: Prentice-Hall, 1967, pp. 116–85; Kessler and McKenna, *Gender*, 1–20; S. Jacobs and C. Roberts, "Sex, Sexuality, Gender and Gender Variance"; Sandra Morgan (ed.), *Gender and Anthropology*, Washington, D.C.: American Anthropological Association, 1989, pp. 438–62.

17 Richard A. Shweder, *Culture Theory: Essays on Mind, Self, and Emotion*, Cambridge: Cambridge University Press, 1984, p. 3.

18 J. Money and A. A. Ehrhardt, *Man & Woman, Boy & Girl: The Differentiation and Dimorphism of Gender Identity from Conception to Maturity*, Baltimore, Ohio: The John Hopkins University Press, 1972, p. 284.

19 Cf. M. Kay Martin and Barbara Voorhies, *Female of the Species*, New York: Columbia University Press, 1975, pp. 84–107.

20 Cf. Anne Bolin, *In Search of Eve: Transsexual Rites of Passage*, South Hadley, Mass: Bergin and Garvey, 1988; Anne Bolin, "Vandalized Vanity: Feminine Physiques Betrayed and Portrayed", in Francis Mascia-Lees and Patricia Sharpe (eds), *Tattoo, Torture, Adornment, and Disfigurement: The Dennaturalization of the Body in Culture and Text*, Albany, New York: SUNY Press, 1992, pp. 79–99; Devor, *Gender Blending*.

21 Victor Turner, "Betwixt and Between: The Liminal Period in Rites de Passage,"

in Victor Turner (ed.), *The Forest of Symbols: Aspects of the Ndembu Ritual*, Ithaca, New York: Cornell University Press, 1967, pp. 93–110; Victor Turner, *Dramas, Fields and Metaphors: Symbolic Action in Human Society*, Ithaca, New York: Cornell University Press, 1974; Mary Douglas, *Purity and Danger: An Analysis of Concepts of Pollution and Taboo*, New York: Frederick A. Praeger, 1966; Mary Douglas, *Natural Symbols: Explorations in Cosmology*, New York: Pantheon Books, 1973; Clifford Geertz, "Deep Play: Notes on the Balinese Cockfight," Clifford Geertz (ed.), *Myth, Symbol, and Culture*, New York: Norton, 1971, pp. 1–33; Clifford Geertz, "The Uses of Diversity," in S. McMurrin (ed.), *The Tanner Lectures on Human Values*, Cambridge: Cambridge University Press, 1986, pp. 253–75.

22 Jeffrey Weeks, *Sex, Politics and Society: The Regulation of Sexuality Since 1800*, New York: Longman, 1981; Catherine Gallagher and Thomas Laqueur, *The Making of the Modern Body: Sexuality and Society in the Nineteenth Century*, Berkeley, California: University of California Press, 1987; Janice M. Irvine, *Disorders of Desire: Sex and Gender in Modern American Sexology*, Philadelphia, Penn.: Temple University Press, 1990.

23 Susan R. Bordo, "The Body and the Reproduction of Femininity: A Feminist Appropriation of Foucault," in Alison M. Jaggar and Susan R. Bordo (eds), *Gender/Body/Knowledge/Feminist Reconstructions of Being and Knowing*, New Brunswick, New Jersey: Rutgers University Press, 1989; Susan R. Bordo, "Reading the Slender Body," in *Body/Politics: Women and the Discourses of Science*, New York: Routledge, 1990, pp. 83–112; Marcus and Fischer, *Anthropology as*; Michel Foucault, *The Use of Pleasure*, New York: Vintage Books, 1985; Michel Foucault, "Technologies of the Self," in Luther B. Martin *et al.* (eds), *Technologies of the Self: A Seminar with Michel Foucault*, Amherst, Massachusetts: University of Massachusetts Press, 1988.

24 Gilbert Herdt, *The Sambia: Ritual and Gender in New Guinea*, New York: Holt, Rinehart and Winston, 1987; Herdt, "The Sambia "Turnim-Man";" Gilbert Herdt (ed.), *Homosexuality and Adolescence*, New York: Haworth Press, 1989.

25 Serena Nanda, *Neither Man nor Woman: The Hijras of India*, Belmont, California: Wadsworth Publishing Co., 1990; Serena Nanda, "The Hijras of India: Cultural and Individual Dimensions of a Institutionalized Third Gender Role," in *Journal of Homosexuality*, vol. 11, No. 3–4 (1985).

26 Money and Ehrhardt, *Man and Woman*, p. 290.

27 Money and Ehrhard, *Man and Woman*, p. 285.

28 W. W. Hill, "Note on the Pima Berdache," in *American Anthropologist*, vol. 40, No. 2 (April–June, 1938) pp. 338–40.

29 Robert B. Edgerton, "Pokot Intersexuality: An East African Example of the Resolution of Sexual Incongruity," in *American Anthropologist*, vol. 66, No. 6, Pt. I (December, 1964), pp.1288–99.

30 Edgerton, "Pokot Intersexuality," p. 1295.

31 Edgerton, "Pokot Intersexuality," pp. 1288–99; also Kessler and McKenna, *Gender*, p. 23; and Martin and Voorhies, *Female*, p. 89.

32 W. W. Hill, "The Status of the Hermaphrodite and Transvestite in Navajo Culture," in *American Anthropologist*, vol. 37 (April, 1935), pp. 273–9; W. W. Hill, "Note;" and Martin and Voorhies, *Female*, pp. 89–93.

33 Martin and Voorhies, *Female*, p. 92.

34 Nanda, *Neither Man nor Woman*, pp. 35–55.

35 Nanda, "The Hijras of India," p. 42.

36 Edward Sagarin, "Sex Rearing and Sexual Orientation: The Reconciliation of Apparently Contradictory Data," in *Journal of Sex Research*, vol. 11, No. 4 (November, 1975), pp. 329, 34.

37 J. Imperato-McGinley, L. Guerrero, T. Gautier, and R. E. Peterson, "Steroid 5a-Reductase Deficiency in Man: An Inherited Form of Male Hermaphroditism," in *Science*, No. 186 (1974), pp. 1213–15.

38 Sagarin, "Sex Rearing," p. 331.

39 John Money, "Gender Identity and Hermaphroditism," in *Science*, No. 191 (1976), p. 872; Hein Meyer-Bahlburg, "Hormones and Psychosexual Differentiation: Implications for the Management of Intersexuality, Homosexuality, and Transsexuality," in *Clinics in Endocrinology and Metabolism*, 11 (1982); and Gilbert Herdt, "Gay Culture in America: Essays from the Field", Boston, Massachusetts: Beacon Press, 1992, pp. 433–46, for a thorough review of the Dominican Republic Syndrome.

40 Gilbert Herdt, "Mistaken Gender: 5-Alpha Reductase Hermaphroditism and Biological Reductionism in Sexual Identity Reconsidered," in *American Anthropologist*, No. 92 (1990), pp. 433–46.

41 Gilbert Herdt and Julian Davidson, "The Sambia 'Turnim Man:' Sociocultural and Clinical Aspects of Gender Formation in Male Pseudohermaphrodites with 5-Alpha-Reductase Deficiency in Papua, New Guinea," in *Archives of Sexual Behavior*, vol. 17, No. 1 (February, 1988), pp. 33–56.

42 Imperato-McGinley, "Steroid 5a-Reductase;" J. Imperato-McGinley, L. Guerrero; T. Gautier, and R. E. Peterson, "Androgens and the Evolution of Male-Gender Identity Among Male Pseudohermaphrodites with 5 Alpha-Reductase Deficiency," in *New England Journal of Medicine*, 300 (1979), pp. 1233–7; J. Imperato-McGinley, R. E. Peterson, M. Leshin, J. E. Griffin, G. Looper, S. Draghi, M. Berenyi, and J. E. Wilson, "Steroid 5 Alpha-reductase Deficiency in a 65-Year-Old Male Pseudohermaphrodite: The Natural History Ultrastructure of the Tests and Evidence for Inherited Enzyme Heterogeneity," in *Journal of Clinical Endocrinology Metabolism*, vol. 54 (1980), pp. 15–22; J. Imperato-McGinley, R. E. Peterson, T. Gautier, G. Looper, R. Danner, A. Arthur, P. L. Morris, W. J. Sweeney, and C. Shackleton, "Hormonal Evaluation of a Large Kindred with Complete Androgen Insensitivity: Evidence for Secondary 5 Alpha-Reductase Deficiency," in *Journal of Clinical Endocrinology Metabolism*, vol. 54 (1982) pp. 931–41.

43 Herdt and Davidson, "The Sambia 'Turnim Man:' Sociocultural," p. 41.

44 Money and Ehrhardt, *Man and Woman*, pp. 150–62.

45 Imperato-McGinley, "Steroid 5a-Reductase;" Imperato-McGinley, "Androgens and the Evolution;" Imperato-McGinley, "Steroid 5 Alpha-reductase Deficiency;" Imperato-McGinley, "Hormonal Evaluation."

46 Evelyn Blackwood, "Lesbian Behavior in Cross-Cultural Perspective," M.S. Thesis, San Francisco State University, 1984; and Evelyn Blackwood, "Sexuality and Gender in Certain Native American Tribes: The Case of Cross-Gender Females," in *Signs*, vol. 10, No. 1 (Autumn, 1984), pp. 27–42.

47 Evelyn Blackwood, "Breaking the Mirror: The Construction of Lesbianism and the Anthropological Discourse on Homosexuality," in *Journal of Homosexuality*, vol. 11, Nos. 3–4 (1985), p. 6.

    For reports of the female two-spirit tradition see Blackwood's "Sexuality and Gender;" Blackwood's "Lesbian Behavior;" and Walter L. Williams's *The Spirit and the Flesh: Sexual Diversity in American Indian Culture*, Boston, Massachusetts: Beacon Press, 1986, pp. 233–51. My discussion is limited to male two-spirit traditions for several reasons: space considerations, my background is in the area of male traditions, and the literature is dominated by reports of male forms. In addition, it is questionable whether female two-spirit traditions are the mirror image of the male (see Blackwood, "Breaking the Mirror"). I have included examples on women's gender variation under the other forms.

Another example, Omer Stewart recorded its occurrence for Alfred L. Kroeber's *Cultural Element Distributions*, University of California: Anthropological Records, 1937–1943, vol. 1–81. G. Devereaux cited in "Institutionalized Homosexuality of the Mohave Indians," in *Human Biology*, vol. 9, No. 4 (1937), pp. 498, 527, reported the case of the *alyha* among the Mohave Indians as a *Berdache* (two-spirit) role. E. Adamson Hoebel also noted in his work, *Man in the Primitive World*, New York: McGraw Hill, 1949, pp. 458, 45–9, that two-spirit institutions were present among Plains Indians groups, as did Robert Harry Lowie in *The Crow Indians*, New York: Farrar and Rinehart, 1935, p. 48. E. E. Evans-Pritchard observed gender variance among the Azande in "Sexual Inversion Among the Azande," in *American Anthropologist*, vol. 72, No. 6 (December, 1970), pp. 1428, 34; Hill among the Navajo in "The Status," pp. 273, 279, and Pima in "Note on the," pp. 338, 340). W. Bogoras described the "softman" of the Chukchee in *The Chuckchee Religion, Memoirs of the American Museum of Natural History*, Leiden: E. S. Brill, 1907, pp. 11,449. See also Anne Bolin, "Transsexualism and the Limits of Traditional Gender Analysis," in *American Behavioral Scientist*, vol. 31, No. 1 (September–October, 1987), pp. 41–65; Will Roscoe, "Bibliography of *Berdache* and Alternative Gender Roles Among North American Indians," in *Journal of Homosexuality*, vol. 14, Nos. 3–4 (1987); Will Roscoe, *The Zuni Man-Woman*, Albuquerque, New Mexico: University of New Mexico Press, 1991, among others.

48 Sue-Ellen Jacobs and Jason Cromwell, "Visions and Revisions of Reality: Reflections on Sex, Sexuality, Gender, and Gender Variance," in *Journal of Homosexuality*, vol. 23, No. 4 (1992), pp. 43–69; Charles Callender and Lee Kochems, "The North American Berdache," in *Current Anthropology*, vol. 24 (August/October, 1983), p. 53; Harriet Whitehead, "The Bow and the Burden Strap: A New Look at Institutionalized Homosexuality in Native North America," in S. B. Ortner and Harriet Whitehead (eds), *Sexual Meanings: The Cultural Construction of Gender and Sexuality*, Cambridge: Cambridge University Press, 1981, pp. 80–115.

49 Williams' *The Spirit and the Flesh*, pp. 273–4; Wainwrig Churchill, *Homosexual Behavior Among Males: A Cross-Cultural and Cross-Species Investigation*, Englewood Cliffs, New Jersey: Prentice-Hall, 1971, p. 81; R. D'Andrade, "Sex References in Cultural Institutions," in L. Hudson (ed.), *The Ecology of Human Intelligence*, Harmondsworth: Penguin, 1970, p. 34; Clellan Stearns Ford and Frank A. Beach, *Patterns of Sexual Behavior*, New York: Harper and Row, 1951, p. 130; Herdt, "The Sambia 'Turnim-Man,'" p. 38.

50 Martin and Voorhies, *Female*, p. 96.

51 Kessler and McKenna, *Gender*, p. 29.

52 Whitehead, "The Bow and the Burden Strap," p. 93.

53 Edwin N. Ferdon, *Early Tahiti: As the Explorers Saw It 1767–1797*, Tucson, Arizona: University of Arizona, 1981; Niko Besnier, "Polynesian Gender Liminality through Time and Space," in Herdt (ed.), *Third Sex Third Gender*, [note 7], p. 300.

54 Robert Levy, "The Community Function of Tahitian Male Transvestism: A Hypothesis," in *Anthropological Quarterly*, vol. 44, (1975), pp. 12–21; Robert Levy, *Tahitians: Mind and Experience in the Society Islands*, Chicago, Illinois: University of Chicago Press, 1973.

55 Levy, "The Community Function."

56 Besnier, "Polynesian Gender," p. 286.

57 Levy, "The Community Function;" and Levy, *Tahitians*.

58 Callender and Kochems, *North American*; Charles Callender and Lee M. Kochems, "Men and Not-Men: Male Gender-Mixing Statuses and Homosexuality," *Journal of Homosexuality*, vol. 11, Nos. 3/4 (1985).

59 Levy, *Tahitians*, p. 34.
60 John Kirkpatrick, *The Marquesan Notion of the Person*, Ann Arbor, Michigan: UMI – University of Michigan Research Press, 1983.
61 For discussion of the *mahu*, see Kirkpatrick's *The Marquesan*; Levy, "The Community Function;" Levy, *Tahitians*; Douglas L. Oliver, *Ancient Tahitian Society*, Honolulu, Hawaii: University of Hawaii Press, 1974; and Anne Bolin, "The Polynesian Islands: French Polynesia," in Robert T. Francoeur (ed.), *The International Encyclopedia of Sexuality*, New York: Continuum Press, 1995; Besnier, "Polynesian Gender."
62 S. Chanteau, *et al.*, "A Serological Survey of AIDS in a High Risk Population in French Polynesia," *The Medical Journal of Australia*, vol. 145, No. 2 (1986), and A. Spiegel *et al.*, "HTLV-I in French Polynesia: A Serological Survey in Sexually Exposed Groups," in *The Medical Journal of Australia*, vol. 155, No. 11 (1991).
63 Unni Wikan, "Man Becomes Woman: Transsexualism in Oman as a Key to Gender Roles," in *Man*, new series, vol. 12, No. 2 (August, 1977), pp. 304–19.
64 See also Judith Shapiro, "Cross-Cultural Perspectives on Sexual Differentiation," in Herant Katchadourian (ed.), *Human Sexuality: A Comparative and Developmental Perspective*, Berkeley, California: University of California Press, 1979, p. 274 for discussion.
65 Oscar Lewis, "Manly-Hearted Women Among the North Piegan," in *American Anthropologist*, new series, vol. 43, No. 2, Pt. I (April–June, 1941), p. 176; Martin and Voorhies, *Female*, p. 101.
66 Martin and Voorhies, *Female*, p. 102.
67 Martin and Voorhies, *Female*, p. 102.
68 Kirkpatrick, *The Marquesan Notion of the Person*.
69 See Kath Weston, "Lesbian/Gay Studies in the House of Anthropology," in *Annual Reviews of Anthropology*, vol. 22 (1993), pp. 339–67.
70 Sabine Lang, *Männer als Frauen-Frauen als Männer: Geschlechstrollen-wechsel be den Indianer Nordamerikas*, Hamburg, Germany: Wayasbah-Verlag, 1990.
71 Blackwood, *Lesbian Behavior*.
72 Denise O'Brien, "Female Husbands in Southern Bantu Societies," in Alice Schlegal (ed.), *Sexual Stratification: A Cross-Cultural View*, New York: Columbia University Press, 1977, pp. 109–26; Salvatore Cucchiari as quoted in Evelyn Blackwood, "Cross-Cultural Dimensions of Lesbian Relations," p. 1984.
73 Edward E. Evans-Pritchard, *Kinship and Marriage Among the Nuer*, Oxford: Clarendon Press, 1951.
74 Evans-Pritchard, *Kinship and Marriage*.
75 Oboler as quoted in Blackwood, "Sexuality and Gender," p. 57.
76 Blackwood, "Sexuality and Gender," pp. 59–60.
77 Regina Smith Oboler, "Is the Female Husband a Man? Woman/Woman Marriage Among the Nandi of Kenya," *Ethnology*, vol. 19, No. 1 (January, 1980), pp. 69–88.
78 Blackwood, "Sexuality and Gender," p. 60.
79 Evans-Pritchard, "Sexual Inversion," pp. 1428–34.
80 Evans-Pritchard, "Sexual Inversion," p. 1429.
81 Evans-Pritchard, "Sexual Inversion," p. 1429.
82 Evans-Pritchard, "Sexual Inversion," p. 1430
83 Gilbert Herdt, *Guardians of the Flute: Idioms of Masculinity*, New York: McGraw Hill, 1981; and Herdt, "The Sambia 'Turnim-Man.'"
84 Gregory Bateson, *Naven: The Culture of the Iatmul People of New Guinea as Revealed Through a Study of the "Naven" Ceremonial*, Stanford, California: Stanford University Press, 1958, pp. 198–203.
85 Bateson, *Naven*, pp. 198–203.
86 Ibid., pp. 198–217.

87 Victor W. Turner, "Betwixt and Between: The Liminal Period in Rites de Passage," in Turner, *The Forest of Symbols*, pp. 93–111.
88 Turner, "Betwixt and Between;" Victor W. Turner, *The Ritual Process: Structure and Anti-Structure*, Ithaca, NY: Cornell University Press, 1977; Turner, *Dramas, Fields*.
89 Turner, "Betwixt and Between."
90 William Young, "The Kába, Gender, and the Rites of Pilgrimage," in *International Journal of Middle East Studies*, vol. 25, No. 2 (May, 1993) p. 296.
91 Turner, *The Ritual*, p. vii.
92 Elizabeth Crouch Zelman, "Reproduction, Ritual, and Power," in *American Ethnologist*, vol. 4, No. 4 (November, 1977) pp. 714–33.
93 E. Westermarck, "Homosexual Love," in *Homosexuality: A Cross-Cultural Approach*, New York: Julian Press, 1956, pp. 101–38.
94 See Hill, "Note on the;" Devereaux, "Institutionalized Homosexuality"; Lewis, "Manly-Hearted Women;" Williams, *The Spirit*; Will Roscoe, *The Zuni*; James Steel Thayer, "The Berdache of the Northern Plains: A Socioreligious Perspective," in *Journal of Anthropological Research*, vol. 36, No. 3 (Fall 1980), pp. 287–93; Martin and Voorhies, *Female*; Kessler and McKenna, *Gender*; Levy, *Tahitians*; Jacobs, "Native American;" and Jacobs, "The Berdache."
95 Imperato-McGinley, "Steroid 5a-Reductase;" Gilbert Herdt, "Cross-cultural Forms;" Herdt, "The Sambia 'Turnim-Man';" Sagarin, "Sex Rearing;" Morris Oboler, "The *Hijar* (Hermaphrodites) of India and Indian Nation Character: A Rejoinder," in *American Anthropologist*, vol. 62 (1960), pp. 505–11; and Nanda, *Neither Man nor Woman*.
96 Evans-Pritchard, *Kinship*.
97 Blackwood, "Lesbian Behavior."
98 Gregory Bateson, *Naven*.
99 Turner, *The Ritual*.
100 See Note 47.
101 Besnier, "Polynesian Gender."
102 Donald Symons, *The Evolution of Human Sexuality*, Oxford: Oxford University Press, 1979; Robin Fox, "In the Beginning: Aspects of Hominid Behavioral Evolution," in *Man*, vol. 2, No. 2 (June, 1967), pp. 415–33; Lionel Tiger, *Men in Groups*, New York: Vintage Press, 1970; Edward O. Wilson, *On Human Nature*, Cambridge, Mass.: Harvard University Press, 1978; Edward O. Wilson, *Sociobiology: The New Synthesis*, Cambridge, Mass.: The Belknap Press of Harvard University Press, 1975.
   For an excellent critique of sociobiological applications to homosexuality and the conceptual muddles embedded in Western scientific categorization of gender variant identities see Dickemann, "Wilson's Panchreston."
103 Bolin, "Transcending and Transgendering," pp. 447–85, 589–96.
104 Weeks, *Sex, Politics*, p. 3.
105 After Linton, see Stanislav Andreski, *Social Sciences as Sorcery*, Harmondsworth, Penguin, 1974.
106 Bryan S.Turner, *The Body and Society: Explorations in Social Theory*, Oxford, England: Basil Blackwell, 1984, p. 28.
107 Jane Flax, "Postmodernism and Gender Relations in Feminist Theory," in *Signs*, vol. 12, No. 4 (Summer, 1987), p. 637; Anne Bolin, "Women Bodybuilders: Relation, Reflection, and Reform." Paper presented at the Annual Meeting of the North American Society for the Sociology of Sport, November 6–9, Milwaukee, Wisconsin, 1991, p. 6.
108 Kessler and McKenna, *Gender*, p. 4.
109 For a discussion of how the Euro-American dual gender paradigm evolved in the

Western scientific imagination see Gilbert Herdt, "Representations of Homosexuality: An Essay on Cultural Ontology and Historical Comparison, Part I," in *Journal of History of Sexuality*, vol. 1, No. 3 (January, 1991), pp. 481–504.

110 Kessler and McKenna, *Gender*, p. 4.

111 Ibid.

112 Herdt, *Third Sex, Third Gender*, pp. 25–6.

113 Bolin, "Transcending and Transgendering," pp. 452–60.

114 See also Bolin, "Vandalized Vanity," pp. 79–82, and Bolin, "Transcending and Transgendering," pp. 482–5.

115 See Herdt, "Introduction: Third Sexes and Third Genders," in *Third Sex Third Gender*, pp. 46–57, for an excellent review of the evolution of scientific discourses on gender variance.

116 Bolin, "Transcending and Transgendering," pp. 452–60.

117 Cromwell, "Not Female *Berdache*."

118 Bolin, *In Search of Eve*.

119 This section includes some research initially reported in Bolin, "Transcending and Transgendering," pp. 475–7.

120 Bolin, "Transcending and Transgendering," pp. 451–2.

121 Cross-dresser is the preferred designation, although at the time of this research transvestite was also used informally by community members. Cross-dresser is considered less stigmatizing than male transvestite. It denotes the medical terminology which equates transvestism with "sexual disorder." The latter is regarded as too restrictive and unrepresentative of the actual diversity within this population. It has been suggested by Denny, Director of AEGIS [American Educational Gender Information Service], in the journal *Chrysalis Quarterly* that transsexuals be referred to as transsexual people and persons with transsexualism for the same reasons in Dallas Denny, "Dealing with Your Feelings," *AEGIS Transition Series* (Decater, Georgia: AEGIS, 1991), p. 3. This terminology provides a deliberate effort on the part of an organization, AEGIS, to engage in social identity management by deflecting the "otherness" associated with the terms transvestite and transsexual. I felt that it was already cumbersome to use the designation male-to-female transsexual in efforts not to contribute to female-to-male transsexual invisibility. To add the term "people" to that designation would have been too cumbersome.

122 Bolin, "Transcending and Transgendering," pp. 461–2.

123 Holly Boswell, "The Transgender Alternative," in *Chrysalis Quarterly*, vol. 1, No. 22 (1991), pp. 29–31.

124 Dallas Denny, "Deciding What to Do About Your Gender Dysphoria," *AEGIS Transition Booklet Series*, Decatur, Georgia: AEGIS, 1990), p. 6.

125 Dallas Denny, "Letter to the Editor," in *Society of Lesbian and Gay Anthropologists Newsletter*, vol. 17, No. 1 (1995), p. 1.

126 For review of research methods, see Bolin, "Transcending and Transgendering," pp. 448–9 and Bolin, *In Search of Eve*, pp. 32–9.

127 For commentary on other sociocultural influences, see Bolin, "Transcending and Transgendering," pp. 462–85.

While gay cross-dressers or female impersonators are not usually included as transgenderists, this is not universal. In addition, since sexual eroticism varies among those identified as transgenderists, discussion of sexual orientation illustrates the limits of a Western biologically based discourses on sexuality. For example, how would one define the sexual orientation of a non-surgical male-to-female transsexual who is married to a physiological female and continues to engage in sexual intercourse?

128 "Historic First: Five National Transgender Organizations to Sponsor Educational Booth at NASW (National Association of Social Workers) Conference," in *AEGIS News Quarterly*, September 2 (1994), p. 1.
129 Denny, "Letter."
130 Boswell, *Reviving the Tradition of Alternative Gender*, Decatur, Georgia: AEGIS, n.d., pp. 1–2.
131 Parker, "Historical Facts of Interest to the Gender Community."
132 Marcus and Fischer, *Anthropology as Cultural*, p. 32.
133 Bolin, "Transcending and Transgendering," p. 477.
134 Michel Foucault, *Barbin: Being the Recently Discovered Memoirs of a Nineteenth-Century French Hermaphrodite*, trans. Richard McDougall, New York: Pantheon, 1980.
135 Fausto-Sterling 1993, p. 24; Foucault, *Barbin*.
136 Midnight Sun, "Sex Gender Systems in Native North America," in Will Roscoe (ed.), *Living the Spirit: A Gay American Indian Anthology*, New York: St. Martin's Press, 1988, p. 33.
137 Roscoe, *Living the Spirit*.
138 Roscoe, *The Zuni*, p. 3.
139 Denny, "Letter," p. 2.
140 Susan Skomal, "Multiculturism in the Quincentennial Year: Highlights of the Ninety-First Annual Meeting," in *Anthropology Newsletter*, vol. 33, No. 8 (November, 1992), p. 1.
141 Roscoe, *The Zuni*, p. 1.

3

SUMER

Gender, gender roles, gender role reversals

Judith Ochshorn

What role reversals signify is contingent on the meaning attached by cultures to gender roles themselves and the latter, though ubiquitous, have obviously varied over time and across and within cultures. Gender role reversals then, like gender roles, both illuminate and are shaped by the fundamental beliefs and practices of the societies that give rise to them.

If we reach back to the literature of ancient Sumer, from that part of the world usually regarded as the cradle of Western religions, if not civilization, there are some tantalizing references to gender reversals among devotees of the fertility goddesses of ancient Mesopotamia. For example, accounts of one cultic celebration of the great Sumerian goddess Inanna refer to what might have been cross-dressing by her worshippers.[1] The *Kurgarûs*, originally guards of Inanna but later assigned to various roles in her cultic service, are said to have been changed by that goddess from males to females, sometimes carrying spindles or symbols of femininity, and typically engaging in bloody war games.[2]

Given the apparently widespread conviction in the ancient Near East that the divine intervened constantly in everyday life, and that some individuals in the human community could mediate between it and the sacred, the likely meaning of these gender role reversals to their own cultures may be inferred from Sumerian conceptions of goddesses and gods, the nature of their cultic worship, and how gender figured in both. However, attempts to reconstruct Sumerian culture and its attitudes toward gender elicit the kinds of concerns present in all reconstructions of the past as well as those specific to Sumer.

How do we move beyond accounts in the written records left to us, perhaps selected to be left, by a literate minority of mostly men whose viewpoints, consciously or not, most frequently coincided with those of the "winners" in history? How might we reconstruct the roles and life experiences of the excluded, of ordinary and lower-class people, of women, of slaves, for all of whom cultural values probably resonated deeply? All of them "made" history,[3] most of them filled prescribed gender roles, some resisted them. But we may infer their experiences and contributions to their cultures only from those written records which, incidentally, are used to corroborate the

52

meanings of allegedly unbiased physical artifacts.[4] And all of these become more of a concern the further back in time we look.

There are other difficulties in reconstructing the meaning of gender role reversals in ancient Sumer. The Sumerian language and literature, indeed its very civilization, were lost to us for more than 2,000 years. Though they provided part of the ambience of biblical monotheism and its views on gender roles, we were ignorant of Sumerian views until cuneiform tablets began to be deciphered in the nineteenth century. Sumer was decisively defeated by its enemies and, except for a brief renaissance, ceased to exist as a political entity around the end of the third millennium BCE.

Nevertheless, its cultural influence was enormous. Sumerian continued to be used as the language of the literary and religious texts of its Semitic conquerors; Sumerian divinities were incorporated into the Babylonian pantheon; the Sumerian language and literature were used by schools that trained scribes, and they continued to be studied in the intellectual and spiritual centers of the Babylonians, Assyrians, Elamites, Hurrians, Hittites, Canaanites, and Eblaites. Despite all this, and the existence by now of a body of hymns, myths, accounts of rituals, and epics, much Sumerian literature is undoubtedly lost to us forever due to the ravages of time, political conquests, and cultural and linguistic shifts in antiquity.[5]

Finally, when we examine data about gender roles from the past through the lenses of the present – as indeed we must and should [6] – how can we be sure that we are doing more than imposing our own familiar assumptions and stereotypes about gender on other times and places? For instance, one contemporary scholar finds the character of the fertility goddess Inanna perplexing, anomalous, even inexplicable since she is, simultaneously, the goddess of love and war, fertility and violence, young bride and raging destroyer.[7] Another portrays the fertility goddess Ishtar, the Semitic counterpart of Inanna, as "the female with the fundamental attributes of manhood" in describing "her being and her cult (where she changes men into women and women into men)." Characterizing fertility goddesses as "manly" because, for instance, Inanna wanders about freely "unlike a proper married woman," and because, even more than men, both Inanna and Ishtar love warfare and seek lovers, this view argues that these goddesses were dangerous because they were not permanently domiciled within the house of a god. Indeed, they were divine prototypes of "the sexually available woman undiverted by domestic preoccupations and unencumbered by children."[8]

The fusion of ferocity and fertility might only *seem* to be an illogical union of opposites, of masculine and feminine traits, if assessed according to the gender stereotypes of our own time. In the ancient Near East, the prosperity, even survival, of human communities from year to year was precarious. They depended on producing enough food in the face of capricious weather, maintaining a sufficient population in the face of little-understood illnesses, and defeating their enemies in a time of frequent warfare. Under such conditions, it may have seemed perfectly logical for these communities to try to assure their survival into the next year and meet their most basic needs – for fertility and victory over their enemies – by reliance for both on the intervention of the same powerful goddess. Certainly the chief god of the pantheon, Enlil, was not noticeably well-disposed toward humans and was often portrayed as violent or capricious. And it is simply not the case that every culture shared or shares our own views of sexuality, family life and domestic bliss.

Beyond that, central to Sumerian conceptions of divine gender roles was the sharing of equivalent, sometimes identical, powers by goddesses and gods. Like Inanna and Ishtar, both the god Enlil and his son Ninurta were portrayed as deities of vegetation and destruction, or as fertility gods, as was the god Ningirsu, son of Enlil (or An), who was the deity of war and annual spring rains and riverfloods.[9] Thus, apart from the arguable issue of whether there was such a close fit between real women and goddesses, there is the question of whether what is being described by modern scholars conveys Sumerian attitudes toward gender or our own.

I shall argue here that, in fact, ancient Near Eastern ideologies of gender were not based on masculine-feminine polarities, or the location of norms of appropriate female and male behavior, in either the divine or secular spheres, at opposite ends of the spectrum of human behavior. It is not that there were no distinctions made on the basis of sex or that hierarchies were unknown or unimportant. Rather, from the third to the first millennium BCE, conspicuously absent from Sumerian and later Babylonian religious beliefs and practices was the assignment of importance to gender and gender differences in those activities then understood as meeting the most basic community and, later, individual needs.[10] Gender was not conceived of as the locus of morality, honor, courage, sin, indeed power itself. Thus, ancient Near Eastern polytheistic attitudes were radically different from those that emerged subsequently in the West, perhaps most notably, but by no means exclusively, in the literature and traditions of biblical monotheism that radically elevated the importance of gender and gender differences.[11]

Even when goddesses and gods did not share identical powers, over say fertility and war, they often shared equivalent ones. For example, the establishment and proper functioning of temples were considered essential to community survival. Among the oldest Sumerian literary works recovered is an early third-millennium "Hymn to Kesh" or temple hymn. The chief deity of this temple was the birth goddess Nintur or Ninhursaga, initially one of the ruling cosmic triad along with the gods An and Enlil. She performs the divination ritual necessary before the construction of a temple to ensure favorable conditions for it. Also described in the hymn are the presence and role of the goddess Nidaba in the establishment of this edifice. Variously referred to as a goddess of vegetation, writing and literature including astronomical texts, the deity of "the house of understanding" (most likely intelligence), and as she who "knows the (inmost) secrets of numbers," Nidaba records Enlil's words of praise in establishing the temple, thus providing the "standard version" of events as they truly happened. In a later myth, Nidaba records or preserves the exploits and triumphs of the fertility god Ninurta over the barrenness of the land.[12]

The god Enlil's words of praise (or decrees) were required for the establishment of the local temple or vehicle for cosmic intervention on behalf of the community. The god Ninurta guaranteed an adequate food supply to the community by overcoming the barrenness of the earth. Both became part of the indispensable cultural legacy articulated and preserved by the goddess Nidaba who, by her intelligence, enabled the survival and prosperity of Sumer. Later, the Sumerian god of wisdom Enki and his Akkadian counterpart Ea were to assume (some say usurp) many of Nidaba's roles.

However, in a myth transcribed as early as 2000 BCE but believed to have been current centuries earlier, "Inanna and Enki: The Transfer of the *Me* from Eridu to Erech," the god Enki, to whose safekeeping as the god of wisdom the *me* or arts of civilization were entrusted by the god Enlil right after creation, in effect permits the goddess Inanna to move them from his cultic center, Eridu, to Erech, her own.[13] Obviously, the significance of this transfer hinges on the meaning of the *me*.

By the time of the second half of the third millennium BCE, Sumerian theologians believed that, at the time of the creation of the universe, Enlil composed the *me*, all of the essential plans, laws, and norms that governed its successful, harmonious functioning, and that provided what was needed for civilized life. In intricate if as-yet-not-fully-understood detail, the *me* consisted of:

> a comprehensive assortment of powers and duties, norms and standards, rules and regulations, rights, powers, and insignia relating to the cosmic realms; to countries, cities, and temples; to the acts of gods and men; and to virtually every aspect of civilized life.[14]

Samuel Noah Kramer characterizes the *me* described in Sumerian literary documents as:

> "good," "pure," "holy," "great," "noble," "precise," "innumerable," "eternal," "awesome," "intricate," "untouchable," they could be "presented," "given," "taken," "held," "lifted," "gathered," "worn" (like a garment), "fastened at the side," "directed," "perfected"; deities could sit upon them, put their feet upon them, ride upon them; they could even be loaded on a boat and carried off from one city to another.[15]

It is precisely the last that Inanna accomplishes, and whatever the full meaning of these complex *me*, it is clear that they were viewed as encompassing, among other things, divine plans and provisions for the most fundamental aspects and laws of civilized life as well as an explanation of divine–human relationships. Hence, the goddess Inanna is the equal of the god Enki in wisdom and power, by virtue of her possession of the all-important *me*, and nowhere in the myth are distinctions made about the fitness to possess them on the basis of the sex of the divine.[16]

At times, divinities of the same sex share identical or equivalent powers. The god Ninurta decides "the country's lawsuits," representing the claims of the just to his father Enlil. Like the latter, Ninurta decrees the fates of deities and humans. Like the god Utu, Ninurta dispenses social justice. At times, divinities of both sexes share equal or equivalent powers. Like Ninurta and Utu, the goddesses Inanna and Nanshe dispense justice; like Enlil, they make far-reaching decisions;[17] and, like Enlil, Inanna in her violence terrifies humans and divinities.[18]

It would seem that at least until the first half of the second millennium BCE, poets and theologians considered the gender of the divine almost irrelevant to the pursuit of what they saw as the most important concerns of their societies, namely divine preservation of their legacies from the past and divine assurances that their communities would continue into the future. Both goddesses and gods were seen as running the universe, and the range and content of their powers did not derive from their sex. Indeed, at times they were imaged as bisexual, or their sex changed as their worship spread to new locales.[19]

In contrast to the later tracing of descent through males, powerful Sumerian divinities were sometimes identified as the offspring of both their parents; for example, the hero Utu is called the child of Ningal and the child of Enlil.[20] Ninshubur was the name of a god *and* a goddess. When s/he is Inanna's handmaiden or page she is female.[21] Likewise, both women and men were seen as appropriate and efficacious servants of and intercessors with divinities for the human community.[22] In "The Nanshe Hymn," the fertility goddess Nanshe installs a female majordomo to run her "house" or temple and eliminate cheating. A majordomo might have been a male or female who headed a household, business, or city.[23] Therefore, with the apparent lack of importance ascribed to gender identity in the accomplishment of social goals, gender role reversals in ancient Sumer and Babylon might have signified something quite different from what they were to mean later and elsewhere.

While there is no way to measure the presence or depth of individuals' religious faith, Sumerian goddesses and gods were routinely invoked for a variety of purposes in both official and popular religion – to assure compliance with laws and diplomatic treaties;[24] to ward off divine punishments for communal transgressions;[25] to assist in the exorcism of sickness and other calamities, both personal and social;[26] and to solicit their intervention in one's personal affairs.[27] Religious beliefs provided not only a fundamental explanatory model for the people of these ancient cultures but were also based on trust in the efficacy of rituals to solicit divine influence or mourn divine intervention in daily life.

One type of religious literature, the *balag*-lamentations, were recited by *gala*-priests from the third through the first millennium BCE. Though most of the lamentations derive from the Old Babylonian period (*c.* 2000–1600 BCE), it is believed that many were preserved from an earlier period, and they continued to be inscribed and translated in the neo-Assyrian period or middle of the first millennium.[28] The importance of these lamentations is that for a few thousand years they expressed enduring human fears and concerns, and solicited divine assistance to ward off adversity and keep chaos at bay for the following year.

Lamentations were recited for specific purposes: to deal with bereavement at funerals; to keep evil demons away at times of change, when a building was to be dedicated or a journey undertaken; and to placate the anger of divinities when their dilapidated temples and shrines or sacred objects were to be dismantled and renovated. Specific recitations by the *gala*-priests were performed as part of a fixed liturgy on certain days each month to prevent the anger of one deity or another over the involuntary transgressions of the community or king. Since the *balag*-lamentations represented efforts to ritually express and deal with uncertainties, anxieties, and tragedies afflicting everyone, from personal bereavement to social disasters,[29] they probably reflected prevailing attitudes about gender and gender differences, and therefore yield information about the probable meaning of gender role reversals.

It is important to note that Sumerian lacks a specific symbol that differentiates between male and female deities. Therefore, by the middle of the first millennium, neo-Assyrian scribes differentiated those lamentations directed to male deities from those directed to female deities by listing, in the former, events or works attributed to Enlil, the chief god of the pantheon; and in the latter, those attributed to Inanna, the chief goddess.[30] And despite the continuing and general decline in status of both women and goddesses in the increasingly masculinized culture of the Near East by the neo-Assyrian period, "God in Sumer never became all male ... Inanna played a greater role in myth, epic, and hymn than any other deity, male or female."[31] That religious conceptions of gender and gender roles in the divine and earthly realms remained surprisingly fluid would not be inconsistent with the frequent disjunctions in time between religious norms and social realities.

At first glance, some of the divine roles in the *balag*-lamentations might appear to have had some basis in notions of gender, for example, the characteristic and raging destructiveness of the god Enlil, virtually a primal force in nature, and the characteristic desolation suffered by goddesses and women who most frequently lament it or plead for relief on behalf of the community or themselves. But even in the midst of Enlil's destruction, goddesses sometimes proudly identify themselves individually and, in the first person, assert their greatness.[32]

In one lamentation, a goddess does not so much mourn her losses as directly accuse Enlil of wasting "my" city. In another, Inanna is the only deity of either sex who apparently dares to approach Enlil to pacify him, and confront him with a "how long?" In yet another, Inanna, identifying herself as "the hierodule [or Queen] of heaven" and "the destroyer of the mountain . . . she who causes the heavens to shake," describes the cultural brilliance of the cities where she was worshiped, mourns their destruction, and accuses the powerful gods An and Enlil of destroying them. In effect, she sets her many and awesome attributes as countervailing powers against those of the greatest gods.[33] Moreover, in this literature and elsewhere, the goddess Inanna is also described as a raging destroyer feared by deities and humans alike.[34]

Poets recorded that when goddesses and gods abandoned their cities and temples, the inhabitants often experienced it as a terrible storm or military defeat that ravaged their communities. On a deeper level, this abandonment signaled the disruption of right relationships and the natural order of things. In the latter, individuals viewed themselves as part of a social group that, in turn, resided in nature, in which divinities were immanent and to be propitiated. The well-being of the community and individual were seen as resting on the well-being of nature.

The slight degree to which divine gender figured in the satisfaction of communal needs or the expiation of communal guilt is found in much of the literature. "The Lament for Ur" recounts the abandonment of that city by the goddess Ningil and her consort, the god Nanna. Ningil laments the ensuing desolation for *her* ravaged city, Nanna laments it for *his* ravaged city, and then both are entreated to return to Ur.[35] Likewise, the destruction of cities is reported to both Enlil and his divine consort Ninlil.[36] The "Hymn to Enlil" praises that god as the source and administrator of all life on earth, preeminent vegetation deity, originator of all moral authority, and benefactor of humanity by his words and decrees. It concludes in praise of the goddess Ninlil who, along with her husband, issues decrees and makes decisions for the world. When Enlil is exalted, Ninlil too is exalted.[37] Even scholars who define ancient Near Eastern polytheism as dimorphic, in which divine roles are grounded in the essential femaleness and maleness of goddesses and gods, describe the rather incidental role of gender in the public functions of Sumerian deities: "In some cases, the sex of a god [*sic.*] makes no real difference to its function. In their control of cities, goddesses and gods play equivalent roles. The god [*sic.*] of the city could be either male or female."[38]

Frequently, both female and male divinities are invoked in attempts to put an end to the rampaging fury of the divine. Both goddesses and gods are begged to persuade Enlil not to abandon his city Nippur by abandoning his shrine there; both attempt to be protective to their cities; both pray to Enlil to "calm his heart," and both bless offerings to pacify him.[39] Divinities of both sexes were seen as so closely involved in human affairs that, in laying the foundations of a temple, the *gala*-priest would set up offering-tables for its general deities and, in addition, tables for the god, goddess and genie of the temple. In one lamentation, the life of the nation is described as placed in the "house" or temple of the god Enlil and his wife, the goddess Ningal.[40]

The very language used in appeals to divinities is marked by ambiguity in terms of their sex. In a lamentation to the god Nergal, he is referred to as cow and bull just as the goddess Inanna describes herself as cow and bison. Divine retribution is experienced by divinities of both sexes. When Enlil turns away from his shrine and city Nippur, the god Enki "goes in tears" as does his son, his daughter-in-law and his mother. In a late third-millennium temple hymn, Gudea, the ruler of Lagash, claims the goddess Ninsuna as his divine mother but refers to her as his mother and father, both implanting "the germ" of him in his mother's womb and giving birth to him "from out the vulva."[41]

Similar fluidity in divine gender roles is evident in some of the creation stories. Goddesses and gods, tired of caring for themselves, create human beings for the specific purpose of ritually feeding them. On the divine plane, goddesses are shown as ritually feeding gods. But in "The Cylinders of Gudea," a hymn to a temple, god Ningirsu serves food to his father (and it is unclear here whether he is An or Enlil), an honor usually bestowed on the eldest son.[42]

Just as prayers for relief from affliction were directed to both goddesses and gods who, in turn, were portrayed as engaged as supplicants to other divinities on behalf of the community or as victims of divine wrath, so when it was feared that a god or goddess had abandoned a city or shrine, explaining or foretelling communal disasters, women and men alike were portrayed as suffering the consequences. When Enlil curses the city's lord he causes the lady's sickness. Both its lord and lady are no longer present in the devastated city, and both depart for the Nether World, or the realm of the dead. When the word (or decree) of the destroyer Enlil is encountered by a man or woman, both moan, both are afflicted "with woe," both sob in their misery.[43] Though repetition marks the form of the lamentations, what is striking is the sexual parallelism, specifically naming men and women as members of co-suffering humanity. Calming the fears of communities and individuals and meeting their needs clearly took precedence over the sex of the divine or the human intermediaries between them and their worshippers.

During the second half of the third millennium BCE, from which some of the *balag*-lamentations are thought to date, there is evidence that at least upper-class Sumerian women occupied positions of public power and influence. That apparently was also true during the first half of the second millennium, or during the Old Babylonian period, in the kingdom of Mari and Sippar, and this public prominence of women as well as men encompassed their many cultic roles as temples reached their long arms out into the economic and political life of surrounding communities.[44]

This apparent comfort with female prominence is reflected in the literature describing one of the oldest and most widespread cults in ancient

Mesopotamia that celebrated the Sacred Marriage of the young shepherd god Dumuzi with the nubile goddess Inanna, and lamented his early and seasonal death. While one of its aspects marked the turn of the seasons and its effects on nature and the food supply, another suggests the possible existence at some point, perhaps by then only a memory, of a matrilineal or relatively egalitarian social structure. Inanna's brother Utu prepares her for marriage; when Dumuzi is pursued by the emissaries of the Nether World who want to drag him to his death, he appeals for help to his brother-in-law Utu and his sister Geshtinanna; and though his death is lamented by women – his wife, mother and sister – Dumuzi asks his mother, not his wife, to mourn him. Informing all of these texts are the contributions of male and female divinities to the ongoing processes of nature. Significantly, Inanna is informed by her mother, the goddess Ningal, that after her marriage she will move into and belong to the household of her husband and his family.[45] If these texts indicate the gradual social transition from matrilyny to patrilyny with obvious implications for attitudes toward gender roles – and that can only be conjectured at this point – it would help to explain the relatively high status and public presence of at least upper-class women in third-millennium Sumer.

When Inanna establishes her main temple, Eanna, in Uruk, she also sets up the *gipāru* temple, the traditional residence of an *en* priest or priestess.[46] A recent study corroborates the cultic presence and importance of one class of women and their several public roles in community life. Challenging the traditional view that the Akkadian *quadištu*, "she who is set apart," was a prostitute, sacred or otherwise (because they were unattached to individual men?), apparently from the Old Babylonian period on, those women instead were cultic functionaries. They participated in temple rituals in the cult of the god Adad and his consort Shala and also acted as midwives, wetnurses and sorcerers.[47]

This was by no means extraordinary. We know from the correspondence of mostly royal women in the second-millennium kingdom of Mari that both women and men served in the priesthood, offered prayers and sacrifices on behalf of the king, interceded with the divine, and interpreted dreams. Both women and men were oracles, diviners, and prophets, significant at a time when major personal, community and military decisions rode on the results of oracles and prophecies.[48] In short, females and males in both the divine and earthly realms were viewed as active agents sharing many of the same attributes, causing and experiencing the same desolation, and few distinctions were made on the basis of gender alone.

Gender role reversals in the worship of Inanna and Ishtar might best be understood, then, in the context of Sumerian conceptions of the divine. Conceived of as plural, no one divinity of either sex was considered omnipotent, possessed of total power over life and death. Rather, each possessed a cluster of non-exclusive attributes that might change over time to accommodate changing human needs, values, and historical circumstances.

The relationships, interrelationships, actions, and interactions of the most powerful goddesses and gods – their alliances, conflicts, triumphs, and defeats – were understood to determine not only the changing face of nature but also the contours of social life, and none of these fell strictly along gender lines. For example, Enki, god of wisdom, might have usurped the functions of Nidaba, goddess of writing and literature, but the struggle for kingship of the gods, in which younger male divinities usurped the roles of older ones, also runs like a *leitmotif* through ancient Near Eastern religious texts.

Goddesses and gods were conceived of anthropomorphically, as both immanent and transcendent, but they were never only just like humans in their behavior, and such comparisons are unwarranted. Poets tell us that their sexual and familial behavior were most often far different from that sanctioned in the human community. For the most part, divinities were non-monogamous. The consequences of divine sexuality, particularly divine female sexuality, were seen as beneficial to human society and its representative, the king. Two thousand years of Sumerian poetry commemorate the Sacred Marriage Rite that, on the sexual initiative of the goddesses Inanna and Ishtar guaranteed (instead of divine offspring) the fitness of the king to rule, his victory in battle over enemies, and the fertility of the land. Divine illegitimacy and incest were alien concepts. There was no mind/spirit-body split or double standard among deities. And goddesses were not more limited in their powers by their reproductive roles than were gods.[49] What is attested in the literature about Inanna and Ishtar, as well as other of the greatest gods preeminent in divine pantheons of hundreds, is that their powers were overwhelming to both divinities and humans who feared their judgment and punishment. Against this backdrop, we have the following kinds of allusions to role reversals in the worship of those goddesses.

One hymn to Inanna[50] opens with a description of her powers as equivalent to those of An, Enlil, and Enki, calling forth the homage of the Anunnaki, the great deities of Sumer. It then describes a monthly ritual engaged in by Inanna's cult personnel and many others from the community who parade before her to honor her prowess as warrior and goddess of war. Part of the parade consisted of a corps of "eminent ladies" armed for battle whose "right arms are clothed with cloth in male fashion,"[51] and this scene (with all the ambiguities of the Sumerian language) is sometimes rendered as "The people of Sumer parade before you. The women adorn their right side with men's clothing . . . the men adorn their left side with women's clothing."[52]

Another explicit reference is in the *balag*-lamentation, "That City Which Has Been Pillaged."[53] Inanna, lamenting the wreckage of the city, catalogues her vast powers, in the midst of which she proclaims:

> I go at the front. I am lofty.
> I proceed in the rear. I am wise.
> I make right into left.

I make left into right.
I turn a man into a woman.
I turn a woman into a man.
I am the one who causes the man to adorn himself as a woman.
I am the one who causes the woman to adorn herself as a man.
I cause the weak to enter the house.
I expel the mighty from the house.
. . .
I am the stairs to the high roof.
I am . . . the low parapets.
I turn white into black.
I turn black into white.[54]

These allusions to gender role reversals by Inanna, as part of a series of other reversals, may reflect the Sumerian view of her enormous power to reverse and effect virtually everything in the universe. For what we have in the remains of the sacred texts of ancient Sumer, regardless of the relative insignificance of gender to the exercise of divine authority, are narratives ascribing a level and scope of power to the activities of goddesses rarely seen in the West before or since.

For example, in one of the earliest extant Akkadian hymns dating from the end of the third millennium BCE, "The Exaltation of Inanna," the poet-high-priestess-princess Enheduanna celebrates that goddess' power over all of heaven and earth in its account of the transfer of the *me*, in this case from the powerful moon-god Nanna to Inanna.[55] The latter, autonomous initiator of the Sacred Marriage, is shown here in another guise as goddess of war, the terror of deities and people alike, the terrible judge of humanity who exacts retribution by devastating the land when she is paid insufficient homage. In the widely-proliferated *Epic of Gilgamesh*, the goddess Ishtar threatens to raise the dead so they will outnumber the living if her father An, the God of heaven, refuses to unleash the Bull of Heaven against Gilgamesh to punish that hero for daring to reject her advances.[56] Similarly, Ereshkigal, goddess of the Netherworld, threatens to release the dead in numbers that would overwhelm the living if her lover, the god Nergal, is not returned to her by the chief gods Anu, Enlil, and Ea.[57] And it is Ishtar who forbids the chief god Enlil to partake of the sacrifices offered to gods and goddesses by the survivors of a terrible flood unleashed by Enlil because she holds him responsible for the destruction of "her" people.[58] In all these instances, the dominant gods bow to the power of the dominant goddesses and agree to their demands.

The meaning of gender and the significance attached to gender differences have always been fundamental to how cultures understand and organize themselves. Thus, gender role reversals, or causing men to dress like women and women to dress like men, could have been merely another demonstration of Sumerian conceptions of the all-encompassing power of the Goddesses Inanna and Ishtar over heaven and earth, love and war, life and death, and, what is basic to all human cultures, gender and gender roles.

NOTES

1 Mark E. Cohen, *The Canonical Lamentations of Ancient Mesopotamia*, 2 vols, Potomac, Md.: Capital Decisions Ltd., 1988, II, pp. 587–603.
2 Thorkild Jacobsen, *The Harps That Once ... Sumerian Poetry in Translation*, New Haven: Yale University Press, 1987, p. 286, n.75 and 76.
3 Cf. Gerda Lerner, *The Creation of Patriarchy*, New York and London: Oxford University Press, 1986.
4 Cf. Bernadette Brooten, *Women Leaders in the Ancient Synagogue*, Atlanta: Scholars Press, 1982; "Early Christian Women and Their Cultural Context: Issues of Method in Historical Reconstruction," in Adela Yarbro Collins (ed.), *Feminist Perspectives on Biblical Scholarship*, Chico, CA: Scholars Press, 1985, pp. 65–91.
5 Samuel Noah Kramer, *Sumerian Mythology: A Study of Spiritual and Literary Achievement in the Third Millennium BC*, rev. edn., Philadelphia: University of Pennsylvania Press, 1972, pp. 28–9; Cohen, *Canonical Lamentations*, I, pp. 11–12.
6 Cf. Elisabeth Schüssler Fiorenza, "Remembering the Past in Creating the Future," in Collins, *Feminist Perspectives*, pp. 43–63.
7 Jacobsen, *Harps*, pp. 17, n.2, 19, n.1.
8 Tikva Frymer-Kensky, *In the Wake of the Goddesses: Women, Culture, and the Biblical Transformation of Pagan Myth*, New York and Toronto: The Free Press and Maxwell Macmillan Canada, 1992, pp. 28–9, 66–9, 80.
9 Jacobsen, *Harps*, pp. 235–72; Cohen, *Canonical Lamentations*, I, pp. 136–43.
10 Thorkild Jacobsen, *The Treasures of Darkness: A History of Mesopotamian Religion*, New Haven: Yale University Press, 1976.
11 Judith Ochshorn, *The Female Experience and the Nature of the Divine*, Bloomington: Indiana University Press, 1981.
12 Jacobsen, *Harps*, pp. 251–2, 271–2 n.81, 86, 377–80, n.11, 382, 394, n.28, 409, n.77, 412.
13 Kramer, *Sumerian Mythology*, pp. 64–8.
14 Samuel Noah Kramer, *From the Poetry of Sumer: Creation, Glorification, Adoration*, Berkeley, Los Angeles, London: University of California Press, 1979, p. 45.
15 Ibid., pp. 45–6. Here Kramer cites the work of Gertrud Farber-Flügge, *Der Mythos Inanna und Enki Unter Besonderer Berucksichtigung der Liste der Me*, Rome: Biblical Institute Press, 1973.
16 Ochshorn, *Female Experience*, pp. 62–4.
17 Cf. Jacobsen, *Harps*, pp. 141–2, 237–8, 327.
18 Enheduanna, *The Exaltation of Inanna*, trans. William W. Hallo and J. J. A. Van Dijk, New Haven: Yale University Press, 1968.
19 Ochshorn, *Female Experience*, pp. 31–3; "Ishtar and Her Cult," in Carl Olson (ed.), *The Book of the Goddess Past and Present*, New York: Crossroad Publishing Co., 1983, p. 16.
20 Cohen, *Canonical Lamentations*, I, p. 217.
21 Jacobsen, *Harps*, p. 207, n.3.
22 Ochshorn, *Female Experience*, pp. 110–26.
23 Jacobsen, *Harps*, pp. 126–42, esp. p. 130, n.17.
24 James B. Pritchard (ed.), *Ancient Near Eastern Texts Relating to the Old*

Testament, 3rd edn with supplement, Princeton: Princeton University Press, 1969, pp. 159–206.

25 Cohen, *Canonical Lamentations*, I and II.

26 Julian Morgenstern, "The Doctrine of Sin in the Babylonian Religion," in *Mitteilungen der Voerderasiatischen Gesellschaft*, Berlin: Wolf Peiser Verlag, 1905, pp. 3–5; Campbell R. Thompson, *The Devils and Evil Spirits of Babylonia, Being Babylonian and Assyrian Incantations Against the Demons, Ghouls, Vampires, Hobgoblins, Ghosts, and Kindred Evil Spirits Which Attack Mankind*, trans. from the original cuneiform texts, Luzac's Semitic Text and Translation Series, vols XIV and XV, London: Luzac & Co., 1903.

27 Jacobsen, *Treasures*.

28 Cohen, *Canonical Lamentations*, I and II.

29 Ibid., I, pp. 13–14.

30 Ibid., pp. 18–19, n.33.

31 Kramer, *Poetry of Sumer*, p. 81.

32 Cohen, *Canonical Lamentations*, II, pp. 436, 521, 534, 594–8, 662–6.

33 Ibid., I, pp. 198–9, 261–2; II, pp. 648–9, 718–25.

34 Cf. Enheduanna, *Exaltation*.

35 Jacobsen, *Harps*, pp. 448–74.

36 Cohen, *Canonical Lamentations*, I, p. 331.

37 Ibid., p. 341; Jacobsen, *Harps*, pp. 101–11.

38 Frymer-Kensky, *In the Wake*, p. 12.

39 Cohen, *Canonical Lamentations*, I, pp. 108, 141–2, 293–7; II, pp 626–7, 477–8, 497–8.

40 Ibid., I, pp. 26, 397.

41 Ibid., I, p. 109; II, pp. 512, 648, 664; Jacobsen, *Harps*, p. 391.

42 Jacobsen, *Harps*, p. 400, esp. n.48.

43 Cohen, *Canonical Lamentations*, I, pp. 112, 137, 139–40, 381, 383–4.

44 Samuel Noah Kramer, "Poets and Psalmists: Goddesses and Theologians; Literary, Religious and Anthropological Aspects of the Legacy of Sumer," in Denise Schmandt-Besserat (ed.), *The Legacy of Sumer*, Bibliotheca Mesopotamica: "Primary sources and interpretive analyses for the study of Mesopotamian civilization and its influences from late prehistory to the end of the cuneiform tradition," Giorgio Buccellati (ed.), vol. IV, Malibu: Undena Publications, 1976, pp. 12–16; Georges Dossin and Andre Finet, *Archives Royales de Mari: Correspondence Feminine*, Paris: Librairie Orientaliste Paul Geuthner, 1978; Rivkah Harris, *Ancient Sippar: A Demographic Study of an Old Babylonian City 1894–1595 BC*, Belgium: Nederlands Historisch-Archaeologisch Instituut Te Istanbul, 1975.

45 Jacobsen, *Harps*, pp. 3–84.

46 Ibid., p. 281 n.8.

47 Mayer I. Gruber, *The Motherhood of God and Other Studies*, USF Studies in the History of Judaism, Atlanta: Scholars Press, 1992, pp. 17–47.

48 Dossin and Finet, *Archives Royales*, pp. 79–139.

49 Ochshorn, *Female Experience*, ch. 2–4.

50 Jacobsen, *Harps*, pp. 112–24.

51 Ibid., p. 116.

52 Diane Wolkstein and Samuel Noah Kramer, *Inanna Queen of Heaven and Earth*, New York: Harper & Row, 1983, p. 99.

53 Cohen, *Canonical Lamentations*, II, pp. 587–603.

54 Ibid., p. 596.

55 Enheduanna, *Exaltation*, p. 15.

56 *The Epic of Gilgamesh*, trans. N. K. Sandars, Middlesex, England: Penguin Books Ltd., 1960, pp. 107–9.
57 A. K. Grayson, "Akkadian Myths and Epics," in Pritchard, *Ancient Near Eastern Texts*, pp. 507–12.
58 *Gilgamesh*, p. 85.

4

CROSS-DRESSING AND CROSS-PURPOSES

Gender possibilities in the Acts of Thecla

J. L. Welch

In the late fourth or early fifth century the Christian pilgrim Egeria visited the "very beautiful" shrine of the protomartyr Thecla in Seleucia, a town on the coast of what is now southeastern Turkey. There she found "countless monastic cells for men and women" and a "holy church," where she prayed and listened to a reading of "the complete Acts of Saint Thecla."[1]

What Egeria heard was the tale of a beautiful young virgin, engaged to be married, who takes to heart a sermon preached by the Apostle Paul and resolves to remain celibate. After many ordeals, she triumphs over her persecutors and goes off, dressed as a man, to preach the word of God.

Thecla's story, which does not seem to be based on that of any historical figure, appears in a text called the Acts of Thecla, one segment in the longer Acts of Paul, a narrative (of which we have only fragments) which begins with Paul's activities in Damascus and Jerusalem and ends with his martyrdom in Rome. The text is dated to the middle or late second century, but incorporates older oral traditions. Like most of the other Apocryphal Acts of Apostles, the Acts of Paul and Thecla probably originated among ascetic Christian congregations in Asia Minor.[2]

The Acts of Thecla circulated widely apart from the Acts of Paul. At the end of the second century, the North African writer Tertullian testified, disapprovingly, to Thecla's popularity.[3] Methodius, Ambrose, Gregory of Nyssa, and Jerome are among the Church fathers who praised Thecla in the following centuries.[4] By the time Egeria visited her shrine in Seleucia, Thecla's cult was well established. She continued to be a popular figure well into the Middle Ages.

Because she is a strong female character who takes on male dress and roles, some modern readers have looked to Thecla for evidence concerning women's experience and access to authority in the early Church, even concluding that the Acts of Thecla may be the work of a female author or authors.[5] But it is obvious that the story of the heroic transvestite also appealed strongly to men. At the heart of Thecla's story is a symbolic alteration in gender; but the notion of simple gender-switching – female into male – does not begin to exhaust its possible meanings. In what follows, I will examine the way the complex gendered imagery of the Acts of Thecla lends itself to multiple, even conflicting, interpretations, and thus to the agenda of diverse audiences, depending on whether the transformation of a virgin female into a male-garbed apostle is understood as acquiring the attributes of maleness, as attaining a state of androgyny, or as annihilating the feminine.

THE STORY

Thecla is a young virgin of Iconium, already betrothed in marriage, who listens from her window to a sermon preached by the Apostle Paul in the house of a neighbor, Onesiphorus. The sermon proclaims "continence and the resurrection."[6] To the great consternation of her mother, Theocleia, and Thamyris, her betrothed, Thecla becomes "dominated by a new desire and a fearful passion" to follow the Apostle and his ideal of chastity.[7] After an angry mob led by Thamyris has Paul thrown into jail for "corrupting our wives," Thecla uses her jewelry and her silver mirror as bribes to escape her home and enter his prison cell.

Thecla, too, is brought before the governor who asks why she refuses to marry Thamyris. When she remains silent, "looking steadily at Paul," her mother cries out, "Burn the lawless one! Burn her that is no bride in the midst of the theatre, that all the women who have been taught by this man may be afraid!"[8] After Paul is flogged and driven out of the city, the "young men and maidens" bring fuel to burn Thecla in the arena. The governor weeps at the sight of her naked body, amazed at "the power in her." Looking into the crowd, Thecla sees "the Lord sitting in the form of Paul."[9] Miraculously, the fire blazes around the steadfast virgin without burning her. A tremendous rain and hail storm quenches the flames, destroying many in the crowd and allowing Thecla to escape.

Thecla flees Iconium and finds Paul fasting and praying for her outside the city. She proposes to cut her hair short and follow him, but he replies, "The season is unfavourable and thou art comely. May no other temptation come upon thee, worse than the first, and thou endure not and play the coward!" Thecla then asks to be baptized: "Only give me the seal in Christ, and temptation shall not touch me." Paul responds, "Have patience, Thecla, and thou shalt receive the water."[10]

Paul and Thecla proceed to the city of Antioch where Alexander, "one of the first of the Antiochenes," sees Thecla and conceives an immediate passion for her. He tries to buy her from Paul, who replies: "I do not know the woman of whom thou dost speak, nor is she mine."[11] Alexander then attempts to "embrace" Thecla on the street, but she resists him, ripping his cloak and hurling the wreath he wears as a sign of rank to the ground. For this impertinence Thecla finds herself once again before a governor, this time condemned to be devoured by beasts in a gladiatorial show Alexander is sponsoring. Women in the audience protest the "godless judgment." The governor grants Thecla's request to "remain pure" until her ordeal, allowing her to become the ward of a rich widow, Tryphaena, whose natural daughter has died.

The next day Thecla, stripped and girdled like a gladiator, is thrown into the arena while the crowd roars, some for and some against her. The beasts are set loose and a fierce lioness defends Thecla, killing off a bear and then a lion, against which the lioness dies fighting. Thecla's female partisans bewail the lioness' death. More beasts are sent in and Thecla, expecting to breathe her last, baptizes herself as she jumps into a pool of water in which ravenous seals wait to devour her. Lightning strikes the animals dead while a cloud of fire clothes Thecla's nakedness. Finally, Alexander has the naked Thecla tied by the feet to his two "fearsome bulls" which are then goaded to a frenzy by flames applied to their genitals. Instead of being ripped in half, however, Thecla escapes once again as, in the nick of time, the fire burns her ropes.

At this point Tryphaena faints and the populace, believing her dead, rises up in alarm because she is related to Caesar, whose retribution against the city they fear. At Alexander's request the governor frees Thecla, who gives a short speech about the saving powers of her God. Taking the garments the governor has commanded be brought to her, she says, "He who clothed me when I was naked among the beasts shall clothe me with salvation in the day of judgment." The city resounds with the voices of women who cry out, "One is God who has delivered Thecla!"[12]

Tryphaena becomes a Christian along with "the majority of her maid-servants." She makes over her fortune to Thecla for distribution to the poor. After instructing Tryphaena's household for eight days, Thecla girds herself and sews her mantle into a cloak "after the fashion of men."[13] Accompanied by a crowd of young men and maidens, she goes to find Paul in the city of Myra. Paul "was astonished when he saw her and the crowd that was with her, pondering whether another temptation was not upon her." She reassures him by telling him of her baptism: "for he who worked with thee for the Gospel has also worked with me for my baptism."[14] Many convert after hearing Thecla's story. When Thecla declares her intention of returning to Iconium, Paul replies, "Go and teach the word of God!"

In Iconium Thecla returns to the house of Onesiphorus, where Paul had preached, and offers a prayer of thanks to God for delivering her from prison, fire, and beasts. Thamyris is dead but Theocleia still lives. Thecla encourages her mother to believe in the God who has manifestly saved her daughter and who will provide (through Tryphaena's donation) for her daily needs. Theocleia's response is not recorded. Thecla's story simply concludes, "And when she had borne this witness she went away to Seleucia; and after enlightening many with the word of God she slept with a noble sleep."[15]

ACQUIRING MALENESS

If one approaches the Acts of Thecla, as many readers and listeners of late antiquity surely did, with the assumption that weakness is an inherently female trait while strength is an attribute of men, then Thecla herself stands out as a splendid exception to nature's rule. Inspired by the word of God, represented in the Acts of Thecla by the sermons of Paul, and thus invested with divine power, she suddenly gains the moral and physical strength to resist her intended husband, escape from her family home, beat up a male attacker, and endure a variety of public tortures. She exhibits, in other words, the courage and fortitude "of a man." So thoroughly is she transformed that even her outward appearance comes to match her new "male" identity.

Thecla's acquisition of this desirable quality, masculinity, is open to several interpretations. First of all, it can be seen as an example of the "reversal" motif well known in early Christian, especially Pauline, literature: the last becomes the first, the victim becomes the victor. The ultimate archetype is Christ's "victory" on the cross.

Martyrdom accounts vividly dramatize the theme. Displaying the exceptional fortitude that comes only from God, the martyr turns the moral tables on his or her adversaries and "wins the crown" of everlasting life. Female heroines, martyrs, and others offer particularly dramatic illustrations of the Christian God's ability to empower even the weakest and most humble.[16] The female martyr's unusual strength is often expressed in masculine metaphors.

So, for example, in what is taken to be a relatively historical second-century martyrdom account, the slave woman Blandina endures frightful tortures before winning the martyr's crown. Her approving chronicler writes that "tiny, weak, and insignificant as she was she would give inspiration to her brothers, for she had put on Christ, that mighty and invincible athlete."[17]

When the Carthaginian martyr Perpetua dreams of her coming ordeal she sees herself preparing to wrestle a ferocious Egyptian. "I became a man," she wrote, and proceeded to defeat him.[18]

Thecla becomes a "man" after she succeeds in tests of her courage, faith, and fortitude. In her case reversal of status – from innate weakness to strength, from a mortal condition to salvation – manifests itself as a complete reversal of gender. Masculinity is her crown, an emblem of her divinely invulnerable state.

But Thecla acquires more than male appearance, she takes on male roles: she baptizes herself and, with Paul's blessing, preaches and converts many. In the Acts of Thecla, as in the real world, maleness confers not only strength but also authority. The "egalitarian" reading of the Acts of Thecla sees it as sanctioning the right of women to occupy positions of authority in the Church, even to exercise authority equal to that of men. Thecla claims the rights and privileges of a male apostle, based on the same access to power. As she explains to Paul, ". . . he who worked with thee for the Gospel has also worked with me for my baptism."[19]

That some of Thecla's partisans did interpret her story this way is evident from Tertullian's efforts to rebut them. He warns:

> If those who read the writings that falsely bear the name of Paul adduce the example of Thecla to maintain the right of women to teach and to baptize, let them know that the presbyter in Asia [Minor] who produced this document, as if he could of himself add anything to the prestige of Paul, was removed from his office after he had been convicted and had confessed that he did it out of love for Paul.[20]

Tertullian's "presbyter of Asia" was certainly not alone in promoting the authority of women. A number of Christian circles, especially in the East, tolerated or encouraged women in leadership positions. The Montanist and Quintillian movements stood out in this respect.[21]

One scholar, Dennis MacDonald, argues that the Acts of Paul and Thecla and the Pastoral Epistles (1 and 2 Timothy, Titus), which come from close to the same date and locale, represent variant, conflicting strains of Pauline Christianity.[22] The Acts of Thecla offers an egalitarian interpretation of Paul of Galatians 3:28: "There is neither Jew nor Greek . . . slave nor free . . . male nor female; for you are all one in Christ Jesus." The Pastoral Epistles, MacDonald suggests, were written specifically to refute this and other positions taken in the Acts of Paul. They exclude women from positions of authority and advise them to be submissive, wear modest and "seemly" apparel, and seek salvation through marriage and childbearing.[23] While there were (and are) pockets of resistance, over time the conservative point of view prevailed.

A more radical view of Thecla's transformation focuses on the issue of female autonomy. Traveling as a woman, Thecla is attacked by a lustful stranger. Clothed as a man, she roams freely, in safety. Maleness is seen to confer more than physical and moral strength or ecclesiastical authority. In "becoming male," Thecla escapes not only the risks, but also the obligations of traditional womanhood: marriage and childbirth. In doing so, she achieves freedom from domination by men.[24]

Thecla's autonomy comes as the result of her rejection of sexual intercourse. Celibacy offered those women who could afford it, or who were "widows" supported by the community, the opportunity to control their own bodies and thus their own place in the world, a fact remarked on by ancient writers as well as modern.[25] By dressing as a man, Thecla publicly declares her freedom from sex and all the social and political consequences it had for women.

In the Antioch episode at least, Thecla saves her chastity by defeating a host of specifically male, overtly or implicitly sexual, aggressors, human and animal. We have no way of knowing if women in late antiquity found, or possibly expressed, in Thecla's story the deep hostility toward men or resistance to patriarchal society that some modern readers see there. Friction between celibate females and male Church authorities did exist, both at the time that the Acts were written and in following centuries.[26] Whatever their attitude toward men, there is no reason to doubt that in the numerous households and communities of "widows" that had begun to proliferate by the end of the second century, Thecla, the woman who rejected traditional female sexuality and seized the rights and privileges of manhood, served as an important model and inspiration.

BECOMING ANDROGYNOUS

". . . [T]he unification of opposites, and especially the opposite sexes," writes Wayne Meeks, "served in early Christianity as a prime symbol of salvation."[27] Unification language was prominent in the ritual of baptism. When the Apostle Paul declares: "There is neither Jew nor Greek . . . slave nor free . . . male nor female; for you are all one in Christ Jesus," he is quoting from a pre-Pauline baptismal formula.[28] Baptism conferred on the new Christian a state of ritual androgyny.

Within the context of baptism, androgyny is subject to various interpretations. It speaks perhaps of a return to the "primal, undifferentiated" reality of humankind's original state;[29] of the union of all Christians in the mystical body of Christ;[30] or of a restoration of the divine image the original Adam possessed.[31]

The dramatic structure of the Acts of Thecla mirrors the steps of the Christian ritual of baptism. Thecla undergoes an initiation, gives up her worldly identity, takes part in a public spectacle involving nakedness, immersion in water, and reclothing/rebirth, and emerges with a new identity in Christ. For the new Thecla "there is no male and female."

When the first century Christian, Hermas, encountered a personification of the virtue Continence (*Enkrateia*) in one of his famous visions, she appeared to him girded, looking like a man.[32] In ascetic Christian circles the figure of the androgynous female transvestite was an image of sexual chastity. In this context, androgyny implies the absolute negation, the canceling out of sexuality. Male and female are no longer separate poles; the "treacherous spark" of desire cannot jump between them.[33]

In the so-called "Encratite" churches, it appears that baptism entailed a life of sexual continence.[34] (Although not necessarily virginity. The Apocryphal Acts offer a number of examples of couples who adopt continent marriages.) This expectation is behind Thecla's request of Paul: "Only give me the seal in Christ, and temptation shall not touch me."

Thecla's story can be read as an allegory illustrating the defeat of sexual desire. Chastity's enemies are gendered male in keeping with the view traditional in the ancient world that the man is the active partner in sexual intercourse. In a variation on the reversal theme, the "victim," the human being prey to the onslaughts of lust (and thus passive/female) overcomes her attackers. So, from the allegorical point of view, can the mortal man or woman, with Christ, resist the demons of sexual desire and achieve androgyny/asexuality.

Why is sexual continence the means and mark of salvation? The answer has to do with the Encratite apocalyptic vision. In the ascetic Christian communities of the East, sexual intercourse and childbearing, traditionally cherished as the frail mortal's best hope of "immortality," came to be seen as the very means by which the demonic rulers of this age maintained their fatal grip on a doomed humanity. The defeat of death and the advent of the New Jerusalem presupposed a halting of the juggernaut of human history. What was required was a "boycott of the womb," a radical rejection of the institutions of marriage and family, the foundations of social and political life in the ancient world.[35] Continence was the key to ending the old age and bringing on the new.

Paul's message to Thecla is clear: he preaches "continence and the resurrection." His accusers claim "he deprives young men of wives and maidens of husbands, saying: 'Otherwise there is no resurrection for you, except ye remain chaste and do not defile the flesh . . .'"[36] When Thecla, accordingly, rejects her intended husband, her persecution begins. The status quo has its defenders.

More than a few Christians did take the apocalyptic message to heart. Much criticism of them, by Christians and pagans alike, had to do with their rejection of social and familial obligations and their implied contempt for city and state. Many, like Thecla, adopted a family "in Christ" to the exclusion of their biological kin. Some became propertyless itinerants as well.[37]

Seen as androgyny, Thecla's triumphal state undermines "a potent symbol for the stability of the world order," the "differentiation and ranking of women and men."[38] In its broadest sense it stands for the collapse of temporal society.

ANNIHILATING THE FEMALE

There were other views in the ancient world about the problem of sexual desire and its solution. "When men thought about it," writes Peter Brown, "they tended to see it in terms of the peril presented to them by the perpetual seductiveness of women."[39]

Beautiful women have the power to infatuate men – as Thecla does Alexander – and fill them with uncontrollable sexual passion. Female beauty is the cause of temptation and beautiful women thus incarnate it. Young virgins are the most tempting of all. As the Christian John Chrysostom wrote in the fourth century, "For even if a man accepts a widow as his wife, it is not as if he had taken her as a virgin, for his amorous desires are more violent and frenzied with the virgin than with the widow – a point, I suppose, that is obvious to everybody."[40]

Possessing this power of attraction constitutes a major portion of a woman's "frailty" and elsewhere in the Apocryphal Acts of Apostles it is a reason for punishment and a source of shame and contrition. The Acts of Peter (which may have been a source for the Acts of Paul[41]) presents the story of Peter's virgin daughter. At the age of ten the girl is "a great harm to men" because of her beauty. When she is paralyzed Peter gives thanks to the Lord. To demonstrate God's miraculous powers, Peter heals her momentarily but then returns her to her invalid state. Another story concerns a virgin Peter reluctantly raises from the dead. When she is "seduced" by a passing stranger, the lesson drawn is that she was better off dead.[42]

In the Acts of John one finds the remarkable story of Drusiana who, having achieved a continent marriage with her husband after much travail, excites the passions of another man. Feeling herself "partly to blame for wounding an ignorant soul," she prays for and receives death. Alas, her dead body continues to arouse her suitor who attempts to desecrate it. In the nick of time a huge snake appears and kills him. When the Apostle and bereaved husband return to Drusiana's tomb they raise up and interrogate the lecher to determine whether he succeeded in his foul plan. Only when they know Drusiana is still pure do they bring *her* back to life.[43]

In exploiting images of sexual attraction and sexual violence, the Apocryphal Acts – including the Acts of Thecla – succeed in representing sex at the same time that they reject it. Writing about antique Jewish, Christian, and pagan popular literature in general, one author points out, "In folklore and fairy tale there is often a frank acceptance of sexual and aggressive feelings. Bourgeois popular literature accepts such material with certain premises, adequately summed up in the thesis 'Crime does not pay.' One can depict nearly any amount of sex and violence as long as transgressors reap their due reward. In cultures where sex is suspect, torture and rape become acceptable outlets, for they reinforce the notion that sex is bad."[44]

That the rejection of sex should entail the torture and rape of *women* seems as self-evident to the author quoted above as it did to men writing in antiquity. In the Acts of John a young man driven to murder because of the lust he feels for a certain woman castrates himself. He is rebuked by the Apostle, who says "it is not those organs which are harmful to man, but the unseen springs through which every shameful emotion is stirred up and comes to light."[45]

It is the female body as symbol of both sin and purity that is the appropriate object for demonstrating the defeat of one by the other. While martyrdom accounts typically focus on the body of the martyr, it is rarely in stories about men that sexual torture and the shame and humiliation of nakedness play an important part.[46] When the second-century bishop Polycarp strips off his clothes in preparation for being burned in the arena, the author concentrates on the detail of the old man stooping to remove his own sandals "although he had never had to do this before: for all the Christians were always eager to be the first to touch his flesh."[47] Here the author uses a synecdoche to represent nakedness, which is not in any case understood to be shameful.

In contrast, when the martyr Potamiaena, a virgin like Thecla, came before her judge we are told that he "subjected her entire body to cruel torments and then threatened to hand her over to his gladiators to assault her physically." She dies by having boiling pitch slowly dropped all over her body.[48] The virgin martyr Irene is sentenced to be placed naked in a public brothel before being burned on a pyre.[49] When Perpetua and Felicitas are brought into the arena in Carthage, "the crowd was horrified when they saw that one was a delicate young girl and the other was a woman fresh from childbirth with the milk still dripping from her breasts."[50] The text's concern with the modesty of the two women merely confirms the fascinating quality of female pain and humiliation.

In none of these accounts is sexual continence a major issue. When the drama turns around the defense of chastity – that is to say, when it concerns sex *per se* – the female martyr's ordeal often consists of explicitly sexual mutilation.[51]

From a few centuries after the Acts of Thecla comes the vivid example of the Syrian martyr, Febronia. Raised in a convent where she has never set eyes upon a man, Febronia is nevertheless required to do extra penance because of her extraordinary beauty. When a persecution of Christians takes place, only Febronia and two old sisters remain at the convent. Expecting to be arrested by soldiers, the older women are distraught thinking that Febronia will yield to their "seducement." They exhort her to remember the prize of virginity. When Febronia is taken prisoner by a pagan nobleman seeking to convert and marry her, her convent sisters greatly fear she will be unable to resist. Febronia's torture focuses on her sexual identity. Her face is disfigured, her teeth knocked out, her buttocks and thighs beaten mercilessly with rods. One at a time, her breasts are cut off and each time she is forced to parade around the city holding the severed organ in her hand. As she suffers this disfigurement and loss of female body parts her strength and her sisters' confidence increase. When Febronia is no longer recognizable as a woman her success as a saint is complete. An interesting feature of the story is that it invokes the name of Thecla and recalls her vision in the arena of "Christ in the form of Paul."[52]

The case for misogyny in the Acts of Thecla relies on some of the same evidence used to illustrate its "hostility toward men." There is first the curious behavior of the Apostle Paul: he vanishes from the scene whenever Thecla is in trouble, rejects her request for baptism, and, on more than one occasion, expresses fear that she will give in to "temptation." This may be, as some suggest, a deliberately negative portrayal of a male character or it may represent another concern – that a "comely" woman poses risks and, until she proves herself a Christian hero, is not to be trusted.

Thecla's Antioch ordeal, by which she proves her trustworthiness, is explicitly sexual in nature. Her travails begin with Alexander's attempt to rape her. Or rather, with her successful resistance to his sexual overture. In the arena she is stripped of her clothing, a condition acknowledged to be shameful by the detail that a cloud of fire hides this nakedness as Thecla baptizes herself in the pool of water. The beasts who threaten her are specifically male and implicitly sexual. The last torture visited upon her is a graphic attempt at sexual mutilation: Alexander's two "fearsome bulls," driven wild by their sizzled genitals, nearly rip the naked virgin apart by the legs. Thecla survives to live into old age. But not as a woman. Before taking up a career as an itinerant preacher, she "sews her mantle into a cloak" and takes on the soothing aspect of a man.

Citing the enormously popular story of Pelagia the Harlot who, after her conversion, dresses in a monk's robe and takes up a life of such extreme isolation and asceticism that she is assumed to be male, Sebastian Brock and Susan Harvey describe the theme of female transvestism as an "annihilation" of femaleness.[53]

The salient point of Thecla's story is that she triumphs by surviving all the threats posed against her. She trounces her attacker. She is invulnerable. But perhaps the author is uncomfortable with the "perpetual seductiveness" of even a consecrated virgin, as long as she remains a woman. Thecla receives Paul's blessing only after a series of tests, after the explosive hazard of her beauty is defused by the male identity she takes on following her baptism and her experience of symbolic rape. It is possible to interpret Thecla's trans-formation as the female equivalent of castration. Achieving "continence and the resurrection," following the misogynist logic, requires annihilating the feminine.

As with celibate women and the feminist interpretation, there is no way to know to what extent Christian men (or women) read the Acts of Thecla this way. The abundant examples of misogyny in similar and related works suggest that even holy women were the objects of deep ambivalence on the part of men.

CONCLUSION

In the diverse Christian communities of late antiquity, some men and women made Thecla's choice, linking themselves to a spiritual family and a heavenly spouse. There were certainly communities of celibate women. The typical continent woman resembled Tryphaena, however, not Thecla. She was a widowed head of a household with property and influence in her com-munity.[54] In the eastern Empire and elsewhere there also lived men and women joined in continent marriages, the objects of respect from many and of occasional condemnation by skeptics.[55] And there were, of course, those heirs to the male Apostles, the "church fathers," as well as an ever-expanding contingent of celibate men. Far outnumbering any of these were men and women of lesser vocation, sexual beings who paid their repects to others' heroic feats of chastity.

There was certainly no single audience for the Acts of Thecla and no single meaning assigned to Thecla's act of putting on male dress. It comes as no surprise that male and female readers or listeners might have had (or continue to have) different interpretations of Thecla's transformation. The question arises, how different? Or, for that matter, how much the same? Looking beyond the simple dichotomy of male/female, one perceives that how an audience was likely to understand Thecla's gender depended, at least in part, on its attitude toward sex, that is, toward sexual desire and the means and consequences of defeating it.

NOTES

1 Egeria, *Diary of a Pilgrimage*, Ancient Christian Writers, New York: Newman Press, 1970, vol. 38, ch. 23, p.87.
2 Wilhelm Schneemelcher, "Introduction to the Acts of Paul,", in Edgar Hennecke, *New Testament Apocrypha*, vol. II (NTA II), ed. Wilhelm Schneemelcher, Philadelphia: Westminster Press, 1965, p. 351.
3 *De baptismo* 17, quoted in NTA II, p. 323.
4 Methodius, *Symposium*; Ambrose, *De virginibus*; Jerome, *De viris illustribus*; Gregory of Nyssa, *Life of Macrina*.
5 See Virginia Burrus, *Chastity as Autonomy*, Lewiston, NY: E. Mellen Press, 1987; Stevan Davies, *The Revolt of the Widows*, Carbondale, Ill.: Southern Illinois University Press, 1980; Dennis R. MacDonald, *The Legend and the Apostle*, Philadelphia: Westminster Press, 1983.
6 Acts of Paul and Thecla, in Hennecke, Schneemelcher, *New Testament Apocrypha*, vol. II, ch. 5, p. 354.
7 Acts of Paul and Thecla, ch. 9, p. 355.
8 Acts of Paul and Thecla, ch. 20, p. 358.
9 Acts of Paul and Thecla, ch. 21, p. 358.
10 Acts of Paul and Thecla, ch. 25, p. 359–60.
11 Acts of Paul and Thecla, ch. 26, p. 360.
12 Acts of Paul and Thecla, ch. 38, p. 363.
13 Acts of Paul and Thecla, ch. 40, p. 364.
14 Acts of Paul and Thecla, ch. 40, p. 364.
15 Acts of Paul and Thecla, ch. 43, p. 364.
16 Davies quotes an excellent example from the Acts of Xanthippe in which a disgruntled demon exclaims, "From this destroyer [Christ] even women have received the power to strike us." *Widows*, 68.
17 Martyrs of Lyons, in Herbert Musurillo (trans.), *The Acts of the Christian Martyrs*, Oxford: Clarendon Press, 1972, p. 75.
18 Martyrdom of Perpetua, Musurillo, *Christian Martyrs*, p. 118.
19 Acts of Paul and Thecla, ch. 40, p. 364.
20 *De baptismo* 17, in NTA II, p. 323.
21 MacDonald, *Legend*, pp. 37–9.
22 MacDonald, *Legend*, in particular, ch. 4.
23 1 Timothy 2:9–15, 5:11–14; Titus 2:3–5.

24 In addition to Burrus, Davies, and MacDonald (fn. 5), see also Jo Ann McNamara, "Sexual Equality and the Cult of Virginity in Early Christian Thought," in *Feminist Studies* 3: 3/4 (Spring/Summer 1976), pp. 145–58; Rosemary Radford Ruether, "Mothers of the Church," in R. Ruether and Eleanor McLaughlin, (eds), *Women of Spirit*, New York: Simon & Schuster, 1979, and "Misogynism and Virginal Feminism," in R. Ruether (ed.) *Religion and Sexism*, New York: Simon & Schuster, 1974.

25 MacDonald quoting Pseudo-Chrysostom on the hard injunctions of Genesis: ". . . the text that reads 'your turning shall be to your husband, and he shall rule over you' is powerless with respect to those not lorded over by husbands. The passage 'she shall bear children in sorrows' does not apply to those who live as virgins, for she who does not bear children is outside the sentence of terrible labor pains." *Legend*, p. 53.

26 1 Timothy 5:3–16. The Council of Gangra, CE 346, forbade celibate women to dress as men. See Robin Lane Fox, *Pagans and Christians*, New York: Harper & Row, 1986, p. 372.

27 Wayne Meeks, "The Image of the Androgyne," in *History of Religions*, vol. 13, No. 3 (February 1974), pp. 165–6.

28 Dennis R. MacDonald, *There is No Male and Female* Philadelphia: Fortress Press, 1987, pp. 5–14; Meeks, "Image," pp. 180–1.

29 Peter R. L. Brown, *The Body and Society*, New York: Columbia University Press, 1988, pp. 49–50.

30 MacDonald, *Male and Female*, p. 128.

31 Colossians 3:9–10 uses the saying in reference to the divine image, but omits the pair male/female. See also Meeks, "Image," pp. 189–95 on diverse Gnostic sources.

32 Meeks, "Image," p.196, fn. 137.

33 Brown, *Body and Society*, p. 100; McNamara, "Sexual Equality," p. 154.

34 Brown, *Body and Society*, pp. 92–3, 96.

35 Brown, *Body and Society*, p. 99.

36 Acts of Paul and Thecla, ch. 12, p. 356.

37 MacDonald, *Legend*, pp. 46–9.

38 Meeks, "Image," p. 180.

39 Brown, *Body and Society*, p. 85.

40 John Chrysostom, "On Not Marrying Again," in Elizabeth Clark (ed.), *Women in the Early Church*, Wilmington: M. Glazier, 1983, p. 155.

41 Schneemelcher, NTA II, p. 345.

42 Acts of Peter, NTA II, pp. 276–7; p. 279.

43 Acts of John, NTA II, pp. 247–51.

44 Richard I. Pervo, *Profit With Delight*, Philadelphia: Fortress Press, 1987, p. 49.

45 Acts of John, NTA II, p. 241. Evidently the practice continued. The Council of Nicaea (CE 325) banned self-castrated men from the priesthood. Lane Fox, *Pagans and Christians*, p. 355.

46 See Margaret Miles, *Carnal Knowing*, Boston: Beacon Press, 1989, p. 57.

47 Martyrdom of Polycarp, in Musurillo, *Christian Martyrs*, p. 13.

48 Martyrdom of Potamiaena and Basilides, *Christian Martyrs*, p. 133.

49 Martyrdom of Agape, Irene, Chione, *Christian Martyrs*, p. 291.

50 Martyrdom of Perpetua and Felicitas, *Christian Martyrs*, p. 129.

51 In her study of religious representations of female nakedness, Margaret Miles notes that, "more than a millenium after Christian martyrdom virtually ceased in the West, texts like Jacobus de Voragine's *Golden Legend* and myriad visual images supplied the popular interest in women's body parts. Devotional texts like the *Golden Legend* graphically describe women martyrs, and such texts are often accompanied by pictures of their torture, dismemberment, and executions . . .

pornography did not become secular until well into the modern period". *Carnal Knowing*, p. 156.

52 Sebastian P. Brock and Susan Ashbrook Harvey, *Holy Women of the Syrian Orient*, Berkeley: University of California Press, 1987, pp. 152–76. See also the very similar martyrdom accounts of Anahid (*Holy Women*, pp. 92–6) and Candida (Brock, "A Martyr at the Sassanid Court under Vahran II: Candida," in *Syriac Perspectives on Late Antiquity*, London: Variorum Reprints, 1984). Of the Syrian martyrs, Brock and Harvey write, "The specifically sexual character of some of the tortures imposed on women martyrs reflects on the fact that men were the torturers. But the gratuitously detailed manner in which these incidents are described (in fictional accounts as well as historically accurate ones) reminds us further that men are also doing the writing." *Holy Women*, p. 25.

53 Brock and Harvey, *Holy Women*, p. 25.

54 Brown, *Body and Society*, p. 150.

55 Helen Waddell, *The Desert Fathers*, Ann Arbor: University of Michigan Press, 1957, p. 49 re: respect; for skepticism, see for example the second Pseudo-Clementine epistle, "On Virginity."

5

MARTYRS, ASCETICS, AND GNOSTICS

Gender-crossing in early Christianity

Karen Jo Torjesen

Gender crossing within early Christianity was determined by the patterns of gender relations and gendered expectations of Roman and Greek societies from the first through the fifth centuries. Both societies took as their prototype for maleness the aristocrat in his role as warrior or statesman-citizen and in either arena, whether war of politics, the quest for honor was integral to masculinity. In the public places where men gathered – athletic fields, the assembly, the courts, and the agora (town square) as well as on the battlefield – claims to male honor could be staked out or contested and either won or lost. The quest for honor was agonistic. Every social interaction between equals witnessed by a "public" could be viewed as a contest for honor – a dinner invitation, a gift, an arranged marriage. The arbitrator of honor was public opinion. Like the Greek chorus, the "public" was the anonymous audience for acts of honor; it deliberated and weighed claims to honor and gave its collective judgment. Ritualized recognition of honor could be secured through military duties, public trials, participating in debates, benefactions, holding public office and participating in assemblies.[1]

Honor was both public and masculine. The aggressive quest for honor, the willingness to compete for it and the determination to avenge dishonor defined the masculine character.[2] Because notions of masculinity evolved first in the context of warfare, the military virtues of courage and loyalty and the quest for glory became the hallmarks of masculinity.[3] The aggressiveness of the masculine personality and the willingness to avenge a loss of honor were correlates of the fact that the "instant willingness to engage in personal combat required a high level of personal aggression."[4] Not surprisingly, those traits which defined a masculine personality – aggressiveness, dominance, a desire for precedence, and a willingness to defend one's reputation – were the traits essential for success in the competition for honor.

The rules which governed the quest for honor in public life were codified into a set of virtues which guided public men in the performance of their civic duties. For the Greeks, these were courage, justice, and self-control; the Romans added a fourth, prudence, to head the list.[5] Although ancient writers treated these virtues as a universal code of virtue, they were gendered masculine because their practice was located in the masculine sphere of public life. The Roman discourse of moral excellence was masculine, the virtues for which a magistrate, a benefactor, a patron, were praised were the civic virtues that defined male achievement. Since there was no language for female achievement, when influential Greek and Roman matrons exercised political authority they were praised for the "manly" virtues of courage and self-control or for having a masculine mind.

FEMININITY AND SHAME

The social construction of femaleness did not preoccupy Greek and Roman intellectuals, but to the extent that it was articulated, the feminine was an antipode to the masculine. The counterpart of the public man was the domestic woman whose activities and domain were classified as private to set them apart from the public spaces and political activities dominated by men. The triad of female virtues, chastity, silence, and obedience were the counterpoint to the masculine virtues of courage, justice, and self-control.[6] Since women were defined by their sexual roles as wives and mothers, the principal virtue of womanhood was chastity; it alone constituted the foundation for a woman's honor.

Although a woman's honor was her reputation for chastity, it was not an honor that could be enhanced or advanced. It was a passive form of honor that must be defended. A woman was constantly at risk for losing her reputation for chastity; so her quest for honor focused on the preservation of sexual reputation. Since a woman's sexual fidelity was difficult to judge (affairs could be kept secret) there were socially prescribed ways that a woman could publicly signal her privately observed chastity, through her simple dress, modest grooming, no makeup and reticence to be seen in public. Girls were socialized to acquire a "feminine" personality, to be discreet, shy, restrained, and timid, qualities that would safeguard female chastity and womanly honor.[7]

A woman with a sense of shame possessed the female version of honor. A shameless woman had no concern for her reputation and therefore had lost her honor. The cultural foundation for a woman's sense of shame was her suppressed sexuality and her knowledge of her inferiority, the basis of her subordination to her husband. Although the virtue of courage is commended to both men and women, men are to show it by commanding and women by obeying.[8] The virtuous woman earned a reputation for her deference to her husband and her intent to please him. The virtue of silence was also a measure of women's subordination to their husbands, but more importantly it was a social value by which women could be discouraged from participation in the political sphere where speech was the primary instrument of power, the vehicle of authority, and means of domination. The defining qualities of womanhood, chastity, passivity, and subordination, could be sustained only as long as women were circumscribed within the world of the household.

FEMALE MARTYRDOM AND GENDER-CROSSING

The passive female virtues of chastity, silence, and obedience were incompatible with the heroic ideal of the aggressive quest for honor. The dilemma for Roman authors and for their Christian counterparts was how to praise women for heroic achievements. The only form in which women's stories have been preserved is in the lives of martyrs and ascetics, written to honor them and to praise the ideals of suffering for the faith and renouncing the world.

The martyrdom of saints Perpetua and her slave Felicity (Felicitas) is a rare piece because it was written by a woman.[9] Vibia Perpetua, a young woman of noble birth, kept a journal of her trial and days in prison and an eyewitness added an account of her death. For those who copied her journal, its religious value lay in her visions, windows on the world to come which the martyrs themselves were about to enter. Shortly before her scheduled execution Perpetua received a vision interpreting her anticipated death in the amphitheater where she would be thrown to wild animals for the entertainment of the crowd. In her vision, as the contest begins, her clothes were stripped off, her body became male and her assistants rubbed her down with olive oil: she had become a gladiator. Her opponent, "an Egyptian of vicious appearance," came out to fight her and the two fought fiercely hand to hand. She pummeled his face until he weakened, then she put him in a head lock. When finally he fell, she placed her foot on his head and the crowd roared. She had won. The trainer awarded her the green branch of victory and "she walked in triumph toward the gate of life." So much for Perpetua's vision.

The eyewitness report tells a different story. Because Perpetua and Felicity refused to wear the robes of priestesses, they were stripped naked, entangled in a net and left in the arena to be mauled by two wild heifers (a perverse pairing off of the gender of the victims and the gender of the beasts). Because the naked female body was such a potent symbol of weakness and vulnerability, even the blood-thirsty crowd was "horrified when they saw that one was a delicate young girl." The two women were then clad in tunics. Although wounded from being thrown and trampled, Perpetua was still alive, and the crowd's lust had been satiated. Perpetua was conducted from the arena to the executioner's sword and died there for her faith.

The significance of Perpetua's gender crossing lies in the way her vision of herself as a gladiator in the arena reverses the meanings of her being thrown to the beasts. Although both events were staged as a spectacle for the crowd, the gendering of Perpetua's body as either male or female shapes the meaning of the event quite differently. In the actual arena Perpetua and Felicity were indeed helpless, tied up in the net and victims of the animals. But Perpetua the gladiator was a fighter, an athlete taking a challenge, engaged in a contest and competing for victory. She faced an opponent with whom she was evenly matched and she could by courage, strength, and skill overcome him. A naked female body in the arena could only suggest a passive victim, not an active, powerful protagonist, but the naked male body of the gladiator of Perpetua's vision was a cultural symbol of courage, power, and strength.

Inscribed on the female body itself were the cultural values of female shame, women's inferiority made visible. In contrast the male body was an icon of honor and dignity, the visual representation of maleness. The dishonor of the female body was heightened when Perpetua was thrown by the wild heifer. She landed on her back, the tunic she was now wearing was torn and her hair was in a wild disarray. These two, the disheveling of the hair and the exposure of the body, were powerful symbols of shame for the female body whose honor could be preserved only by keeping it hidden and ordered. Here Perpetua is shamed, but Perpetua the gladiator wins honor through her victory, which is affirmed in the cheers of the crowd. In her male body she is awarded the victory branch and led through the gate of life. In her female body after being thrown to the animals she is led to the executioner's sword and dies as a spectacle.[10]

By seeing herself as male gladiator, athlete and contestant – an identity only possible in a male body – Perpetua takes the measure of the physical courage and strength she will need for the very physical spectacle that will play out in the arena. It is the very physicality of the experience of the martyrs, the brutal forms of torture during interrogation and the physical suffering of their slow deaths that call forth such masculine imagery.[11]

The naked female body itself is a spectacle signifying weakness and shame, the sexualized object of the male gaze. Perpetua in the arena in her female body is twice a spectacle, first of the dishonored female body, then of the humiliated prisoner first tortured by the beasts and then executed by a soldier. The gender-crossing of her vision makes possible a reversal of the meaning of her execution. She is a combatant not a victim; she is honored, not shamed; she is victorious rather than executed. To inscribe these meanings onto her experience as a martyr she needs a male body.[12] Women martyrs often reinterpret the meaning of their nakedness, they refuse the shame society attempts to inscribe on their bodies and they use the body itself as a visible symbol of their spiritual power.[13] This is equally true of the women ascetics.

THE GENDER-CROSSING OF THE FEMALE ASCETICS

Up until the conversion of the emperor Constantine (CE 313), the heroism of the martyrs eclipsed that of the ascetics. But after the trauma of persecution was over Christians celebrated the heroic virtues of courage, justice and self-

control in the lives of ascetics who renounced property, household respons-
ibilities, and family to seek Christian perfection in withdrawal from the world.
The disciplines they undertook, the practice of fasting, vigils of prayer, sexual
abstinence and the suppression of desire, were heralded by their biographers
as heroic feats. Because the inferiority of women and their subordination to
men was directly linked to their reproductive sexuality, by renouncing the
body and sexuality and following the ascetic life, women seemed to transcend
their femaleness.[14] Since the heroic ideals of mastery of the body and the
passions had long been enshrined in the figure of the warrior, women who
could sustain the physical rigors of fasting, the sleeplessness of the vigil, and
the deprivation of poverty were praised for demonstrating masculine virility.

Male hagiographers used the figure of Thecla as a bridge between the
woman martyr and the woman ascetic, for in Thecla's story the heroism of
the martyr was endured on behalf of asceticism.[15] In this way the masculine
heroism of martyrdom could be used to frame female asceticism. The story
of Thecla was already recounted in the preceding chapter. But some points
bear reiteration and development.[16] Of especial interest is Thecla's condemnation to death at Alexander's tribunal – a condemnation which led directly to
her being thrown naked into the arena where, it was expected, she would be
devoured by wild animals. Instead, Thecla was defended by a fierce lioness,
who fought and killed the other beasts. Saved, thus, in an ostensibly
miraculous fashion, Thecla was freed and thereupon, set out once more as a
traveling teacher, now in a man's cloak and accompanied by a retinue of
young men and women. When she finds (St) Paul, he confirms her in her
vocation to teach and baptise by saying, "Go and teach the word of God."

Neither Thecla's cutting of her hair in the style of a man nor her dressing
in a man's cloak receives any narrative development, but each stands at the
conclusion of a longer process of a change in identity. Although the process
begins with Thecla's rejection of a social identity as wife, as she breaks off
her engagement with Thamyris, it reaches its critical point when she refuses
also the role of loyal daughter, rebelling thus against the authority of her
mother even when it is backed by the state. This resolute act of self-assertion
is at the same time a repudiation of the female virtues of obedience and
submission. Her rejection of her familial social identity is the most radical
stage of her gender crossing, for in this one moment she changes from rich
to poor, from heiress to disinherited, without family, home or even city.

What is her new social identity? That of a traveling philosopher or teacher.
The story develops this new identity with significant narrative detail. Her
passion for the new teaching is underscored in the picture of her sitting
transfixed at her window for three days without moving or eating, captivated
by " the discourse of virginity." She has "fallen in love" with the teachings
on chastity in the words of the story. Her devotion to Paul as her teacher is
highlighted by her clandestine visit to him, purchased at the price of her
feminine adornments which she sheds as she casts off her old identity. In

prison she sits at Paul's feet in the position of a disciple receiving instruction. Finally she becomes his companion and accompanies him on his tour of preaching and teaching. Having refused to model her life on that of her mother, she has chosen to model it on that of Paul, the apostle, evangelist and teacher. In the framework of the narrative this change of identity is so radical that Paul himself is not yet prepared to acknowledge it and refuses to baptize her.

The rich detail in the story of the martyrdom, emphasizing the brutality, shame and suffering of death in the arena, highlight her strength, courage and fearlessness. These "manly" virtues prove the completeness of her identity change; she is no longer frail, weak and passive female. Not only was courage gendered male, but the freedom to choose was as well. Her defiance of family is, in fact, a masculine act of self-determination. She rejected the identity set by sociobiological necessity – that of wife and mother – and entered into her new identity by an act of willfulness.[17] The element of the miraculous in her martyrdom attests to divine approval of her new identity and, of course, saves her for the next episode.

When Thecla enters Antioch as a traveling companion and disciple of Paul, she has already assumed her new identity. However her identity as a traveling teacher is immediately contested by Alexander who sees in her not a traveling teacher of chastity, but a kept woman. At this point she is in danger of being reduced to her sexuality, her gendered identity at its most elemental. In this episode she must literally fight for her new identity in what is almost hand to hand combat with Alexander. She defends her chastity and her female honor by dishonoring him. The chastity she defends is quintessentially female, but her mode of defending it is aggressively masculine. She asserts her new identity as bearer of the message of Christian chastity before the governor and he becomes the first to publicly acknowledge it by releasing her into the custody of queen Tryphaena instead of sending her to prison. Once again her martyrdom reveals her (masculine) courage, strength and honor and seals this new identity in Antioch as the first one had in Iconium. When she sets out from Antioch she is no longer a disciple of Paul, but a teacher in her own right, accompanied by young men and women, presumably those she had converted to Christian chastity. By the end of the story she has also become an apostle, evangelist and teacher. Her donning of the male cloak signals that this transformation is complete.[18]

Women like Thecla had appeared earlier in the Greek philosophical schools. Diogenes Laertius describes the gender crossing of Hipparchia (300 BCE) who chose to become a philosopher. Her story has similarities with that of Thecla, Laertius reports, "She fell in love with the discourses and the life of Crates and did not pay attention to any of her suitors." When her parents failed to dissuade her from this new passion, they appealed to the philosopher Crates for help. He is reputed to have stood in front of her naked with his philosopher's cloak lying beside him and to have declared, "This would be your bridegroom and these would be your possessions." To choose for philosophy meant to choose against property, wealth, and comfort, all that a young woman stood to gain by accepting the right suitor. In Laertius' story, as in Thecla's, to choose the vocation of philosophy meant assuming a male identity. Thecla put on a cloak and traveled in public, male space. Laertius' story of Hipparchia follows a similar plot, "So the girl chose and adopting the same dress went about with her husband and lived with him in public."[19]

Nor did the gender-crossing of this female philosopher go unchallenged. Hipparchia, as a practising philosopher, took part in symposiums, all-male collegial affairs held in a private home with food and much wine in which the only women who were normally present were slaves and courtesans.[20] When she bested a colleague in an argument he attempted to recover his honor by reducing her to her femaleness, by ripping off her cloak. Hipparchia, although a woman, had by now transcended femaleness, and thus Laertius reports approvingly, "But Hipparchia showed no sign of alarm or of the perturbation natural in a woman." She could not be shamed by having her body exposed like the bodies of the courtesans and slaves who were there for sexual service. She had achieved a "manly" mastery over the emotions, and her body could not be sexualized by the male gaze.

Again her opponent tried to silence her argument by invoking her femaleness, "Is this she who quit woof and warp and comb and loom?" A woman was destined for the social identity of household manager and the domestic woman was always portrayed at her loom. Hipparchia responded by appealing to a premise of the Platonic school that both men and women could be seekers of wisdom, "Shouldn't I instead of wasting further time on the loom spend it in education?" Because the work of women in the domestic sphere was valued less than the activities of men in the public sphere, Hipparchia's opponent could have only answered her question with a "yes." The women philosophers crossed the boundaries of their gender by donning the philosopher's cloak, abandoning women's domestic work, taking up the masculine activities of study and by demonstrating a masculine mastery over the emotions. In crossing gender boundaries ascetic women exchanged their female socio-sexual identities as fiancé, wife, mother, courtesan, or prostitute for male social identities as teacher, philosopher, pilgrim, hermit.

The donning of a male cloak and tunic was often literally a flight from female sexual identity. The Christian ascetic Matruna escaped her retinue by disguising herself as a man in order to become a hermit and evade the authority of her family over her person.[21] Pelagia fled her life as a wealthy courtesan by expropriating the cloak and tunic of the bishop who converted her while he slept.[22] Apollinaria, a daughter of the emperor, also fled her retinue and her worldly life in the cloak of a man.[23] A female ascetic who took on the male identity and joined a male monastic community could represent herself as a eunuch, who for either religious or social reasons is castrated. Nonetheless even a eunuch has a masculine identity. Anastasia became Anastasius, Eugenia, Eugenius, Euphrosune, Esmeraldus. These were not gender-crossings in name only, the female ascetic also demonstrated a masculine character. "You are rightly called Eugenius," says a bishop who has discerned that the monk before him is female, "for you act in a manly (courageous) way."[24]

The female body suffered in the hands of male hagiographers for whom the effacing of female sexuality also represented the transition from sin to holiness. In converting to asceticism these women made a life commitment to chastity. To signal this transformation they cut off their hair and donned male clothes. For their biographers it was equally important that the beauty of the female body (or the femaleness of the body) was also effaced through the ascetic disciplines. Fasting disfigured the beauty of the wealthy courtesan Pelagia so that she was not even recognizable as a woman.[25] The fountain of tears associated with women's ascetic piety washed away Demetria's beauty, and the natural appeal of the female sexual body was obscured by Syncletica's refusal to bathe.[26] Fasting and exposure to the elements had made the naked body of Mary of Egypt unrecognizable to the holy monk Zosimus.[27] For their male hagiographers the effect of the ascetic disciplines in rendering the sexual body of the female asexual was more significant than their heroic renunciations.

The male admirers of ascetic women who praised their "manly" courage and boldness possessed only a masculine terminology for excellence, but for ascetic women gender-crossing meant more than becoming male, it meant in some way transcending gender altogether. This female perspective on gender-crossing is captured in a speech for Eugenia:

> I shall make known the truth, not in the pride of human rhetoric but for the glory of Christ. So great is the power of his name that women who stand in fear of it achieve the dignity of men. Nor can either sex claim the superiority in faith, the instructor of all Christians says that in the Lord there exists no distinction between male and female for we are all one in Christ. His rule I have wholeheartedly embraced, and out of the faith I have in Christ, not wishing to be a woman, but preserve an immaculate virginity I have steadfastly acted as man. For I have not simply put on a meaningless appearance of honor such that while seeming a man I might play the part of a woman, but rather, although a woman, I have acted the part of a man by behaving with manliness, by boldly embracing the chastity which is alone in Christ.[28]

Christian ascetic identity which raised a woman to the dignity of a man, erased the natural shame and inferiority of woman. However, this movement to masculine dignity and social worth was based on the idea that Christian identity transcends gender, that "in Christ there is neither male nor female."[29] The superiority of male over female was abolished. Eugenia did not aspire to womanhood when she embraced the traditionally female virtue of virginity, nor did she aspire to the honor accorded to maleness. Her claim to male dignity is not to an empty masculine honor, she is not a woman who appears to be a man, but a woman who acts like a man boldly embracing virginity. It is a masculine dignity, because it liberates her from feminine shame and inferiority, but she retains her female identity, which now freed from female shame is enacted in her bold and courageous embrace of virginity.

GNOSTICS

In the use of gendered imagery to express notions of sin and salvation in early Christian writing, such as the *Gospel of Thomas* and the *Gospel of Philip*, we find what we might call cosmic gender crossing. In some of the earliest versions of Christianity, salvation was expressed as the overcoming of sexual difference. When Peter challenges Mary Magdalene's right to be counted among the apostles, saying: "Let Mary leave us because women are not worthy of the life." Jesus responds: "Behold, I myself will lead her so as to make her male that she may become a living spirit like you males, for every woman who makes herself male will enter the kingdom of heaven."[30] Peter was asserting the social hierarchy of men over women. Since women were social inferiors, intellectually and morally deficient, they would not be appropriate candidates for the spiritual teachings which Jesus will disclose. But the reply of Jesus at one and the same time acknowledges, contests, and reframes this notion of gender. Jesus' rejoinder is that woman, qua woman, is indeed worthy of "the life," because her social identity as woman is not a hindrance to a spiritual identity. Social femaleness is radically different from cosmic femaleness. In fact, both men and women are symbolically female until they have entered a state of salvation.

Femaleness here signifies a spiritual state in which difference has not yet been overcome, a state of multiplicity.[31] Here unity symbolizes perfection, while multiplicity and difference is understood as an inferior or deficient mode of being. Becoming male signifies attaining a spiritual state in which difference is overcome and unity is restored: "When you make the two into one, when you make the inner like the outer and the outer like the inner . . . and when you make the male and the female into a single one so that the male will not be male and the female will not be female, then you will enter the kingdom."[32]

Another text, the *Gospel of Philip*, uses androgyny rather than "becoming male" as a metaphor for overcoming sexual difference. Here androgyny does not mean transcending masculine and feminine characteristics, but a restoration of the primal unity through union with the missing and separated part of the primal self. "When Eve was still in Adam, death did not exist. When she was separated from him, death came into being. If he again becomes complete and attains his former self, death will be no more."[33] Both Adam and Eve, both male and female, must be reunited with their alter ego, their lost companion, in order to be restored to their original nature.

Christians following the Thomas tradition celebrated an individual's entry into this state of primal perfection through a ritual of the bridal chamber.[34] In this gendered imagery the bridal chamber symbolizes the union attained in the final state of perfection, the restoration of that original unity that preceded the fall into gender difference. "Christ came to repair the separation which was from the beginning and again unite the two and to give life to those who died as a result of the separation and unite them. Indeed those who have been united in the bridal chamber will no longer be separated."[35] In the Acts of Thomas a couple, newly converted to asceticism and abandoning sexual relations, is promised "an incorruptible and true marriage" in which each will be united to a heavenly mate and will thereby be restored to his or her original androgynous nature.[36] Death itself is the consequence of the alienation of the self, symbolized in the original differentiation of the two genders.

Gnostic Christians used gendered imagery in their myths to challenge the conventional social meanings of masculinity and femininity and to push their boundaries to suggest a different and radical understanding of maleness and femaleness. The *Gospel of Philip* attempts to explain it like this:

> Whereas in this world, the union is one of husband with wife – a case of strength complemented by weakness. In the aeon the form of the union is different, although we refer to them by the same names. There are other names, however, they are superior to every name that is named and are stronger than the strong. These are not separate things, but both of them are this one single thing.[37]

In this world the union of husband and wife is not understood to be a union of equals. Masculinity was characterized by strength and femininity by weakness. It was precisely the hierarchical ordering of male and female that made the gendered imagery ultimately inadequate in its conventional form. This other way of naming masculinity and femininity was superior to the way they are named "in this world." Once masculinity and femininity have been understood in this superior sense, it is possible to grasp the nature of the primal self that "both of them are this one single thing." Notwithstanding, even gnostic writers continued to speak of the "perfect man" as the metaphor for the final state, just as the *Gospel of Thomas* speaks of "becoming male."

The assumption here is that male is generic on the cosmic level and that socially gendered men and women can become cosmic males. The fact that it is male, rather than female, which symbolizes generic humanity, reflects of course the cultural assumption of the natural superiority of males. Although the social construction of gender roles is challenged and done away with, the same gendered meanings are reinscribed in the symbolic order.[38]

As in Greco-Roman society, so also in the ideological world of Christianity moral excellence was described in masculine terms. In the social world of aristocratic Roman society moral excellence must be achieved in the public, political arena. Therefore the cultivation of moral excellence was viewed primarily as a male pursuit. In the countercultural world of early Christianity, however, the quest for moral excellence was urged on every Christian because the disciplines of fasting and praying, of scripture reading, and meditation were practiced beyond the boundaries of the public male domain. Men and women alike committed themselves to the quest for Christian perfection. Nonetheless the metaphor used to describe perfected humanity was the perfect man, *vir perfectus*.[39] Clement, the influential Alexandrian theologian of the second century, urges, "We should make haste to become like the gnostic, manly and perfect" for "the Perfect are rendered more masculine by the virginal spirit."[40] Since most early Christian writers viewed sexual differentiation as part of the fallen state, to become a perfect man meant to transcend differentiation altogether. The metaphors of a woman turned into man and the manly woman do not so much signify gender crossing as the intention to push beyond the categories of gender themselves. The tragedy is that this metaphorical discourse remains trapped within the discredited gender system, because gendered imagery is continually used to praise this progress toward perfection. So the effect of the gendered imagery on the symbolic level is to reinforce the social hierarchy of the world order or male dominance and female subordination. To praise the ascetic Olympias by saying "What a man!" celebrates her transcendence of gender distinctions, but at the same time underlines the social fact that female metaphors cannot be used for excellence or perfection.[41]

To the extent that generic human being is male, that is rational soul, every description of the Christian process of salvation is a form of gender crossing for women. To be saved out of the world of body, flesh, and sexuality to become an incorporeal, rational soul is to become symbolically male. In the light of these traditional notions of salvation, the cosmology of a female founder of a Gnostic school, Phloumene, is quite striking. She posits that in the original creation souls were already gendered. Since gender distinctions exist on the cosmic level, the rational soul cannot be gendered masculine in the symbolic order, as it is in Greek philosophy and early Christian theology. Since it was masculine and feminine souls that fell into bodies, the process of salvation will restore men and women to their primal gendered identity. Only in her system of thought can a woman be saved without undergoing symbolically some form of gender crossing.[42]

NOTES

1 David Cohen, *Law, Sexuality and Society: the Enforcement of Morals in Classical Athens*, Cambridge: Cambridge University Press, 1991, pp. 70–97
2 For anthropological studies of Mediterranean notions of male honor and female shame, see David Gilmore (ed.), *Honor and Shame and the Unity of the Mediterranean*, Washington, DC: Special Publication of the American Anthropological Association, No. 221, 1987.

3 Karen Torjesen, *When Women Were Priests: Women's Leadership in the Early Church*, San Francisco: Harper, 1993, pp. 115–18.

4 John H. Kautsky, *The Politics of Aristocratic Empires*, Chapel Hill: University of North Carolina Press, 1982, pp. 170–7.

5 See Cicero's *De Officiis* for the catalogue of civic virtues.

6 Torjesen, *Women Priests*, pp. 118–21.

7 Carol Delaney, "Seeds of Honor, Fields of Shame," in Gilmore (ed.), *Honor and Shame*, pp. 35–48.

8 Aristotle, *On Politics*, 113 and 198.

9 *The Acts of the Christian Martyrs*, trans. Herbert Musurillo, Oxford: Clarendon Press, 1972, pp. 108–31.

10 Perpetua interprets her own vision as revealing that the contest on the day of execution will not ultimately be with the beasts, but with the devil. By remaining faithful to death she will defeat him.

11 Maureen A. Tilley, "The Ascetic Body and the (Un)Making of the World of the Martyr," *Journal of the American Academy of Religion* vol. 59, No. 3 (Fall 1991), pp. 467–79.

12 Elizabeth Castelli points out that in Perpetua's story she progresses through several stages of divesting herself of her female social identity. She repudiates her gender identity as daughter when she rejects her father's desperate order to renounce her dangerous Christian faith and she surrenders her gendered identity as mother when her infant son is taken from her and is miraculously and instantaneously weaned. That her female body has been replaced by male body is the culmination of this process. "'I Will Make Mary Male:' Pietes of the Body and Gender Transformation of Christian Women in Late Antiquity," in *Body Guards*, Julia Epstein and Kristina Straub (eds), New York and London; Routledge, 1992, pp. 35–42.

13 Margaret Miles, *Carnal Knowing*, Boston: Beacon Press, 1989, pp. 58–62.

14 Kerstin Aspergen, *The Male Woman*, Stockholm, Sweden: Almqvist & Wiksell International, 1990, pp. 139–43.

15 The ascetic Olympius walked in the footsteps of Thecla, Elizabeth Clarke, *Life of Olympius* I, in *Jerome, Chrysostom, and Friends*, p. 127; the ascetic Syncletica was the true disciple of Thecla. See Elizabeth Castelli, "Life and Activity of Syncletica," in *Ascetic Behavior in Greco-Roman Antiquity*, ed. Vincent Wimbush, Minneapolis: Fortress Press, 1990, p. 269.

16 For the Acts of Paul and Thecla see *New Testament Apocrypha*, ed. E. Hennecke, vol. 2, ed. W. Schneemelcher, London: Lutterworth press, 1965.

17 Miles, *Carnal Knowing*, p. 55.

18 Both hair and clothing were important signifiers for female identity and more importantly for female virtue. A woman wore a veil over her hair and a plain white stolla to signal her chastity. These externals of dress and grooming were the cultural codes for making status and virtue public and visible. The cutting of the hair and the wearing of a man's cloak are critical to the story because they make visible and publica private conversion. They become the cultural insignia of her new identity.

19 Diogenes Laertius, *Lives of Eminent Philosophers* VI. Other women as well were members of the Platonic schools, e.g. Lastheneia of Mantinea and Axiothea of Philius. See Prudence Allen, *The Concept of Woman*, Montreal: Eden Press, 1985, pp. 127–63.

20 The gender segregation in the Greek-speaking Mediterranean required that the matron and daughters of the home retired to the woman's quarters during a banquet. Hipparchia belonged to this social class.

21 *Patrologia Orientalis*, vol. 3 (Paris, 1900), pp. 289–91.

22 Joyce Salisbury, *Church Fathers, Independent Virgins*, London: Verso, 1991, pp. 99–103.

23 *Acta Sanctorum* Jan. 1, pp. 257–61.

24 John Ansom, "The Female Transvestite in Early Monasticism: The Origin and Development of a Motif," *Viator, Medieval and Renaissance Studies*, vol. 5 (1974), p. 22.

25 Salisbury, *Independent Virgins*, pp. 99–103.

26 Karen Jo Torjesen, "In Praise of Noble Women: Gender and Honor in Ascetic Texts," *Semeia*, vol. 57 (1992), pp. 41–64.

27 Salisbury, *Independent Virgins*, pp. 68–73.

28 Ansom, "Female Transvestite," p. 23.

29 Galationa 3.28 quoted here is an early baptismal formula that women often appeal to to argue that they had transcended the shame, inferiority, and subordination of their female identity by becoming Christians.

30 *Gospel of Thomas*, Logion 114, in *The Nag Hammadi Library*, ed. James Robinson, San Francisco: Harper, 1978, p. 130.

31 In the *Gospel of the Egyptians* femaleness refers to lust, birth, death, and decay. See Aspegren, *The Male Woman*, p. 123ff.

32 *Gospel of Thomas*, 22, in *The Nag Hammadi Library*, p. 121.

33 *Gospel of Philip*, II, 3, in *The Nag Hammadi Library*, p. 141.

34 I am grateful to Donna Wallace for calling attention to a tradition of salvation as androgyny in the *Gospel of Philip*, *Gospel of Thomas* and *Acts of Thomas* in an unpublished paper, "From Thomas to Thecla: Androygyn as Salvation in Early Christianity."

35 *Gospel of Philip*, II, 3, in *The Nag Hammadi Library*, p. 142. See also p. 139.

36 *Acts of Thomas*, 12–15, in *New Testament Apocrypha* vol. 2, ed. Wilhelm Schneemelcher, Louisville, KY: Westminster/John Knox, 1992, pp. 339–441.

37 *Gospel of Philip*, II, 3 in *The Nag Hammadi Library*, p. 145.

38 Karen King, "Ridicule and Rape, Rule and Rebellion: Images of Gender in *The Hypostasis of the Archons*," in *Gnosticism and The Early Christian World*, ed. James Goehring, Charles Hedrick, Jack Sanders, Hans Dieter Betz, Sonoma: Polebridge Press, 1990, pp. 3–24.

39 Kari Vogt, "Becoming Male: One Aspect of an Early Christian Anthropology" in *Women Invisible in Theology and Church*, ed. Elizabeth Schussler Fiorenza, Edinburgh: T. T. Clark, 1985, p. 74–5.

40 Clement, *Strommateis*, IV. 132, V.6.

41 A male's movement toward perfection is not described as gender crossing. A Christian man is described as feminine only when he becomes morally degraded. Gender crossing for men signified a loss of status in the social order and a loss of moral virtue in the Christian order.

42 Anne Jensen, *Gottes selbstbewusste Toechter: Frauenemanzipation im fruehen Christentum*, Freiburg: Herder, 1992, pp. 365–426.

6

CROSS-DRESSING, GENDER ERRORS, AND SEXUAL TABOOS IN RENAISSANCE LITERATURE

Winfried Schleiner

In the Renaissance, cross-dressing appears as festive and ritual practice during seasons when ordinary rules of behavior are suspended (carnival, the Twelve Days of Christmas), as a transgressive act whose severity is discussed in legal, religious, and medical contexts, and – most notably in England – as theatrical practice, since here (as on the classical Greek stage) women's roles were played by male actors. If one asks where the imaginative center of Renaissance accounts of cross-dressing lies, the writers' veiled language, their suggesting while withholding, or their muting of existing sources can point the direction for an answer, for in the realm of the sexual they are sure indications of taboos at work: what is not *really* said or said with seeming resistance or difficulty is worthy of focal attention. Before considering cross-dressing in imaginative literature, we may glance at how the topic was treated in some prose accounts of the period.

CROSS-DRESSING IN GENERAL ACCOUNTS OF THE PERIOD

As a way into this topic, I will consider a story often cited in the Renaissance that originated with the second-century writer Hyginus. A young woman of Athens, in order to circumvent a supposed Athenian law forbidding slaves and women to exercise the art of surgery, cuts her hair, puts on male clothes, and enters the service of a physician. Although modern translations are available, I quote this passage from Thomas Heywood's compendium on women, *Gynaikeion* (1624), starting from the point at which she has learned the art of medicine from her male mentor:

> By her industrie and studie having attained to the deapth of his skill and the height of her own desires, upon a time hearing where a noble ladie was in child-birth, in the middest of her painfull throwes, she offered

her selfe to her helpe, whom the modest Ladie (mistaking her Sex) would by no persuasion suffer to come neere her, till she was forced to strip her selfe before the women, and to give evident signes of her woman-hood. After which she had access to many, prooving so fortunate, that she grew verie famous. In so much that being envied by the colledge of Physitians, she was complained on to the Areopagitae, or the nobilitie of the Senat: such in whose power it was to censure and determine of all causes and controversies. *Agnodice* thus convented, they pleaded against her youth and boldnesse accursing her rather a corrupter of their chastities, than any way a curer of their infirmities: blaming the matrons, as counterfeiting weaknesse, onely of purpose to have the companie and familiaritie of a loose and intemperate yong man. They pressed the accusations so far, that the Iudges were readie to procede to sentence against her; when she opening her brest before the Senat, gave manifest testimonie that she was no other than a woman: at this the Physitians the more incenst made the fact the more heinous, in regard that being a woman, she durst enter into the search of knowledge, of which their Sex by the law was not capable. The cause being once more readie to goe against her, the noble matrons of the cittie asembled before the Senat, and plainely told them, they were rather enemies than husbands, who went about to punish her, that of all their Sex had beene most studious for their generall health and safetie. Their importance so far prevailed, after the circumstances were truely considered, that the first decree was quite abrogated, and free libertie granted to women to imploy themselves in those necessary offices, without the presence of men. So that Athens was the first cittie of Greece, that freely admitted of Mid-wives by the meanes of this damosell *Agnodice*.[1]

The story would merit analysis on a number of levels: the historical and mythical were both addressed to some extent by Campbell Bonner, who claimed that the statement that the ancients had no midwives was absurd and was convinced that "wise women" treated minor ailments with impunity. He considers the story therefore a *novella* of popular origin, sharing, for instance, with the Christian legend of Saint Eugenia the elements of cross-dressing and "exposure as apotropaeic gesture."[2] A different level of interest, and one much closer to my concerns, would be the reception of the Hagnodice story in the Renaissance. For it seems to have been quite well known and taken for fact, as appears from Girolamo Bardi's (1600–67) inclusion of Hagnodice among famous female physicians.[3] Heywood emphasizes the envy and even malice of her male colleagues and renders with apparent satisfaction the successful class or sisterhood action of the Athenian women. It is doubtful that Bonner would have arrived at his ideas of the apotropaeic and aischrological core of the story on the basis of the English version, for Heywood does not have Hagnodice lift her tunic twice, but has her demonstrate her sex considerably more modestly.[4] Be that as it may, there is no doubt that Heywood's muting of sexual detail as well as the core of the story for him (the Athenian lady's "modesty" and the nature of the envious physicians' original allegations) are based, in our terms, heterosexually. Perhaps there is also a touch of something else when, as Heywood puts it, the physicians, after realizing that a woman has been treating women, "make the fact the more heinous," but since at best (or worst) this seems to him a pretext and thus an inauthentic reaction, I will not press the point. With reference to our range of topics, this "something else," that is, a different kind of phobia, is not hard to find.

When Jacques Duval, a professor of medicine, writes his book *Des hermaphrodites* (Rouen, 1612), which contains an account of how the physician rescued Marie le Marcis from prison and ignominious death by persuading the court that the accused was really *Marin*, a male, Duval early in his account comments that he is not writing on the subject of hermaphrodites "for any lascivious emotion [of his] whatsoever."[5] This rejection of questionable motive not sufficing, he adds that he has led a long and happy married life. His addition clarifies what kind of critique an author in the period, particularly one writing in the vernacular – since Duval was writing his work in French, partly addressed to *obstetrices et matrones* – had to anticipate when taking up a certain range of problems, namely hermaphroditism, crossdressing, gender errors, and gender change. In Latin, the physicians of the period express themselves more freely on such subjects because their addressees are the learned (and would necessarily have excluded most women).[6] The physician Rodrigo a Castro, for whose style Robert Burton expressed his admiration in his longish disquisition in Latin on "unnatural acts," annotates in his famous work on women's diseases the word *masturbatores* in a learned "scholion" defining four kinds of masturbation, but then adds: "This I would like to have written only for the learned, and it is certainly to be omitted if someone should translate this book of [medical] praxis into the vernacular ... "[7] It would seem that all these topics are dangerous because they variously stand in some relation to the subject most tabooed of all, that of same-sex sexuality.

It is hardly surprising that the topic of cross-dressing, in the period conceived as the proper use or the "abuse" of clothing, is located in the same tension field. In Philipp Camerarius' book *Operae horarum subcisivarum, sive meditationes historicae*, first published in Latin, then translated into vernacular languages and reaching its most expanded form in the French edition of 1610, there are several sections on clothing including one entitled "Sçavoir si l'habillement d'homme est sans distinction defendu au sexe feminin, ou non?" This is a rather roughly "historicized" account of the subject that cites the famous passage from Deuteronomy 22:5 ("The woman shall not wear that which pertaineth unto a man, neither shall a man put on a woman's garment; for all that do so are abomination unto the Lord thy God"), council decrees threatening specifically cross-dressing women with excommunication, and the Thalmudists' praise of conservative Jewish dress. Change of clothes, like all change (notably in speech and in forms of government) is conceived of as dangerous and potentially fraudulent. Interestingly, however, the second half of the chapter proposes a non-literal understanding of the interdiction in Deuteronomy, for here the author summarizes a couple of dozen "judicial" cases or instances of justified cross-dressing, divided into ancient and "modern." The most detailed case of the latter is that of a Christian taken prisoner by the Turks in 1595, who after being recognized to be female, under interrogation boldly revealed that she had all along fought the Turks in the Emperor's army; another case is that of Joan of Arc. Following the exposition of Nicholas of Lyra, Camerarius explains the Biblical interdiction as growing out of Jewish opposition to pagan practices: in sacrifices to Mars, Pagan women were armed as men, and in sacrifices to Venus, men cross-dressed as women. (Modern scholars have pointed to similar practices during Dionysian festivities.)[8] On the basis of the famous exegist, Camerarius' conclusion seems simple: the biblical text is about "ordinary" use of clothes, *l'usage confus*, and abuse, for it gives rise to vice. "For dressed as a man, a woman could with greater freedom abandon herself to men: as also a man in women's clothes would have freer access to the quarters and rooms of women" (pp. 324–5).

Answering a query about cross-dressing by Ben Jonson (whose specific question does not seem to have been preserved), the distinguished Hebraist John Selden, in a letter to the poet of 28 February 1615, takes the reading of the passage from Deuteronomy to a considerably higher level, namely to the level of a historical critique of mythology. He begins by retranslating it, as he puts it, "word for word:" "'man's armour shall not be upon a woman, and a man shall not put on a woman's garment.' In Deut xxii.5 so it is and not as the vulgar hath it, that *a woman shall not wear a man's garment, nor a woman's*."[9] He omits to say that the King James version (which I inserted above, somewhat anachronistically, into my translation of Camerarius) is quite close to the "vulgar" or Vulgate. With the help of Maimonides and others, Selden's point is historical: that the focus of the interdiction is not prevention of some indecency, but "avoiding of a superstitious rite used to *Mars* and *Venus*, which was, that men did honour and invoke *Venus* in *Woman's* attire, and women the like to *Mars* in man's armour" (col. 1692). This practice, to which, as we saw, Camerarius had alluded in passing, is then elucidated with a wealth of detail about the mythological ancestry particularly of Venus (whose origins, according to Selden, were worshipped in the Palestine deities Dagon or Astarot and who is ultimately identical with "the *Mater Deum* in mythology"). Baal, Dagon, Moloch, Atargatis, powerful names in the mythology of the Middle East, "were expressly noted by both sexes, and according to that mystery of community of sexes, were worshipped" (col. 1696). His concern is neither the "trifles" of grammatical genders (an interest with which he reproaches the great contemporary classicist Isaac Casaubon), nor any moral evaluation, but the "mystery of their theology concluding upon the masculine-feminine power." Unlike most Renaissance writers using the passage from Deuteronomy, including Camerarius, Selden seems to dismiss moral speculations deriving from it as equally trivial: "With what ancient fathers, as *Cyprian* and *Tertullian* specially have of this text or others dealing on it, as it tends to morality, I abstain to meddle."

This letter, by one of the most learned scholars of the period to a poet priding himself on his learning, puts into perspective Camerarius' topic of the freedom, and sometimes license, that male dress gives to women when they approach or seek out men and reveals the topic to be considerably more standard or even "commonplace" – in fact the genre of his work can be identified, in a descriptive and non-evaluative way, as a commonplace book. But we may probe a little deeper by focusing on what is *not* said in this section. First, in view of the many reported justified cases of women dressing as males, it is striking that Camerarius in this chapter does not here give a single "judicial" case of a man disguised as a woman. It is true that the title of the chapter narrows the focus to only half of the question regarding gender disguise, but he is quite aware that Deuteronomy forbids both male and female cross-dressing. In fact the negative example of the reign of "the young Andronicus" and his debauched court at Constantinople seems to suggest, if not identify, both kinds (p. 321).

That Camerarius has no example of justified cross-dressing of a man as woman unquestionably has to do with the Renaissance gender hierarchies that have been pointed out with respect to "hermaphroditism" and sex change: according to most (but not all) physicians of the period, the "one-sex model," as Thomas Laqueur has called it (that the female genitalia were the inversion of the male sex organs), seemed to exclude the possibility that a man could turn into a woman, but it was thinkable, possible, and documented in the medical literature of the period that occasionally a female changed to the "higher" gender and became male.[10] It would seem, first, that for Camerarius the question of whether a male is ever allowed to wear women's clothes need not even be asked – the possibility is unthinkable or at least unmentionable. (If he had lived in England, where boys regularly played women's roles on the stage, he might have sided with those radical Protestant attackers of the theater who found this practice abominable.)[11] Second, it is clear that something unmentionable lurks generally behind the passages most insistently presenting the dangers of cross-dressing: "If there is so much danger and bad portent in the change of clothes from one area to another, how much more frightful (*redoutable*) is the change from men's clothes to women's and from women's to men's? For apart from the lightness which is found there, followed by change in custom, honesty and shamefulness are lost, and there is danger of horrible confusion . . . For if one sex could not be distinguished from the other, such an abominable mix would open the door to all dishonest and shameful acts" (321–2). It would seem that behind such a phrase as "horrible confusion" lurks the fear of same-sex sexual acts.

MEN DRESSED AS WOMEN IN IMAGINATIVE LITERATURE

Renaissance romances contain quite a few episodes in which a male prot-agonist for reasons of intrigue, love stratagem, or escape from danger, puts on female clothes and baffles the bystanders by his beauty, a situation quite in contrast to the male macho prototype of the hero typically presented in modern romance, whether from the screen or the newsstand.[12]

In *The Honour of Chivalrie*, a romance Elizabethans could have read in translation from Italian, Don Belianis puts on a female disguise to facilitate escape,

> wherewith he became so fair that the damsels not a little wondered to see him so beautiful, that Persiana cryed out. Is it possible oh gods; such beautie should be on earth, you have been better served to glorifie your imperial thrones, unlesse heere you will inhabit to manifest your great powers among us.
>
> And truely (Sir knight) such beauty was never seene but in the Princesse *Florisabella* our Lady Mistresse: And well it is for all knights, you are not of our sexe, else so many would by you perish, as by the Princess our Mistresse, whose onely sight killeth (though not outright, yet with living death) like the murthering eyes of a slaying baselike.[13]

Similarly, when in the sequel to the "French" *Amadis de Gaule*, a work of paradigmatic importance for the entire Renaissance romance tradition, Amadis de Grèce changes clothes and becomes the slave girl Nereide, the narrator exclaims that anyone who then had seen Amadis in that Turkish taffeta interwoven with gold would have been as elated as was Aeneas by the appearance of Venus.[14]

Before we decide that such scenes might describe a fictional world entirely divorced from our own, we need to be reminded – as, for instance, Emmanuel Forde's romance *Ornatus and Artesia* (written *c.* 1598) makes clear – that the male heroes in such romances are conceived of as very young. Ornatus "attired himself like a virgin of a strange country (which he might well be esteemed to be, by his youth)."[15] There are at least two ways in which we may historicize this conception of beauty: it can be seen as the ultimate consequence of the "one-sex model" said to dominate Renaissance sexology; and it may relate, in some cases, if not in all, to the Renaissance notion that love makes a man (in a particular Renaissance sense) "effeminate" or, to use Sir Philip Sidney's term, applied to his cross-dressed hero Pyrocles in *Arcadia*, "womanish." (In fact, Pyrocles donning Amazon attire has been read as the visual or iconic expression of this Renaissance commonplace.)[16]

Cross-dressed often in order to prove themselves male (that is, to gain access to their beloved), these young romance heroes, after adopting female "bashfulness" and female discourse, appear to think of themselves as phallic "women," as is noticeable in a curious permutation of intrigue to which the cross-dressing often leads: another male in some way "tricked" by the cross-dressing will make overtures to the disguised male. This happens to Pyrocles, who is wooed by King Basilius; to Ornatus who, disguised as Sylvia, is wooed by the tyrant Floretus; and, perhaps most strikingly, in the sequels to the *Amadis*. I quote one of several passages describing how Amadis de Grèce (disguised as Nereide) is assaulted sexually by an aging Sultan:

> But inasmuch as impotent age had taken from him the strength of arm, it had left him even less of the force of excess. Since he knew this, Nereide was biting his tongue to the blood to keep himself from laughing ... In any case, the [Sultan's] knife, unbridled and out of the stable, falters constantly, since it was so weakened through years past, that the more he stirs the bridle or works it the less he finds it responsive, without even pretending to bounce or to kick, always keeping its head lowered: for a weak body does not respond to such desire at all.[17]

"Nereide's" laughter is *à la dérobée* and voyeuristic. At the same time, his reaction is eminently male: the smirk of the powerful and potent at the have-not and would-be. The passage depicting the attempted assault is one of the most sexually outspoken in this literary genre. The directness of sexual reference (only slightly veiled by the extended rider-horse metaphors) is not an accident but intimately connected with the topic we are considering. The occasion of cross-dressing allowed the narrator to write about sex while hiding behind a distancing *as it were* or *ut ita dicam*. His language was proper since he was speaking improperly. He created for himself an area of *Maskenfreiheit*, for he could pretend (and even say against better knowledge) that he was not really writing about sex at all, since at least one character and the reader knew that it was all a mistake. While on the one hand a passage such as this therefore approaches satire, its homosexual implications cannot be entirely denied. In fact, if we switch perspective from the cross-dresser to the assailing Sultan, would we not have to ask how it was possible that he was so deluded? (Renaissance accounts of "unnatural acts" ascribe same-sex love to the religious and cultural other, the Turk.)[18] Could it be that in a literary genre that could represent subtleties of male friendship and even what we may call unconsummated homoeroticism, this manner, *à la dérobée* and indirect, was the only one in which a version of homosexuality could be presented?[19]

WOMEN DRESSED AS MEN

Scenes of Renaissance fiction describing gender disguise constitute moments of high gender consciousness, and so it is with episodes of women cross-dressing. The purported motives for such disguise range from practical (to enter a castle or jail [*à la* Fidelio]) to what may loosely be called feminist (to explore a world of power, usually military – or at least to escape weakness).[20]

In different parts of the episodic continuations of the *Amadis*, two women in male clothes, Oronce and La Belle Sauvage, do stunning deeds of valor, sometimes by physical force, sometimes by intelligence. With all the carnage of battle and their superior strength in any duel, the author is careful to insist on their beauty and delicacy, and they are thus further examples of a Renaissance idea and ideal of beauty in which the erotic charge does not derive, as it were, from the genders being apart or diametrically opposed, but from their similarity: this similarity becomes the source of erotic titillation.[21]

In their disguise as males, Oronce and La Belle Sauvage are so good-looking that all women, including duchesses, princesses and queens, marvel at their beauty and may even fall in love with them. When a duchess, for whose cause Oronce has valiantly borne arms, sees her taking off her armor, the duchess is both surprised and excited by the warrior's face, since she still thinks Oronce is male. She had expected someone "robust and strong, because of the high degree of valor; when she saw such a delicate, rosy, and beautiful face, she was overcome not only by much wonder but also by a wonderful pleasure: and as she felt the pleasure, she fell in love as if she had never seen or hoped to see such a handsome and graceful knight."[22] Thus Oronce's delicacy and beauty, those traits that the reader, aware of her cross-dressing, knows to be feminine, are the prime stimuli of the duchess's sudden infatuation. A little later, the Infanta Licinie, who until then has been absorbed by her attempts to free her imprisoned brother, experiences a similar emotion. Licinie,

> who until that hour had not felt how powerful love is, felt her heart so much burn with the beauty of the person she thought a knight that leaving any concern for her brother, the prince, it seemed to her that she wanted to lose her eyesight looking at Oronce and to see the image of herself in her beauty.[23]

Like Oronce, who travels in the company of a lady (and therefore acquires the surname "Chevalier de la Damoiselle"), La Belle Sauvage has sought out a young lady called Lucence (thus being named "Chevalier de Lucence"), and naturally Lucence falls deeply in love with her "chevalier." In fact, for La Belle Sauvage, we have the narrator's statement that she possesses a certain grace that will attract males and females to her, not at the same time, but according to the gender that she professes by her clothes.

When a queen, smitten with the handsome Chevalier de la Damoiselle (Oronce) "si jeune et sans poil de barbe" finds out to her distress that the beloved is a woman, her friend the duchess (who has gone through the same experience before) tries to console her: "O how well have we done not to reveal our love! Else it would be all over with us."[24] The fear of making a mistake (a fear I will provisionally and tentatively call homophobic, that is, a fear of the homosexual) is shown even to traumatize a character. Thus the princess Licinie, who, as we saw, was so infatuated with Oronce, is emotionally traumatized upon learning of her error and paralyzed by the suspicion of further possible gender ambiguity after Oronce's female identity has been revealed. She is most reluctant to enter an emotional relationship with a young man with whose good looks she is impressed, for she is afraid that he will turn out to be a cross-dresser, too!

Rather than pursuing in more prose romances the subject of Licinie's shudder at the possibility of a same-sex act (for closer analysis, see my essay referred to in fn. 18), I would like to end with a glance at a brief segment of Shakespeare's *Twelfth Night* that some interpretors and editors, possibly unaware of the tradition I have been describing, have found enigmatic.

Viola (in Shakespeare's time of course played by a boy), after shipwrecking has entered, in men's clothing, the services of Duke Orsino, who has sent her as his messenger to plead his case with the seemingly hard-hearted Lady Olivia. Unlike other messengers before her, Viola as Cesario has succeeded in delivering a message to the lady, and Olivia, fooled by the cross-dresser, has taken a strong liking to the unusual servant. As Viola is on her way to return to Duke Orsino, she is pursued by Lady Olivia's servant Malvolio, at her behest "returning" a ring to the messenger.

> *Mal.* She returns this ring to you, sir. You might have sav'd me my
> pains, to have taken it away yourself. She adds moreover, that you
> should put your lord into a desperate assurance she will none of
> him. And one thing more, that you be never so hardy to come
> again in his affairs, unless it be to report your lord's taking of this.
> Receive it so.
>
> *Vio.* She took the ring of me, I'll none of it.
>
> *Mal.* Come, sir, you peevishly threw it to her; and her will is it should
> be so return'd. If it be worth stooping for, there it lies, in your
> eye; if not, be it his that finds it.
>
> *Exit.*
>
> *Vio.* I left no ring with her. What means this lady?
> Fortune forbid my outside have not charm'd her!
> She made good view of me; indeed so much
> That methought her eyes had lost her tongue,
> For she did speak in starts distractedly.
> She loves me sure, the cunning of her passion
> Invites me in this churlish messenger.
> None of my lord's ring? Why, he sent her none. . . .
> Disguise, I see thou art a wickedness
> Wherein the pregnant enemy does much.
>
> (II.ii.5–28, Riverside edn)

The seeming contradiction between Viola's affirmation to Malvolio that Olivia took the ring from her ("She took the ring of me, I'll none of it") and her subsequent denial ("I left no ring with her") at the beginning of the soliloquy has stimulated much discussion among interpreters, one of whom even suggests that the former line ought to read "She took NO ring of me!" Another one chronicled in the *New Variorum Edition* did not want to change the words, but thought that "a note of admiration after 'me' best expressed the author's intention, which was no doubt to make Viola utter an exclamation of surprise, equivalent to saying, is it possible any one can say she took the ring of me?"[25] But according to yet another view recorded there, "this passage always appeared to us one of the finest touches of the play," primarily because Viola is immediately seen to grasp "that the message [from Olivia] contained a secret of some kind which had not been confided to the messenger."

Licinie's traumatic experience (in the *Amadis*) of falling in love with someone who turns out to be a woman, Licinie's "homophobic shudder," as I may provisionally, although debatably, call it, can serve as the context for Viola's immediate reflex to shield and protect Lady Olivia through her lie ("She took the ring from me") from the prying and possibly malevolent servant. Potential same-sex love is the secret only Viola is able to grasp at this point.[26] When she is alone and full realization of what is happening sets in, she is presented as shocked, a state in which Shakespeare has her tap into the kind of harsh and ideologically loaded "discourse" which was common in his time on the subject of cross-dressing and with which we are familiar from Camerarius's commonplace book: "Disguise, I see thou art a wickedness / Wherein the pregnant enemy does much."

EPILOGUE

About a century after the period of my primary interest, the notorious printer Edmund Curll published an anonymous work (now attributed at least in part to Giles Jacob, 1686–1744) entitled *Tractatus de Hermaphroditis*.[27] That the title is in Latin in this case only serves as spice, because the work is in English and belongs to the genre soon to be called "curious." Its center section is called "Intrigues of Hermaphrodites and Masculine Females, and of the outward Marks to distinguish them" and contains stories, ostensibly set in Italy, depicting from a decidedly male–prurient perspective the most out-spokenly "lesbian" behavior presented in English and in print until then. One of them is about two young women who after losing their male lovers are described as taking up a practice of satisfying one another with artificial penises and instruments spraying moisture to simulate ejaculation. A young man falls in love with one of the women and in order to gain access to his beloved has not only to cross-dress but to simulate same-gender preference: he puts on women's clothes and makeup and carries a dildo in his hand. At one point he walks away from the ladies and, "pulling up his petticoats," pretends attaching "the instrument in a furbelow of his gown" (p. 44). He is said to deceive his beloved successfully "'till the moment of Ejaculation, which was not usual with the same Instrument in her Embraces with *Amaryllis*," the lady's female lover. "Prodigiously surpris'd," the young woman, "experiencing a material Difference between Art and Nature" (p. 45), then abandons her lesbian ways and rewards the ingenious gallant for his stratagem by marriage.

In some ways this episode of cross-dressing is the natural extension of the ones from the Renaissance we have considered. But some differences are obvious and bring into focus the specifics of the Renaissance versions. These two lesbian women most decidedly are not of the kind that figure in Renaissance books on "hermaphrodites," women (often called *tribades*) with a clitoris so large that it resembles a penis and makes them close to incapable of heterosexual intercourse. What remains unmentionable in Renaissance romances is named in these early eighteenth-century narratives. Whereas the character Licinie was emotionally paralyzed – traumatized – by the thought of the unmentionable, these women are described as acting out the previously unsayable, and this, in turn, is the result of a trauma received in their heterosexual life. Therefore the male cross-dresser can appear as the healer returning the women through his male pharmakon to comforting hetero-sexuality. The topic of cross-dressing may be said to have sunk to the level of pornography; the unmentionable has been tamed, domesticized, and even erased.

NOTES

1 Thomas Heywood, *Gynaikeion: Or Nine Bookes of Various History, Concerning Women*, London, 1624, p. 204.

2 Campbell Bonner, "The Trial of Saint Eugenia," in *American Journal of Philology*, vol. 41, (1920), No. 3, p. 260. Margaret Alic assumes the story to be historical – I do not know on what authority; see *Hypathia's Heritage: A History of Women from Antiquity to the Late Nineteenth Century*, London: Women's Press, 1986, pp. 28–30.

3 Girolamo Bardi, *Medicus politico Catholicus*, Genoa, 1644, p. 278.

4 For the Latin version, see Hyginus, *Fabularum liber*, Basel, 1535, where the story, no. 274, is on p. 63. For a modern translation, see *The Myths of Hyginus*, trans. & ed. Mary Grant, Lawrence, Kansas: University of Kansas Press, 1960, pp. 175–6.

5 Sig. A7: "pour aucune affection lascive qui soit en moy . . ." Stephen Jay Greenblatt has called attention to Duval in *Shakespearean Negotiations – The Circulation of Social Energy in Renaissance England*, Berkeley and Los Angeles: University of California Press, 1988, ch. 3, "Fiction and Friction."

6 See, e.g. Caspar Bauhin, *De hermaphroditorum natura*, Frankfurt, 1614; Amatus Lusitanus, *Curationum medicinalium centuriae*, Burdigulae, 1620, particularly centuria secunda, curatio 39; Estavão Rodrigues de Castro, *Tratatus de natura muliebri*, Frankfurt, 1668, particularly p. 55; Johann Georg Schenck, *Historia monstrosa*, Frankfurt, 1609; Isaac Cardoso, *Philosophia libera*, Venice, 1673, particularly lib. 6, quaestio 14, "De sexus mutatione."

7 Castro, *De universa mulierum medicina*, Hamburg, 1603, pars 2, lib. 1, c. 15, p. 69.

8 See Arthur Evans, *The God of Ecstasy: Sex-Roles and the Madness of Dionysos*, New York: St Martin's Press, 1988.

9 John Selden, "To my honoured and truly worthy Friend, Mr. Ben Jonson," in John Selden, *Opera omnia*, ed. David Wilkins, London, 1726, II, cols. 1691–6. I am grateful to Jason Rosenblatt for pointing me to this letter.

10 Thomas Laqueur, *Making Sex: Body and Gender from the Greeks to Freud*, Cambridge, MA: Harvard University Press, 1990, p. 65 (on the one-sex model); p. 141 quoting Zacchia as saying that nature is turning "to the more perfect." However, Isaac Cardoso is one of a small group of physicians thinking that sex change in either direction is possible *(Philosophia libera*, p. 462). In a very detailed account of the most famous Renaissance case of sex change, Patricia Parker has presented a differentiated account of medical and popular ideas on the subject; see "Gender Ideology, Gender Change: The Case of Marie Germin," in *Critical Inquiry*, vol. 19, No. 2 (Winter 1993), pp. 337–64.

11 On the anxiety in England about the consequences of cross-dressing young boys, see Vern L. Bullough and Bonnie Bullough, *Cross Dressing, Sex, and Gender*, Philadelphia: University of Pennsylvania Press, 1993, pp. 76–7.

12 I have treated these matters at greater length in my essay "Male Cross-Dressing and Transvestism in Renaissance Romances," in *Sixteenth Century Journal*, vol. 19, No. 4 (Winter 1988), pp. 605–9.

13 *The Honour of Chivalrie Set Downe in the Historie of Don Bellianis*, London, 1598, p. 132.

14 *Le huitiesme livre d'Amadis de Gaule*, Lyon, 1575, p. 526.

15 Emanuel Forde, *Ornatus and Artesia*, in *Shorter Novels: Seventeenth Century*, ed. Philip Henderson, London: Dent, 1930, p. 21.

16 See Mark Rose, "Sidney's Womanish Man," in *Renaissance Essays and Studies*, n.s. 15 (1964), pp. 353–63.

17 *Le huitiesme livre*, p. 541, my translation.

18 See my essay "Burton's Use of *praeteritio* in Discussing Same-Sex Relationships," in Claude J. Summers and Ted-Larry Pebworth (eds), *Renaissance Discourses of Desire* Columbia and London: University of Missouri Press, 1993, pp. 159–78.

19 This is raised here as a question of literary decorum. The most important works in this general field are Alan Bray, *Homosexuality in Renaissance England*, London: Gay Men's Press, 1982 and Bruce R. Smith, *Homosexuality in Shake-speare's England: A Cultural Poetics*, Chicago and London: University of Chicago Press, 1991. See also my essay "'That Matter Which Ought Not To Be Heard of:' Homophobic Slurs in Renaissance Cultural Politics," in *Journal of Homosexuality*, vol. 26, No. 4 (Winter 1994), pp. 41–75.

20 The literature on this subject in different cultures is immense. I have chronicled some of it in f n. 3 of my essay *"Le feu caché:* Homosocial Bonds Between Women in a Renaissance Romance," in *Renaissance Quarterly*, vol. 45, No. 2 (Summer 1992), pp. 293–311.

21 Marianne Novy has observed something similar in Shakespeare's plays: "Among the young lovers in the romances, as in the comedies, the genders are not polarized in their activities," *Love's Argument: Gender Relations in Shakespeare*, Chapel Hill and London: North Carolina Press, 1984, p. 189. Stephen Orgel instructively compares the urgency of Elizabethan warnings of the dangers of being enthralled to women with warnings against "sodomy." See his "Nobody's Perfect: Or Why Did the English Stage Take Boys for Women?" in *South Atlantic Quarterly*, vol. 88, No. 1 (Winter 1989), pp. 7–27.

22 *Le vingtiesme livre*, fol. 192ᵛ, my translation.

23 Ibid., fol. 211^v (misnumbered 122^v).

24 *Le vingtiesme livre*, fol. 78^v.

25 *The New Variorum Edition of Shakespeare*, ed. H. H. Furness, vol. xiii: *Twelfth Night, or, What You Will*, Philadelphia and London: Lippincott, 1901, p. 101.

26 See also Valerie Traub, "The (In)Significance of 'Lesbian' Desire in Early Modern England," in *Queering the Renaissance*, ed. Jonathan Goldberg, Durham and London: Duke University Press, 1994, p. 62–83; particularly p. 70: ". . . Viola's articulation of anxiety . . . is more appropriately viewed as the expression of the *dominant* discourse on *tribadism* and *sodomy*."

27 (London, 1718). The Folger copy is bound with Johann Heinrich Meibom, *A Treatise of the Use of Flogging* and has the no. 184284. For the attribution, see Ralph Straus, *The Unspeakable Curll*, London: Chapman & Hall, 1927, p. 253. I have written about the latter work in *Medical Ethics in the Renaissance*, Washington, DC: Georgetown University, in press.

7

ELENA ALIAS ELENO
Genders, sexualities, and "race" in the mirror of natural history in sixteenth-century Spain

Israel Burshatin

For three weeks in the summer of 1587, the women's quarters of the municipal prison of Ocaña housed two prisoners who were husband and wife. They were Eleno de Céspedes, a surgeon by trade, and María del Caño, his spouse. No, prison officials did not flout the rules separating male and female prisoners for the sake of bringing husband and wife together. On the contrary, this uncommon arrangement was emphatically orthodox in its intended aim of putting Eleno in the place where the governor and chief magistrate of Ocaña ruled that he – or, rather, she – belonged:

> In the town of Ocaña, 7 June 1587, the licentiate Felipe de Miranda, chief magistrate of this province, ordered that said Elena de Céspedes be removed from the room where she is now, for men frequent it, and that she be taken to one of the rooms in the same jail, which are at the stairway in the first patio, to the left of the hearing room, and that it be locked and the key handed to said chief magistrate. And that her wife, María del Caño, be put in another room in the women's section, distinct and apart from where said Elena de Céspedes might be, and likewise be locked so that no one may speak with her. (And this was thus instructed, commanded, and signed [etc.]
> [Signed:] Licentiate Felipe de Miranda.)

> En la villa de Ocaña, en veynte e siete días del mes de junyo de myll e quinientos y ochenta e siete años, el licenciado Felipe de Miranda, alcalde mayor desta probyncia, mandó que la dicha Elena de Céspedes se quite e saque del aposento donde está, por ser frequentado de onbres, y se ponga(n) en uno de los aposentos que están en la dicha cárcel, en una escalera que está en el primero patio della, a mano izquierda de adonde se hace audiencia, y se cierre con llabe y se le entregue al dicho alcalde mayor. Y la dicha María del Caño, su muger, se ponga en otro aposento en el quarto de las mugeres, distyncto y apartado de donde estubiere la

dicha Eleno de Céspedes, y ansy mysmo se cierre con llabe de manera que nynguna persona la hable. Y ansy lo probeyó e mandó e firmó [etc.] [Signed:] El licenciado Phelippe de Myranda.)[1]

The prisoner's relocation captures the vehemence – as well as the futility – of official attempts to peg Eleno's protean genders according to the ruling model of dimorphic sex and gender. Having heard from the physicians and midwives who examined Eleno's genitalia, the Ocaña tribunal orders Eleno's move from one side of the jail to the other. The accused is now legally – and grammatically – a female subject. But still impinging on this court-ordered gender reclassification is Eleno's rather smart male attire, a vivid reminder of more than twenty years of successful cross-dressing. Eleno's relocation to the female prisoners' quarters is also meant as a prophylactic of sorts, for men "frequent" her room. This easy association with men smacks of immodesty, at the very least. But after being pronounced female, Eleno's alleged feminine chastity also needs to be safeguarded. According to the report filed by the midwives who examined Eleno's genitalia, her vulva is so tight and resistant to the candle and fingers utilized to explore its constitution, that the midwives conclude that Eleno's virginity is intact:

> She stuck the candle up her female sex, and it entered a bit, with difficulty, and this witness was suspicious, so she also introduced her finger, and it entered with difficulty, and the witness, therefore, does not think that a man has ever been with her.

> La qual le metió por su natura de muger la dicha bela, la qual entró premyosa e poco, y esta testigo no se confió y tanbién le metió el dedo [. . .], y entró premyoso, y con esto esta testigo no entiende que aya llegado barón a ella.

The midwives conclude that she is not only female, but a virgin as well. Reclassified and relocated, Eleno would be among her kind.[2] But what kind is that? The regime of bipolar gender and compulsory heterosexuality shows its limits as it produces a classic moment straight out of a "women-behind-bars" B-movie. Having received the midwives' reports that Eleno is a woman who has never been penetrated by a male and that her wife María "is corrupted and wide and roomy" ("La qual está corronpida e ancha y anplia"), Eleno's sexuality acquires mythical proportions. The chief magistrate takes precautions and isolates Eleno from both male and female contact; yet he brings Eleno nearer to his beloved María, who is also under arrest in the same women's quarters.

By reclassifying Eleno as Elena and situating her among the women, the authorities produce a dissident female subject vulnerable to prosecution for offenses "against nature." With medical proof of what they suspected all along, Eleno is to be tried for her unruliness as a female.[3] The record of her first hearing in Ocaña (18 June 1587) shows the extent of official displeasure over the name *Eleno*. Rather than furnishing a masculine veil, the altered name seems to proclaim a defiant gender reversal, a deliberate statement of transitivity that challenges the rigid limits of the bifurcated world of masculine versus feminine:

> She was asked if they named her "Eleno" at her baptism, and how was it possible to give her that name and call her thus, since the name "Eleno" is neither customary nor is it used, while "Elena" is a well-known woman's name and is not used by men, nor is it so considered.[4]

> Preg[unta]do si le pusieron este nonbre Eleno en el bautismo, y cómo es posible selo pusiesen y llamasen ansí, pues este nonbre de Eleno no es acostumbrado ni se usa y el de Elena es nonbre conoçido de muger y no de onbre usado y guardado por tal.

The physical examination enables the court to (re)feminize Elen*o* as Elen*a* and restore her name's grammatical gender according to its putative feminine source. The prisoner enters the women's side of the prison and is led to the rooms located to the left side of the courtroom – the side, which, coincidentally, is also the body's feminine side, according to Renaissance medical discourse.

The Ocaña authorities thus produce the conditions for lesbian desire. Penal sexual etiquette confines Eleno among the women, and soon thereafter (4 July 1587) she is formally indicted for committing sodomy with the aid of a dildo: "with a stiff and smooth instrument she committed the unspeakable crime of sodomy" "con un instrumento tieso y liso con el qual cometió el delito enefando de sodomya." The proscribed sexuality is a figure of deception. It is an artifice, an impersonation of male-female relations; the alleged dildo fetishizes the phallic order of things that Eleno is accused of transgressing. Eleno must be kept among women, but she may not consort with them. Indeed, the precautions taken by the chief magistrate to sequester Eleno bespeak official discomfort with Eleno – that his transgendered persona displaces "true" masculinity and serves as a magnet for lesbian desire.[5] Female Elena will be held in solitary confinement in the women's quarters. And no one but the chief magistrate himself will hold the key to the female surgeon's cell. A woman with medical knowledge, who also happens to be married to another woman, contradicts the ruling ideology of the household, and it is therefore not surprising that this brown-skinned surgeon – her mother was an African slave – is also under suspicion of having made pacts with the devil, as some have alleged. Her wife, María, is under strict orders to be kept "distinct and apart" from this seductive and capable surgeon.

In addition to the midwives' report, chief magistrate don Felipe de Miranda also receives learned confirmation of Eleno's female genitalia from three physicians (doctors Alonso Gutiérrez, Villalta de Carbajal and Vázquez) who concur that Eleno is a woman and that her body shows no signs of hermaphroditism. Their working medico-legal definition of sex is mainly genital. But, unlike the midwives' physical sketch, the physicians' portrait of

Eleno slips into the more ambiguous areas of cultural style and performance. They first list genital conformation, the primary measure of Eleno's correct location in the hierarchy of gender. But most interesting from the point of view of the history of sexualities is that two out of the three physicians include along with the expected physical characteristics ("vagina" and "breast"/ "vasso" and "pecho"), language and other unspecified cultural markers ("speech and all the rest"/"habla y de todo lo demás"), and that most polyvalent and malleable of all visible corporeal signifiers, "face" ("rrostro"):

> They found that, in reality, she is not nor has she ever been a man, but a woman, which they saw and found in her natural vagina, similar to and properly that of a woman, and all the signs of woman, like breast, face, speech, and all the rest, from which it is inferred that she is female [Dr. Villalta's testimony].
>
> Having looked at and examined him [sic], there was not nor does she have any sign of being a man, but only the female sex, **and in the composure of body, face, and speech she has the appearance of a woman, as she is, and not a man** [Dr. Vásquez's testimony].

> Hallaron que realmente no es ni a sido honbre, sino muger, lo qual vieron y constó de su vasso natural, semejante e proprio de muger, e todas las señales de muger, como son pecho y rrostro y habla y de todo lo demás, de que se ynfiere ser muger [Dr. Villalta's testimony].
>
> A el qual aviendo vido e miradole no tenía ny tiene ni a tenido señal nynguna de hombre, sino solamente sexo de muger **y en conpastura** [sic] **de cuerpo, de pecho, y rrostro, e fabla pareçe ser tal muger como lo es e no hombre** [Dr. Vázquez's testimony].

As these physicians would have it, Eleno's feminine *conpostura* ("composure") belies her attempts at masking her true gender.

In a medico-legal setting, the concept of *conpostura* renders the code of gender and sexuality as an unproblematic system of correspondences: body, speech, body-language, humoral complexion, voice, and the site within which all of these corporeal and cultural signs of gender are articulated are taken unambiguously as statements of the feminine. The experts conclude that Eleno is, after all, just Elena. The Book of Nature is transparent when it comes to gender. It is, as Pliny would have it, a world in which bodies, even in death, continue to articulate the division of cultural roles that makes patriarchy possible:

> Males are heavier than females [. . . .] The dead bodies of men float upon the back, those of women with the face downwards, as if, even after death, nature were desirous of sparing their modesty.

> Virorum cadavera supina fluitare, feminarum prona, velut pudori defunctarum parcente natura.[6]
>
> (Book VIII, Ch. 18; vol. 2, pp. 158–59)

The male body and ethos represent a completed process of development, "weightier" in every respect. Drier and hotter in complexion, male composure orients the body upwards, superior and supine, facing the sun. The female body, on the other hand, its complexion cold and wet, communicates modesty and shamefulness by its prone position, looking down toward the depths of the watery medium that informs its personal constitution and temperament.

What was Eleno's true *conpostura*? In view of Eleno's astounding record of twenty years of successful "passing" as a man, we may properly question the uninflected femininity that physicians and midwives read into Eleno's *conpostura*. They would picture Eleno floating in a prone position. But the story of her/ his life, which reads like a picaresque narrative of fluctuating "fortunes and adversities" ("fortunas y adversidades"), would trace a free-floating body mirroring the ebb and flow of willed and imposed gender inflections, as well as the multiplicity of readings generated by those constructions.[7] Contrary to the Ocaña decision, a year and a half earlier the Madrid court of the archbishop of Toledo had ruled that Eleno was a man and not a hermaphrodite, thus clearing the way for Eleno and María's union. But before arriving at a singular, masculine identity for Eleno, his/her rather more complex intergendered *conpostura* left its mark in the legal record. In December of 1584 the vicar of Madrid, Juan Baptista Neroni, was struck by the ambiguity of Eleno's beardless face: "The vicar, seeing her without a beard or facial hair, asked her whether she was a capon, and she replied, no" ("Y el vicario biendo a ésta sin barba y lampiña la dixo que si hera capón, y ésta respondió que no"). A capon is a castrated male, a eunuch. Eleno has no facial hair, but her skin is not smooth. Eleno's face bears the brand of slavery, which was burned into both cheeks when she was a little girl and a slave.

Born into slavery, Eleno's manumission occurred, at age twelve, following the death of her mistress, the "original" Elena de Céspedes, in whose memory the freed slave was (re)named. Is there a truly personal history to Eleno beyond the laconic record of the transfer of human chattel she presents to the court? The bits and pieces scattered throughout the court documents give no account of a name prior to the one bestowed at age twelve "in contemplation" of the deceased owner. As far as the legal system of slaveholders is concerned, the name Elena – an archetype of femininity if there is one – locates the prisoner's gender antecedents in servitude, which is itself a paradox, for the intensely phallocratic regime of slavery calls into question gender as a naturalized category. The whip and the branding iron ungender the slave's body and transform it into a living and breathing ledger-book entry.[8] Is it really possible to examine Eleno's face and not interpret the slave brand? Or, rather, do the physicians construe the mark of ungendering as a sign of feminization when they include "rrostro" ("face") in their list of feminine markers of Eleno's *conpostura*?

Confronted with Eleno's history of gender ambiguity, the ability to translate the mark of slavery as a sign of feminine gender furnishes a convenient advantage for a tribunal seeking to feminize and punish "her" for gender dissidence and sexual irregularity. The name *Elena* becomes synonymous with the slave brand on the subject's face, which remains intelligible according to the ruling code of Castilian hegemony nearly thirty years after manumission. The standard autobiographical testimony portion of trials of the Inquisition, "Discourse of her/his life" ("Discurso de su vida"), is for Eleno a narrative that subjugates by its sequential and linear disposition. And, thus, in the act of narrating her slave origins Eleno rearticulates a slave positionality in a society obsessed with documenting honorable and "untainted" origins and the so-called "purity of blood" ("limpieza de sangre"). At the time of Eleno's birth *c.* 1545, Habsburg Spain was turning increasingly ruthless in its extirpation of the multicultural elements of medieval Spain, whose porous frontiers prior to 1492 and the conquest of Granada offered fertile ground for extraordinary cultural and human achievements amidst its three constitutive religious cultures of Christians, Muslims, and Jews. Eleno's birth in Alhama de Granada placed her at one of the principal sites of an Islamic culture increasingly proscribed and in swift decline, but vibrant, still, in its resistance to Christian and Castilian hegemony.[9]

To what extent do culture and "race" figure in the calculus of gender, sex, personal constitution, and complexion that comprise Eleno's *compostura*? Eleno's history is an important document in this regard since *hermaphrodite* emerges not just as a designation for disruptive sexuality and unusual corporeal morphology, but as "nation" or "race." Eleno's chief defense to the triple charge of sodomy, contempt for the sacrament of marriage, and demonic affiliation is that he is a hermaphrodite, even though at the time of her trials, first in Ocaña and then, after 14 July 1587, in the court of the Inquisition at Toledo, her body bears no actual "facts" of hermaphroditism. Although physically a female, her subjectivity remains that of the hermaphrodite he claims to have been from the age of sixteen until just twelve days prior to his imprisonment in Ocaña. He describes how his full set of male genitals withered from a cancer that developed following a traumatic riding accident. From Eleno's own perspective – that of a licensed and literate medical practitioner – his or her hybrid *compostura* is assimilated to the male subjectivity that he overestimates, even after losing the male member that he and others testify was present at the time of his physical exams prior to his marriage to María. As a mode of filiation with history, hermaphroditism stands as a metaphor for race that displaces slavery/femininity. In claiming the status of hermaphrodite, Eleno transforms the meaning of her brown skin. Facing the Inquisitors, Eleno's only felicitous point of origin is the transformation to hermaphrodite that he describes.

Although some medical theories lent weight to the notion of female to male transformations, Eleno would find little support for her assertion that her body was more than the bearer of slave "stygmata."[10] But there is something numinous about her body's transformation in the course of giving birth to her first and only child, the event that led to her subsequent adoption of masculine dress, her passage from typically female to male professions (weaver, hosemaker, shepherd, tailor, soldier, surgeon) and to her becoming a husband, the ultimate "confirmation" of superseded femaleness. Her description of the effects of childbirth transforms the body of a former slave into the mirror of the other, as in an Ovidian tale translated into a "Christian" language[11]:

> When she gave birth, as she has said, with the force that she applied in labor she broke the skin over the urinary canal, and a head came out [the length] of about half a big thumb, and she indicated it so; in its shape it resembled the head of a male member, which when she felt desire and natural excitement it would come out as she has said, and when she wasn't excited it contracted and receded into the place where the skin had broken.

> Quando ésta parió, como tiene dicho, con la fuerça que puso en el parto se le rompió un pellejo que benía sobre el caño de la orina y le salió una cabeza como medio dedo pulgar, que ansí lo señaló, que parecía en su hechura cabeça de miembro de hombre, el qual quando ésta tenía deseo y alteración natural, le salía como dicho tiene, y quando no estava con alteración se enmusteçía y recogía a la parte y seno donde estava antes que se le rompiese el dicho pellejo.

She had married about a year earlier, at age sixteen (c. 1561), and had lived with her husband, a stonemason from Jaén, for a scant three months, until he left her. She never saw him again, but soon thereafter she received news of his death. Their son, who was named Christóval after his father, was thought to be living in Seville, where she had left him as a little boy in the care of a foreigner who operated a bread oven in the city, and she apparently had no further contact with her son. Eleno thus gave birth to a son and to a penis.

But the newly acquired male genitalia were imperfectly formed, in that the sexual arousal ("alteration") Eleno felt in the company of women was impeded by the skin covering his penis, which prevented him from having a full erection. Within a year after his metamorphosis, while living in Sanlúcar de Barrameda, Eleno underwent a surgical procedure to remove the impediment. The operation was performed by a certain licenciate Tapia. Eleno credits this surgeon with the first medical diagnosis of his condition – that Eleno was a hermaphrodite. The operation left Eleno with a fully working member: "and she was left with the aptitude to have relations with women" ("y esta quedó con abtitud de poder tener quenta con muger"). His female to male transformation finally complete, Eleno, who was working as a hose maker at the time, was properly endowed to carry on a love affair with his employer's wife for the next four or five months.

In his own defense and in answer to charges of sodomy and the sin against nature, he submits to the Toledo tribunal of the Inquisition a learned letter contextualizing his body's metamorphosis in the discourses of medicine and natural history.[12] He pleads innocent to all the charges. Nothing he ever did – dressing as a man, being aroused by and having sexual relations with women, marriage to María, and medical practice as a male surgeon – was contrary to nature, since nature itself produced his altered form. He reasons that his physical transformation, though unusual, parallels the metamorphoses and unusual births recorded in natural history by such eminent authorities as Cicero, Saint Augustine, and Pliny:

> But neither with tacit nor explicit pact with the devil did I ever pretend to be a man in order to marry a woman, as has been alleged. And what happens is that since in this world many times people have been seen who are androgynous, who, in other words, are called hermaphrodites, who have both sexes, I too have been one of these, and when I intended to marry I prevailed more in the masculine sex and was naturally a man and had all that was necessary for a man to be able to marry. (And I informed them about it and gave visual proof to the physicians and surgeons expert in the art, who saw and touched me and testified under oath that I was a man and could marry a woman, and with such judicial proof I married as a man [. . .]
>
> As for the other [charge], regarding the testimony by women questioned in this case, with whom I have had carnal coupling, they have given evidence that I was a man and had the effect of such at the time that such coupling occurred, and I was considered a man, and that is what the first of the four witnesses says, whose testimony was given to me. And this is not denied by saying that I had no effusion of seed, since this did not occur due to my not being a man, but for some of the same reasons that other men fail to do so [. . .]
>
> As for the other [charge], I am not hindered by the testimony of three of the four witnesses who declare in the declaration given to me, that I naturally could not have been a man, but that if I have given the impression of one, it has been due to devilish illusion or artifice, as these said witnesses have claimed, and they speak thus of appearances and vain beliefs, and they do not harm me in particular because **I have quite naturally been a man and a woman, and even though this may seem like a prodigious and rare thing that is seldom seen, hermaphrodites, as I have been one myself, are not against nature** [emphasis added].

> Por que yo con pacto expresso nj tácito del demonio nunca me fingj honbre para casarme con muger como se me pretende imputar. E lo que pasa es que como en este mundo muchas veçes se an vjsto personas que son andróginos, que por otro nonbre se llaman hermafroditos, que tienen entramos sexos, yo tanbién e sido uno de estos. Y al tienpo

que me pretendí casar incalecía e prevalescía más en el sexo masculino e natural mente era honbre e tenja todo lo necessario de honbre para poderme casar, y de que lo era hiçe información e probanza ocular de médicos e zirujanos peritos en el arte, los quales me vjeron e tentaron e testificaron con juramento que era tal honbre y me podía casar con muger y con la dicha probanza hecha judiçial mente me casé por honbre [. . . .]

Lo otro por que por dichos de mugeres que están en esta causa examjnados con quien yo e tenjdo ayuntamjento carnal constara yo ser honbre y tener efectos de tal al tiempo que tenja el djcho ayuntamjento, y tenerme por tal honbre. Y ansí lo dize el primero testigo de los quatro que se me dieron en publicación. Y no obsta el deçir que no tuve effusión semynys, por que aquello no fue por falta de ser honbre, sino por alguna de las causas por las quales otros honbres caen en esta falta[. . . .]

Lo otro por que no obsta lo que diçen los tres testigos de los quatro que se me dieron en esta ultima publicación, que natural mente yo no e podido ser honbre, sino que si lo e parecido a sido por illusión del demonio o arte suya, por que estos dichos testigos vjenen a conclujr que esto les paresçe, y así hablan de parezer y vanas creençias, y en espeçial no me dañan por que **yo natural mente e sido honbre y muger, y aunque esto sea cosa prodigiosa y rrara que pocas veces se ve, pero no son contra naturaleza los hermafroditos como yo lo e sido.**

On the margins of the passage quoted Eleno cites his classical sources: Cicero, *De Divinatione*, Augustine, *Civitatem Dei*, and Pliny, *Naturalis Historia*.[13] Among these, his citation of Book VII of Pliny's *Natural History* is an especially pertinent reference, and one that would have an uncanny relevance to Eleno's place in historiography.

Organized acording to Pliny's customary principle of "chaotic enumeration,"[14] Book VII ranges across "Man, his birth, his organization, and the invention of the Arts." Echoing Eleno's own concerns we find the following chapter headings: The wonderful forms of different nations (Ch. 2); Marvellous births (Ch. 3); Some remarkable properties of the body (Ch. 18, which contains the excerpt quoted above regarding the "physics" of gender in the bodies of the supine male and the prone female); and Slaves for which a high price has been given (Ch. 40). In citing Pliny, Eleno casts himself as one more instance in a long chain of nature's marvels: "Individuals are occasionally born, who belong to both sexes; such persons we call by the name of hermaphrodites; they were formerly called Androgyni and were looked upon as monsters, but at the present day they are employed for sensual purposes" (Book VII, Ch. 3, 2: 136). In some, the transformation occurs after birth, as implausible as it may seem: "The change of females into males is undoubtedly no fable" (Book VII, Ch. 3, 2: 138). Even in the *locus classicus* cited by Eleno in order to naturalize her sexual variance, two questions immediately arise regarding the preternatural, which will also haunt Eleno: what are marvelous "facts" and what sort of agency produces them?

In her searching study of the epistemology of miracles and marvels in early modern thought, Lorraine Daston outlines the operative "distinctions between marvels and miracles, and the related distinctions between natural, preternatural, and supernatural causation." Daston contrasts Augustine's "profusion of marvels, ordinary and extraordinary" with Aquinas's Aristotelian framework, within which "nature [is] considerably more orderly and autonomous [. . .]." For Aquinas, the supernatural consists in "God's unmediated actions"; the natural is "what happens always or most of the time"; and the preternatural is "what happens rarely, but nonetheless by the agency of created beings [. . . .] Marvels belong, properly speaking, to the realm of the preternatural." Preternatural effects can therefore be produced by "unaided nature," as well as by spirits, angels, and demons. In the sixteenth century "the preternatural came to be ever more closely associated with the dubious and possibly demonic activities of magic and divination."[15] While the Spanish Inquisition was remarkably rationalistic in its rejection of demonic agency, the charge alone of having made pacts with the devil could have devastating consequences for the accused, and it was often used to quell dissident women, Moriscos, *conversos* and other marginal groups.[16] Viewed in this wider context, Eleno's citation of Pliny is a well considered move, since she insists that nature, and not sorcery, is the agent of her metamorphosis. "Hermaphrodites like myself are not contrary to nature, even though this is a prodigious and rare thing, seldom seen." Her body belongs to the temporal and logical sequence of the preternatural. Pliny's text furnishes the record of these unique deviations. In the words of Gian Biagio Conte, while the order of nature is indisputable, it also "abandon[s] itself to play [. . .] experimenting with multi-form productivity." The supreme agent of artifice is nature itself, *natura artifex*.[17]

Pliny's hermaphrodites inhabit a peripheral geographic region on the edges of the empire, which is also home to people of darker colored skin. Eleno's own genealogy – furnished to the Inquisitors as a requisite portion of the "Discurso de su vida" – links Eleno to these other "gentiles."

> In response to the question, he said that he thinks both parents are Old Christians, although his mother was a slave who was black and she must have been of the caste of Gentiles. And that neither she nor her parents have ever been penanced by the Holy Office.

> Preguntada, dixo que éste y sus padres cree son christianos viejos, aunque su madre era esclava que era negra, y devía de ser de casta de jentiles, y que ésta ni sus padres no an sido presos ni penitençiados por el sancto officio.

114

Despite an Old Christian and Castilian father – a shadowy and ultimately absent figure in Eleno's upbringing and legal status – it is through her black African mother that Eleno taps into the discourse of "race" and Europe's others. Natural history designates Aethiopia and India, regions of extreme heat, as the breeding ground of monsters and wonders. If heat is the superior form-inducing agent of the masculine–feminine polarity of humoral physiology, in a geographic and imperial context it produces races to be wondered at as their bodies instantiate disseminated forms and exceptions to nature's predictable order:

> It is not at all surprising that towards the extremity of this region the men and animals assume a monstrous form, when we consider the changeableness and volubility of fire, the heat of which is the great agent in imparting various forms and shapes to bodies. Indeed, it is reported that in the interior, on the eastern side, there is a people that have no noses, the whole face presenting a plane surface; that others again are destitute of the upper lip, and others are without tongues [. . . .]
>
> (Pliny, Book VI, Ch. 35, 2: 101)

The Androgyni are amongst these creatures of torrid volubility:

> Above the Nasamones and the Machlyae, who border upon them, are found, as we learn from Calliphanes, the nation of Androgyni, a people who unite the two sexes in the same individual, and alternately perform the functions of each. Aristotle also states, that their right breast is that of the male, the left that of a female.
>
> (Pliny, Book VII, Ch. 2, 2: 126)

One of the most influential works in the wonder literature of sixteenth-century Spain is Antonio de Torquemada, *Jardín de flores curiosas* (1570), which is written in the form of a philosophical dialogue. In the section on hermaphrodites, Luis, one of the interlocutors, refers to the case of a hermaphrodite in Burgos who was burned at the stake because of her bisexuality – she first "chose" to use her female nature, but it was later discovered that she was also secretly availing herself of her male genitalia. After adducing another example of a hermaphrodite burned to death, this time in Seville, Antonio introduces the concept of a nation of hermaphrodites whose geographic location might some day be charted. Thus, even what is unnatural sexuality at home, may have a proper place abroad. The notion of "strategic location," which is crucial to the imperial gaze on subordinated cultures, also comes into play in imagining sexual dissidence.[18] The connection between sexuality and "race" is a powerful and effective one – as it is in Eleno's own defense against the charge of sodomy. Citing Pliny, Antonio relativizes the figure of the hermaphrodite by linking it to the notion of sympathy – the connection between peoples, places, climate, personal constitution, and humoral complexion. There is a place in which the phenomenon is not scandalous, as "we" think of it here, "as it is in these lands" (that is,

Spain; "en estas tierras"). Although the details derived from Pliny are garbled, Antonio further historicizes the Roman writer's imperial musings on an exotic homeland for androgyny and sexual variance, which is situated at the edge of the known world:

> In these lands it would be considered a great marvel for men to have a female sex, or women that of men; but look at Pliny, attributing to the philosopher Calliphanes, who accompanied Alexander the Great at the conquest of India, who says that in the far reaches of the Nasamones there is the province of a people called the androgyni, who are all hermaphrodites and have no respect for any sort of order or concert in coitus; rather, they use [their pudenda] willy-nilly with same and other.

> En estas tierras por muy gran maravilla se ha de tener que los hombres tengan natura de mujeres, o las mujeres de hombres; pero ved a Plinio alegando al filósofo Callifanes, que se halló en la conquista de la India con el grande Alejandro: el cual dice que en los confines de los Nasamones hay una provincia de gentes, llamadas andróginas, que todos ellos son hermafroditas, sin guardar orden ni concierto alguno en el coito, sino que los unos y los otros usan de ello igualmente.[19]

A third interlocutor, Bernardo, is astonished by all this talk of hermaphrodites and, presumably, their ability to "choose" sexual partners of either sex. The hermaphrodite is the erotic other – witness the peculiar social standing of hermaphrodites as sexual workers in Pliny: "at the present day they are employed for sensual purposes" (Book VII, Ch. 3, 2:136). Bernardo puts aside his doubts about these sexual marvels because they are "authorized by such grave authors" ("la autoridad de autores tan graves que la afirman por verdadera," Torquemada 117).

But it is the fact of empire, in the end, that furnishes the proper epistemological framework within which sexual and racial variance find their "true" place. Bernardo is confident that these reports must be accurate, for our time and place ("in these lands") daily receives news of wondrous places and peoples. The far-flung Portuguese and Spanish empires provide new insights into natural history. In an expansive age the wonderment induced by marvels will be a spur to epic conquest and adventure. Bernardo's comments show precisely the complementarity of both imperial expansion and archival accumulation and revision. His dialogue with his fellow amateurs of nature and science occurs in the privileged space of the metropolis, which commissions adventures to distant lands and receives not only material evidence and news of such exploits, but slaves by the thousands, imported from those lands and employed in domestic labor. That is the political framework for the accumulation of goods, wealth, peoples, facts, and other material to be marketed, displayed in rarified cabinets of curiosities, enumerated and contextualized in encyclopedic works like *Jardín de flores curiosas*, "captured" in the archives of the Inquisition, and then turned into spectacles of cruelty and scorn in an *auto da fé*. Bernardo's openness to difference is the liberality of the conqueror, enabled by the politics of imperial expansion and its necessary revision of the concept of natural agency. Adventure and archive operate in Torquemada's dialogues not as alternatives, as Conte suggests is the case in Pliny, but as secret sharers of natural history. Although a nation of androgyni strains all belief, Bernardo is confident, nevertheless, that it does exist in India: "The way things are today, I still consider it possible" ("según las cosas que hay en el mundo, no dejo de tener ésa por posible," 117). In the metropolis, hermaphrodites have no proper place and are burned for their transgressions. But, in theory, at least, regardless of how unusual the products of *natura artifex* in the colonies and periphery of known civilization may seem, they can systematically be given a proper place in harmony with their land of origin or the political needs of the metropolis.

When such cases appear in Europe, however, the notion of natural "sympathy" produces a rational and beneficent nature. Bernardo is intrigued by a report by the physician Andria Matiolo Senés (*Epístolas medicinales*), that he saw in the kingdom of Bohemia three he-goats with teats like a female, and that he found their milk an effective remedy in treating certain diseases. This bit of fantastic stuff is just too much to accept, but Bernardo observes that underneath apparent transgressions of the natural order may lie un- suspected reasons: "There must not have been a lack of cause for nature to depart from its order in a thing like this" ("No debió faltar causa para que naturaleza saliese de su orden en una cosa como ésta [. . . .]," Torquemada 115). The hermaphrodite nation lies very, very far away (much farther than Bohemia!); indeed, its remoteness accentuates an unsuspected "sympathy" of land and people that would account for their frenetic and orgiastic sexuality. In those *other* lands there is a hidden harmony that would account for their frantic – and titillating – sexual acrobatics: they "have no respect for any sort of order or concert in coitus; rather, they use [their pudenda] willy-nilly with same and other ("sin guardar orden ni concierto alguno en el coito, sino que los unos y los otros usan de ello igualmente," Torquemada 117). Pliny's hermaphrodite nation will surely come under Spanish imperial sway, which confidently retraces the glories of Alexander the Great and shall, no doubt, pinpoint the geographic location of the Androgyni; their land may yet be "discovered," as other regions of India are at this very moment charted and explored: "even though this province must be remote from those which are now again being discovered in India" ("aunque esta provincia debe estar bien apartada de las que ahora en la India de nuevo están descubiertas," Torquemada 117).

While Eleno served the empire most loyally as a soldier in the War of the Alpujarras (1568–70), the Toledo tribunal of the Inquisition does not accord her any special treatment on that account. Neither is it moved by Eleno's belonging to the "caste of Gentiles" to accept her narrative of transmutation.

Indeed, all the medical experts who examine Eleno at Toledo agree with the findings in Ocaña that Elena is, and always has been, female. The tribunal's final sentence insists on that point and condemns her for the crime of bigamy–bypassing a direct ruling on some of the other, legally messy accusations leveled against her by the tribunal's prosecuting attorney.[20] Elena's bigamy consists in her failure to obtain proper documentation of the death of her husband prior to her marriage to María. As a bigamist, Elena receives the standard punishment of two hundred lashes and ten years of confinement. But her case is given a higher profile by the Inquisitors themselves, when they also make her appear in an *auto da fé*, held in Toledo on Sunday, 18 December 1588, in which she publicly abjures her crimes *de levi* (reconciliation for minor crimes) and is forced to parade around the central square wearing the requisite mitre and robes (*sambenito*), with insignias "appropriate" to her crime of bigamy. But the text of the sentence issued by the Inquisitors to accompany her public lashing goes beyond the narrow legal principles applied in her conviction and encompasses the closeted charges of sodomy.[21] True to their misogyny, the Inquisitors vent their contempt for and anxiety over the sexuality of a woman-identified woman. With the physical punishment occurring on the streets of the two principal sites of her transgressions – Toledo, where the trial was held, and Ciempozuelos, where the "same-sex" betrothal occurred – Eleno's notoriety as a "woman who fooled other women" (and not a few men as well) grows stupendously. The last document in her dossier in the archives of the Inquisition shows precisely the almost mythical proportions that her powers acquire in the popular imagination. Elena, now, presumably, in female attire, serves out her sentence in the Hospital del Rey (King's Hospital) at Toledo, where she heals the indigent sick. Her sentence is, in effect, ten years of "community service." But on 23 February 1589, the hospital administrator files a petition with the Inquisition of Toledo for Elena's transfer to another, more remote facility, on account of the disruption that attends to Eleno's medical practice:

> The presence of Elena de Céspedes has caused great annoyance and embarrassment from the beginning, since many people come to see and be healed by her.

> Que es grande el estorbo y enbaraço que a causado la entrada de la dicha Elena de Céspedes por la mucha gente que acude a verla y a curarse con ella.

A reputed hermaphrodite, a woman who has lived, loved and married as a man, has become a surgeon, and has even been suspected of possessing magical healing powers, this *mulata* is now a local *cause célèbre*. Of Eleno's many bodies, none is as powerful as this latest incarnation. Thanks to the formidable Toledo Inquisitors, Elena alias Eleno is a pilgrimage site. Her transfer to the hospital at Puente del Arzopbispo, however, does not extinguish interest in Eleno's numinous persona, even when that interest aims to discredit Eleno's claims to the preternatural.

In 1599, ten years after Eleno's ouster from Toledo, the physician and lay agent ("familiar") of the Inquisition, Jerónimo de Huerta, publishes his annotated translation of Pliny, *Natural History*. Eleno has cited Book VII in his own behalf, but it now becomes the place of *her* insertion into the annals of natural history. If nature is the supreme artificer (*natura artifex*), then woman is the wiliest counterfeiter – and none more so than a female slave. This baroque Pliny shifts attention from the hermaphrodite to the slave, from nature's wonders to the counter-natural deceptions that the servile castes are capable of.[22] In the table of contents Elena is the unproblematic *she* who deceives: "Deceit by a female slave who pretended to be a man" ("Engaño de una esclava que se hazia hombre" folio 5*v*). Eleno's account is fraudulent, a desperate lie told by a slave. If Pliny narrates the preternatural, Eleno instantiates lesbian sexuality as duplicity and as history:

[. . . .] invention and deceit, as the one that occurred in Castile, with that Andalusian slave, named Elena de Céspedes, who having abandoned female dress, for many years pretended to be a man [and] gave indications of being one, though badly sculpted, and without a beard and with some deceitful artifice; and it was so natural in style that after being examined by several surgeons and declared a man, she was married in Cien Poçuelos.[23]

[. . .] inuencion y engaño, como fue el que sucedio en Castilla, con *aquella esclaua Andaluça*, llamada Elena de Céspedes, la qual dexado el habito de muger, fingio muchos años ser hombre, mostraua serlo aunque mal tallado, y sin barba con cierto artificio engañoso, y era tan al natural que despues de auerle mirado algunos cirujanos, y declarado ser hombre, se caso en Cien Poçuelos[. . .]

Along with his fellow Inquisitors, Huertas reads Eleno's femaleness as slavery in the mirror of natural history. To peg Eleno as "an Andalusian woman slave" is to produce an overdetermined subordinate subject, whose "sympathy" with the land bespeaks cheap labor and "sensual purposes," but not wonder.

NOTES

1 This and all subsequent citations from the trial summaries of Elena de Céspedes are from my transcription and translation of the dossier at the Archivo Histórico Nacional, Madrid (Sección Inquisición: Legajo 234, Expediente 24). The documents are written in various sixteenth-century hands. I give no page numbers, since the originals lack consistent page or folio numbers. My transcriptions show some slight modifications to facilitate reading. I resolve all abbreviations (e.g. *dho=dicho*, *Mª=María*), furnish accent marks and punctuation, and regularize the

use of *u* and *v*. Recent studies of Eleno can be found in Marie-Catherine Barbazza, "Un caso de subversión social: el proceso de Elena de Céspedes (1587–89)," in *Criticón*, vol. 26 (1984), pp. 17–40; Michèlle Escamilla, "A propos d'un dossier inquisitorial des environs de 1590: les étranges amours d'un hermaphrodite," in *Amours légitimes, amours illégitimes en Espagne (XVIe–XVIIe Siècles)*, Paris: Publications de la Sorbonne, 1985, pp. 167–82; Guillermo Folch Jou and María del Sagrario Muñoz, "Un pretendido caso de hermafroditismo en el siglo XVI," in *Boletín de la sociedad española de historia de la farmacia*, vol. 93 (1973), pp. 20 – 33. See also, Vern L. Bullough and Bonnie Bullough, *Cross Dressing, Sex, and Gender*, Philadelphia: University of Pennsylvania Press, 1993, pp. 94–6, who cite, apparently, from an unpublished paper by Richard A. Kagan, which I have not seen.

2 On the role of physicians in establishing the legal status of hermaphrodites in sixteenth-century France, see Lorraine Daston and Katharine Park, "Hermaphrodites in Renaissance France," in *Critical Matrix: Princeton Working Papers in Women's Studies*, vol. 1 No. 5 (1985), pp. 1–19.

3 On women and the law, see Mary Elizabeth Perry, *Gender and Disorder in Early Modern Seville*, Princeton, NJ: Princeton University Press, 1990.

4 The Spanish indirect object pronoun, *le*, ("to him" or "to her") is not gender specific, but the authorities already believe Elena to be female – hence my translation, "her."

5 Daston and Park, p. 7, emphasize the homophobic reaction to hermaphrodites in sixteenth-century France. Among many recent studies on the history and meaning of the hermaphrodite, see, e.g., Emma Donoghue "Imagined More than Women: Lesbians as Hermaphrodites, 1671–1766," in *Women's History Review*, vol. 2 (1993), No. 2, pp. 199–216; Julia Epstein, "Either/Or – Neither/Both: Sexual Ambiguity and the Ideology of Gender,' in *Genders*, No. 7 (March 1990), pp. 99–142; Ann Rosalind Jones and Peter Stallybrass, "Fetishizing Gender: Constructing the Hermaphrodite in Renaissance Europe," in Julia Epstein and Kristina Straub (eds), *Body Guards: The Cultural Politics of Gender Ambiguity*, New York-London: Routledge, 1991, pp. 80–111; Georgia Nugent, "This Sex Which is Not One: Deconstructing Ovid's Hermaphrodite," in *Differences: A Journal of Feminist Cultural Studies*, vol. 2, No. 1 (Spring 1990), pp. 160–85; Lauren Silberman, "Mythographic Transformations of Ovid's Hermaphrodite,' in *Sixteenth-Century Journal*, vol. 19, No. 4 (Winter 1988), pp. 643–52.

6 This and all subsequent English citations from the *Natural History* are from Pliny, *The Natural History of Pliny*, vol. 2, London: Henry G. Bohn, 1855; the Latin text is from C. Plini Secundi, *Naturalis Historiae (Libri VII-XV)*, Leipzig: B.G. Teubner, 1909. I cite in the text the book and chapter number, along with the volume and page number from the Bostock and Riley translation.

7 I refer to the rogue protagonist of the sixteenth-century picaresque novel, *Lazarillo de Tormes*, ed. Francisco Rico, Barcelona: Editorial Planeta, 1988.

8 The cultural meanings that attach to the whipping and dismemberment of female African slaves in the Americas is the subject of Hortense J. Spillers, "Mama's Baby, Papa's Maybe: An American Grammar Book," in *Diacritics*, vol.17, No.2 (Summer 1987), pp. 65–81. On slavery in Spain, see Jose Luis Cortés López, *La esclavitud negra en la España peninsular del siglo XVI*, Salamanca: Ediciones Universidad de Salamanca, 1989; Alfonso Franco Silva, *Los esclavos de Sevilla*, Sevilla: Diputación Provincial de Sevilla, 1980; Alfonso Franco Silva, "La mujer esclava en la sociedad andaluza de fines del medioevo," in Angela Muñoz Fernández and Cristina Segura Graiño (eds), *El trabajo de las mujeres en la Edad Media Hispana* (Madrid: Asociación Cultural Al-Mudayna, 1988) pp. 287–301.

9 On Moriscos, see Antonio Domínguez Ortiz and Bernard Vincent, *Historia de los moriscos: vida y tragedia de una minoría*, Madrid: Revista de Occidente, 1978.

10 Daston and Park observe the shift away from the "Aristotelian complexion view of sexuality ... to a Hippocratic-Galenic view based upon the proportions of male and female seed present at conception," p. 4. See also Danielle Jacquart and Claude Thomasset, *Sexuality and Medicine in the Middle Ages*, trans. M. Adamson, Princeton: Princeton University Press, 1988; Ian MacLean, *The Renaissance Notion of Woman: A Study in the Fortunes of Scholasticism and Medical Science in European Intellectual Life*, Cambridge: Cambridge University Press, 1980; Thomas Laqueur, *Making Sex: Body and Gender from the Greeks to Freud*, Cambridge, Mass.: Harvard University Press, 1990; Katharine Park and Robert A. Nye, "Destiny is Anatomy; Review of *Making Sex: Body and Gender from the Greeks to Freud*, by Thomas Laqueur," in *The New Republic* (18 February 1991), pp. 53–7; Joan Cadden, *Meanings of Sex Difference in the Middle Ages: Medicine, Science, and Culture*, Cambridge: Cambridge University Press, 1993; Gilbert Herdt (ed.), *Third Sex, Third Gender: Beyond Sexual Dimorphism in Culture and Society*, New York: Zone Books, 1994.

11 On the numinous aura of the Ovidian tale, see Leonard Barkan, *The Gods Made Flesh: Metamorphosis and the Pursuit of Paganism*, New Haven-London: Yale University Press, 1986.

12 Unlike Aragon, the Inquisition in Castile did not have jurisdiction over sodomy cases. While Eleno was also charged with sodomy, her principal offense was "mockery of the sacrament of marriage," which was a matter for the Inquisition. On the prosecution of sodomy, see Bartolomé Benassar, "El modelo sexual: la Inquisición de Aragón y la represión de los pecados 'abominables,'" *Inquisición española: poder político y control social*, ed. Benassar, Barcelona: Editorial Crítica, 1981; Rafael Carrasco, *Inquisición y represión sexual en Valencia. Historia de los sodomitas (1565–1785)*, Barcelona: Laertes, 1985; Mary Elizabeth Perry, "The 'Nefarious Sin' in Early Modern Seville," in Kent Gerard and Gert Hekma (eds), *The Pursuit of Sodomy: Male Homosexuality in Renaissance and Enlightenment Europe*, New York-London: Harrington Park Press, 1989, pp. 67–89; Francisco Tomás y Valiente, "El crimen y pecado contra natura," in *Sexo barroco y otras transgresiones premodernas*, Madrid: Alianza Editorial, 1990, pp. 33–55; William Monter, *Frontiers of Heresy: The Spanish Inquisition from the Basque Lands to Sicily*, Cambridge: Cambridge University Press, 1990, pp. 276–99.

13 Left margin: "A. Cicero lib..1. de diuy natu. Diuus Agustinus Lib. 16. de civitate dei.c.8. Pli[n]j lib. 7. natur. histor." Eleno possessed a library, numbering twenty-seven volumes, which was inventoried by the Inquisition. The contents of the catalogue – books on medicine, surgery, rhetoric, and natural philosophy in Spanish, Latin, and Italian – and her testimony indicate that she purchased it in its entirety from a medical humanist.

14 Gian Biagio Conte, "The Inventory of the World: Form of Nature and Encyclopedic Project in the Work of Pliny the Elder," in *Genres and Readers: Lucretius, Love Elegy, Pliny's Encyclopedia*, trans. Glenn W. Most, Baltimore and London: The Johns Hopkins University Press, 1994, pp. 67–104, quotation at p. 72.

15 Lorraine Daston, "Marvelous Facts and Miraculous Evidence in Early Modern Europe," *Critical Inquiry*, vol. 18, No. 1(Autumn 1991): 93–124, quotations at pp. 96–8.

16 See, e.g., Jaime Contreras and Gustav Henningsen, "Forty-Thousand Cases of the Spanish Inquisition (1540–1700): Analysis of a Historical Data Bank," in Gustav Henningsen, John Tedeschi, and Charles Amiel (eds), *The Inquisition in Early*

Modern Europe: Studies on Sources and Methods, Dekalb, Ill.: Northern Illinois University Press, 1986, pp. 100–29; Monter, *Frontiers* pp. 255–75; Mary Elizabeth Perry and Anne J. Cruz (eds), *Cultural Encounters: The Impact of the Inquisition in Spain and the New World*, Berkeley: University of California Press, 1991.

17 Conte, pp. 84 and 86; see, also, Paula Findlen, "Jokes of Nature and Jokes of Knowledge: The Playfulness of Scientific Discourse in Early Modern Europe," in *Renaissance Quarterly*, vol. 43, No. 2 (Summer 1990), pp. 292–331.

18 I borrow the notion of "strategic location" from Edward W. Said, *Orientalism*, New York: Vintage, 1979, pp. 20–1.

19 Antonio de Torquemada, *Jardín de flores curiosas*, ed. Giovanni Allegra, Madrid: Castalia, 1982, pp. 116–17. Subsequent citations of this work will appear in the text, with page numbers in parentheses. All English translations from this and other Spanish works cited above are mine.

20 Bigamy was a major concern for the Inquisition after the Council of Trent, see Enrique Gacto, "El delito de bigamia y la Inquisición española," in *Sexo barroco*, pp. 127–52.

21 Reading the sentence in an *auto da fé* "was an instrument of propaganda and popular education consciously used by inquisitors to mold opinion. As such, it is interesting for the purpose of recovering the image that the tribunal wished to give of itself and of the beliefs it attacked," Jean Pierre Dedieu, "The Archives of the Holy Office of Toledo as a Source for Historical Anthropology," trans. E. W. Monter, in Hennigsen *et al.* (eds), *The Inquisition*, p. 180.

22 By the term "baroque" I refer to the "cult of (and anxiety about) the artificial" that obtained in post-tridentine Spain, John R. Beverley, "On the Concept of the Spanish Literary Baroque," in Anne J. Cruz and Mary Elizabeth Perry (eds), *Culture and Control in Counter-Reformation Spain*, Hispanic Issues, vol. 7, Minneapolis: University of Minnesota Press, 1992, pp. 216–30.; quotation at p. 223.

23 Gerónimo de Huerta, *Tradvcion de los libros de Caio Plinio Segvndo, de la historia natvral de los animales. Hecha por el licenciado Geronimo de Huerta, medico, y filosofo. Y anotada por el mesmo con anotaciones curiosas*, Alcalá: Justo Sánchez Crespo, 1602, folio 20*v*, my emphasis.

8

BECOMING MALE

Salvation through gender modification in Hinduism and Buddhism

Cynthia Ann Humes

Numerous world literatures share the motif of humans experiencing a change of sex. In some cases, a gender reversal may be desirable for personal reasons. In some religious circles, on the other hand, changing one's sex – particularly if born female – is considered essential for salvation. Some Hindu and Buddhist soteriological texts, for instance, argue the necessity of females to adopt male bodies before complete emancipation can be reached. Further, even when actual physical transformation of sex is deemed unnecessary, in both Hindu and Buddhist scriptural traditions, key spiritual concepts of transcendence are linked with symbology that has been likened "male" or "masculine," such that women are specifically admonished to purge themselves of "women's" characteristics and "become male" in gender orientation to become enlightened.

I am interested here in offering a broadly drawn picture of why this religious gender transformation, whether in body or in mind, is or was thought to be necessary, and how such concepts have influenced both men's and women's experience. In doing so, I also seek to demonstrate certain Hindu and Buddhist theories of embodiment in general, and gendered embodiment in particular. Throughout, I will discuss a number of pertinent themes interwoven in both traditions. These include perceived dichotomies of gender, matter and spirit, ascetic/philosophical and devotional approaches to salvation, and immediate or distant salvation. In the first section I explain Hindu religious theories. In the second, in addition to describing Buddhist theories, I draw conclusions comparing and contrasting Buddhist and Hindu concepts of gender and salvation.

GENDER AND SALVATION IN HINDUISM

Belief in the superiority of male birth undergirds most Hindu salvation schemes. Hindu literature even up to today accepts that a change from woman to man is virtually always desirable, while the reverse is undesirable: paradoxical exceptions merely tend to prove this rule.[1]

"Hinduism" is a widely accepted heuristic term which encompasses within it a variety of South Asian-based traditions, but virtually all of them claim as their common heritage four sets of Sanskrit literature they view to be sacred: the *Saṃhitās* (c. 1400–1000 BCE), *Brāhmaṇas* (c. 1000–700 BCE), *Āraṇyakas* (c. 800–600 BCE), and *Upaniṣads* (c. 800–500 BCE). Those people of north India who composed the earliest set of scriptures agreed today to be Hindu actually called themselves *Ārya*[n]s, followers of the "superior" path. Aryan religion is also known as Vedic, so named after its literature, collectively referred to as the *Veda*[s], repository[ies] of "knowledge."

I must introduce at this point an immediate caveat. Although they are now perceived as significant contributors to concepts of gender and salvation for all Hindus, these sets of scriptures were in fact popularized only in the modern era by non-Indian Orientalists and Indian Nationalists, who used them as resources to facilitate their own group's divergent agendas. Further, the texts reflect a minority view from their very creation. Their authors omitted discussion of the religious experience of those that did not fall within their self-conceived elite groups, and, even today, most of their passages hold little import for the vast majority of those people who have come to be called "Hindu." Since, however, the texts have assumed such vast importance in the construction of a Hindu identity since the nineteenth century, examining them for their views on gender change remains a significant task in its own right.[2] Thus, while they give insight to a dominant view, this view derives from what was originally a minority, nevertheless, and its value is still contested.

The Aryans did promote patriarchal traditions (for example, elevation of males, patrilineality, and patrilocality), but women could themselves attain salvation. As wives and mothers, women were important to men's religious goals as well. Their first set of texts are the collections of hymns or *Saṃhitās* (c. 1400–1000 BCE). The *Saṃhitās* suggest an appreciation of both femininity and the complementarity between husband and wife.[3] Both domestic and public rituals, for instance, depended on the copresence of husband and wife, and pairing of them was believed to be divinely ordered. No Hindu scripture henceforth offered an alternative view of sexuality and gender construction other than natural heterosexuality.[4] The maintenance of harmony between husband and wife was a primary concern of Vedic verses, one which perdures into the present as a major feature of later *strī dharma*, or women's religious duty.

Human women appeared often in didactic scriptures as good wives who contributed importantly to the *trivarga*, or three modes of worldly life which together constituted a mode of salvation. Through their ideal behavior, women supported *dharma*, the divine order of the family, society, and the cosmos. In producing sons, they contributed to *artha*, material wealth. Through their aesthetics, they symbolized the well-being of the family as a whole, and inspired the third aim of worldly life, *kāma* or desire and pleasure. Such affirmative evaluations of women's contributions continued into later ages. At least within the *Saṁhitās*, salvation was conceived as a joint venture of husband and wife. A woman's gender, while it defined her contributions, did not render her incapable of salvation *per se*.

This positive evaluation of women shifts somewhat in the more hierarchical religious concepts recorded in the second set of Hindu texts, the *Brāhmaṇas* (c. 1000–700 BCE). The *Brāhmaṇas* posited greater disparities between birth-groups (*jātīs*) and the increasing importance of a son as the deliverer of his father to heaven. Later *Brāhmaṇas* proposed that one must be "born again" through initiation into Vedic ritual to be saved. Initiation was reserved for members of the top three classes or *varṇas* (literally "color"), thus excluding from heaven the fourth *varṇa* – the *Śudras*, or members of the servant class. Further, one had to undergo rigorous training at the home of a teacher after initiation to gain the expertise necessary to perform rituals and hymns properly. Although domestic and public rituals continued to be performed for various goals, including the acquisition of wealth, progeny, and health, domestic rituals were increasingly seen as inferior to the more elaborate rituals directed towards the maintenance of the universe which required professional overseers to complete properly. Greater stress came to be placed on the need for elaborate ritual intervention to attain life after death in heaven, which was coupled with the emphasis that males perform such sacrifices, sponsored by and presided over by legitimate sons with the aid of priests. This led to a considerable widening of the gulf between men's and women's educational levels. For instance, while boys of the highest (*Brāhmin*) class were enjoined to study and accommodated, girls were educated only optionally.

Given the new prerequisite for legitimate sons in the quest for heaven, greater emphasis was also laid on controlling women's sexuality. Eventually, women's chastity was equated with "purity," which came to be viewed as a proper substitute for female education. A man's status became closely related to his wife's purity/chastity, increasing further need for greater control of women's sexuality. These developments contributed to the increasingly more common view that women were ignorant and incapable – even if chaste and honored – by their very nature. By the late *Brāhmaṇa* era (c. 800–700 BCE), women came to be viewed as a source of pollution through menstruation and childbirth; hence, their dangerous nature was both physical and temperamental.

The third and fourth sets of Hindu texts, the *Āraṇyakas* (c. 800–600 BCE) and *Upaniṣads* (c. 800–500 BCE), introduced new religious goals and philosophical concepts of the material and spiritual which had great repercussions on salvation theories for women. Most of these promoted a new vision of human destiny: all persons are subject to continual rebirth, and hence are trapped in *saṁsāra* (the perpetual, cyclical rounds of phenomenal, worldly existence). Concomitantly, the religious goal shifted. The *trivarga* was expanded to include a fourth dimension: *mokṣa*, or release from rebirth. In some cases, *mokṣa* was escape to a heaven with a/the god(s), not all that unlike visions found in earlier Hindu scripture, but more commonly, *mokṣa* meant escaping the cycle of rebirth entirely.

The many *Upaniṣads* accepted as authoritative expound various views; some are deeply theological, others speculative and monistic. Most *Upaniṣads* incorporated early Sāṃkhya dualism (variously dated, but the seeds of which date *c.* 500 BCE) which posited two eternal principles: matter or *prakṛti*, which was feminine and the material cause of the universe, and spirit or *puruṣa* (literally, "man") which was the masculine consciousness. These *Upaniṣads* devalued *prakṛti*, which came to be viewed as an aspect of the *puruṣa*. The *puruṣa* was identified with the *ātman* or individual soul, which was ultimately identical with the immaterial, spiritual essence of the universe, *Brahman*. *Brahman* was an all-pervasive, eternal, and fully real principle; the world was material, temporary, and therefore, to a degree, a lower level of reality which should be transcended in *mokṣa*. Female fertility came to be equated with sexuality, which itself was deemed the delusory force or power of *prakṛti*. If left uncontrolled, sexuality/*prakṛti* would obstruct the path to enlightenment.

In the highly regarded and influential Advaita [non-dual] philosophy, which is rooted in the more monistic *Upaniṣads*, *prakṛti* and *puruṣa* are not distinguished from the highest point of realization, and gender, too, is ultimately irrelevant. Gendered constructions are ephemeral, or in philosophical or ascetic approaches, serve as tools or ideological hooks meant to assist one to eventually transcend distinctions.[5] Yet this ideal realization is known by the tradition to be a rare insight, and Advaita philosophical discourses still employ gendered terminologies and values. Thus, philosophical treatises admonish followers to destroy attachment to the "female" material element and hold fast to, and become, fully spirit or *puruṣa* – literally, "male." Thus, while the word *brahman* is a neuter noun, the epitome of human behavior or the spirit, in addition to underlying the dominant modes of action for its realization, is directly modeled on the masculine and male experience.

Classical Hinduism attempted to synthesize all four sets of texts even as it added new elements. It affirmed the necessity of traditional Vedic study, but its purpose was to prepare the student for greater tasks in the enlightenment quest, such as philosophical rumination, asceticism, and meditation, which together lead to enlightenment. Realization succeeds in attaining the ultimate goal: freeing the individual soul from a cycle of rebirth in material worlds (including rebirth in heaven). Classical Hinduism thus deemphasizes family and early Vedic ritual performance conducted in pursuit of worldly aims and a life in heaven with the gods.

Women's participation in Classical Hinduism gradually grew increasingly restricted. During the early Upaniṣadic age, upper class women could be initiated into Vedic learning and devote themselves to study. By the time of the *dharma* texts (*c.* 400–100 BCE), women were classified into two categories:

brahmavādinīs and *sadyodvadhās* or *sadyodvāhās*. *Brahmavādinīs* were those women who remained lifelong students, becoming "knowledgeable in *Brahman*." Ordinary renunciation involved wandering celibate alone, and by definition, an unprotected woman was unchaste. Thus, *Brahmavādinīs* underwent initiation, and conducted their study, fire rituals, and begging, but within the confines of the parental home, leaving later interpreters to debate as to whether they had actually attained complete enlightenment. The *sadyodvadhūs* also underwent initiation, but their study lasted only eight or nine years until their marriage. By *c.* 300–200 BCE, the initiation ritual for women came to be only a formality, and girls were immediately married. For instance, Manu, the prominent codifier of law whose work has held an enviable position of enormous authority in Hinduism, recommended that no Vedic mantras be recited on the occasion of girls' initiations.[6] Initiation without Vedic mantras being recited therein or taught after the ritual was a contradiction in terms, of course, and so more straightforward authors of *dharma* texts such as Yājñavalkya began to simply prohibit the ceremony altogether for girls. By the first century BCE, marriage was interpreted to be the equivalent of initiation for women, serving her husband came to be equated with residing with a teacher, and household duties were substituted for the service of the sacrificial fire. Women's proper religious behavior (*strī dharma*) was *patiyoga*. *Patiyoga* is union with, or discipline under, one's husband or *pati*, literally "ruler" or "lord." It combined sacrifice, asceticism (*yoga*), and devotion (*bhakti*), all under the auspices of *strī dharma*, that is, directing all one's religious actions to the worship of the husband.

Once women's marriage became equated with initiation, a widespread belief developed by the first century BCE that women who were unlearned, unable to recite so much as the hymns of daily prayer – even if of *Brāhmin* birth and marriage – were not unlike *Śudras*, who were automatically excluded from Vedic sacrifice. This association may have been facilitated in part by the rise of inter-caste marriages between twice-born (hence "Aryan") males and *Śudra* females; once these men married them, tensions with *Brāhmin* priests arose as to whether the non-twice-born women could co-sponsor Vedic sacrifices. Perhaps in part to by-pass the potential problem of distinguishing between "Aryan" and "non-Aryan" women, *c.* 200 BCE the *dharma* scholar Atiśāyana declared that all women were ineligible to participate so that none would be offended.[7] His view eventually came to be the dominant one.

However, this negative view of women in Vedic ritual and initiation into study and renunciation was tempered by the continued appreciation of woman as wife and mother, and the positive evaluation of female chastity and purity.

Marriage came to be seen as a far more transformative event for women than men. When women marry, their lineage and bodies are believed literally to change; they become members of their husband's lineages.[8] While for men marriage is important to sire a legitimate son to repay the debt he owes his ancestors (*putradharma*, or the *dharma* of [siring] a son) and to light his own cremation pyre to save him from hells reserved for the issueless, marriage does not effect essential changes of his nature.[9]

The inescapable link of women to marriage and consequently, *patiyoga*, led to dramatic consequences regarding Hindu concepts of gender and soteriology. Women's lives were henceforth divided into three phases: maidenhood, marriage, and – should the husband die first – either self-immolation on the husband's funeral pyre (becoming a *satī*, a "truthful/virtuous woman"), or widowhood.[10] In contrast, the ideal life-cycle of upper-caste Hindu males had four stages or *āśrama*s: studentship, householdership, forest dwelling, and renunciation. The only time period when males and females shared a complementarity was householdership, although women were to share vicariously the benefits of a husband's asceticism during the latter two stages, and more rarely, if allowed by her husband, by ascetic practice conducted alongside him. Women were taught to prolong and value householding, whereas men were taught to escape and devalue it. Indeed, a man's depreciation of the world was in many ways symbolized by woman: she embodied sexuality, reproduction, and family, in essence, embodiment itself, the major obstacle to liberation. Yet even though male celibacy is a major religious virtue, to become an ascetic without first having experienced marriage and parenthood is to act contrary to the even more stringent social and religious norms of *putradharma*. Thus, men were caught between two opposing values: marriage was obligatory, but renunciation was a higher calling.

Almost all Hindu philosophical systems which stressed asceticism and wisdom viewed women as either ineligible by nature, or incompetent, for the higher stages of discipline necessary for complete release. Thus, women's best option became either heaven, understood at this point as a temporary reward for good behavior, or a higher rebirth, that is, accompanying her husband in later births and eventually becoming male herself in a distant future life when she would finally be capable of pursuing final liberation.

Bhakti, or devotional worship, soon eclipsed Classical Hinduism's fusion of Vedic sacrifice, learning, and *Upaniṣad*ic renunciation. *Bhakti* for women stressed devotion not only to one's husband, but also to a benevolent, all-powerful deity. In contrast to the postponed freedom necessitated by a woman's gender in Classical Hinduism, *bhakti* admitted the possibility of immediate, ultimate deliverance. And unlike the temporary heavens stylized for good wives in the *Upaniṣads*, the deity's heaven was not merely a temporary reward for good conduct, but salvation itself. The prerequisites necessary for pursuing release in the *Upaniṣads* (lengthy education, male gender, and twice-born status) were unnecessary in *bhakti*. In addition, unlike Vedic sacrifice, women and low-caste persons could offer food, songs, and prayer in private worship services. Indeed, the most famous female *bhaktas* or exemplary devotees were those who refused to marry, and thus could focus on their chosen deity without the distraction of husband-worship still deemed incumbent on the good wife.

Bhakti and *patiyoga* do not necessarily conflict, however, and they continue to coexist as the dominant forms of women's religious experience in Hinduism. They effectively by-pass exclusivist, male-dominated forms of asceticism even as they integrate self-abnegation, which is a form of renunciation. Thus, while women have been devalued and excluded by their nature from certain paths, alternate, gender-geared forms of Hindu soteriology allow for their release as women. Further, the majority of people who fall in "lower-caste" group categories now called Hindu were relatively unaffected by what the scriptures had to say in the first place. They practiced their own unique forms of religion, with often widely varying experiences for both genders, many of which held far less oppressive views of women.

Descriptions of gender reversal in Classical Hinduism almost always depict change as a progression from inferior female to superior male in later lifetimes as a reward or outcome of good behavior, or a regression from superior male to inferior female in later lifetimes as a punishment or result of bad behavior. In *bhakti*, gender reversals may actually occur where male devotees adopt feminine modes of being to become closer to the divine. This type of gender reversal is predicated on the common belief in Hindu culture that women are more emotional, and therefore capable of deeper love for the deity. Males within the *Vallabha* sect in southern India, for instance, impersonate women to win the attention of the god Krishna, recalling tales of his affairs with the milkmaids, and imagining physical union with Krishna in an erotic symbolization of the union of the soul with its lord.[11] Thus, whereas women's temperament is a detriment for ascetic paths, it can be an advantage in devotional ones, so that a female mind is deliberately inculcated – restricted, of course, to relating with the divine.

In worship of female deities, males may adopt feminine dress and mannerisms, either in imitation, or in some cases, because of possession by the goddess. Legend has it that when the famous nineteenth-century Bengali saint Ramakrishna became a woman in his blissful devotion to the goddess, he began to menstruate, but such bodily transformation is clearly an exception.

Gender reversals described in *bhakti* are not in physical or bodily form, but in the sense of play-acting: men really are not expected to become women. This type of salvific cross-dressing is in keeping with Hindu notions of *līlā*, or "divine play." The term *līlā* connotes both amusing diversion or sport, and drama or game playing. *Līlā* refers both to the divine imitating human form or taking on manifestations unlike their true nature, and humans imitating divine form. The universe itself is often considered to be divine *līlā*, or the sport of gods and goddesses, simultaneously being and not being "divine." Likewise, in their own *līlās*, human actors might imitate the divine, and by so doing, actually "become" them, even without any specific physical transformation. This transformation is regarded as "true" enough such that, in certain contexts, other devotees worship these players as divine embodiments. Formal *līlā* performances intended for public viewing may stipulate that only males may act out the parts of the gods and goddesses. Since there are both male and female deities in India, male human actors imitating the divine may adopt either gender. However, I have not found many instances of women becoming male in imitation of male deities; rather, because of the elevation of women as the more emotional of the two genders, female *bhaktas* focus on male divinities through various modes of intense male-female interaction, whether acting as the mother, lover, servant, and so on, of the male deity. In the case of goddess worship, women may respond to her as their mother, or less commonly, act as her vehicle for possession, becoming themselves "mothers."[12]

Hindu Tantric philosophy (originating CE *c.* fifth century), posits that one need not escape from the world to be enlightened, nor undergo asceticism which denies sexuality. Indeed, the very aspects of the phenomenal world held by mainstream Hindus to be polluting or liminal are valorized as essential means to attaining enlightenment. Thus, its religious practice utilizes wine, meat, fish, symbolic hand gestures and figures, and sexual intercourse.[13] In this system, since women's bodies are not obstacles to enlightenment, changing sex is not a prominent theme. Hindu Tantra underscores the fact that perceptions of the world, sexuality, and women's bodies are consistently linked in Hindu religious thought.

GENDER AND SALVATION IN BUDDHISM

Buddhism originated within the same general cultural milieu as the *Āranyakas* (*c.* 800–600 BCE) and *Upaniṣads* (*c.* 800–500 BCE), the third and fourth sets of scriptures which introduced new religious goals and philosophical concepts in Hindu salvation schemes.

The Buddha (*c.* ?563–483 BCE) formulated Four Noble Truths which even today remain the core Buddhist teaching. The first explains that "everything is *dukkha*, unsatisfactory or suffering." *Dukkha* is the first of three characterizations of the world, and connotes the misery of human existence: unfulfilled desire, anxiety, pain, disease, old age, and death. The world and humans are also transitory; they have no abiding permanence. All things in the world are composed of a mixture of five components, the combination of which shift and change from one moment to the next. One's whole being is in a state of constant flux, hence there can be no permanent, abiding, unchanging soul. No permanent entity transmigrates from body to body. Rather, the Law of Karma (literally, "action") teaches that each act of thought, word, or deed causes an accumulation of volitions to further action. These volitions to further action result in future thoughts, words, and deeds. The nature of each individual is thus the result of past action by the karmic impulses carried by that individual, and what one will become is conditioned by action undertaken in the present. Rebirth is merely the result of karmic impulses, not the transmigration of an essential self, as it is perceived in Hinduism. The second truth explains that the reason why people are unsatisfied with existence is because they desire a multitude of things, continued life, and a permanent essence that might remain after death. The third truth affirms that where there is no desire, there is no suffering. This absence of suffering is *nirvāṇa*, the "extinction" of desire. The fourth truth explains the eightfold path to achieving *nirvāṇa* which causes the cessation of *dukkha*.

In Hinduism, the world and material themselves, and attachment to them, are often symbolized by the feminine and by women; so it is in Buddhism. Buddhist texts use women as a metaphor for the karmic energy that maintains suffering in the world because they embody birth, thus representing suffering, death, and rebirth. Further, women are believed to be more grossly implicated in the ensnarements of the world than men, and are thus reasoned to have a more difficult time untangling themselves from it.[14]

Buddhism is usually split into two major divisions: Theravada (Way of the Elders) and the later Mahayana (Great Vehicle). Within the Mahayana, a third branch developed called Vajrayana, a form of Buddhist Tantra (originating CE *c.* fifth–sixth century). Like Hindu Tantra, it also posits that one need not escape from the world to be enlightened nor undergo celibate asceticism, and its religious practice thus also utilizes wine, meat, fish, symbolic gestures and figures, and sexual intercourse. Again, as with Hindu Tantra, since women's bodies are not obstacles to enlightenment in Buddhist Tantra, changing sex is not a prominent theme.[15] Mahayana adds many other works to the Theravadin scriptural corpus and departs from earlier doctrine in ways that have important implications for our topic. I will briefly sketch some outlines of both divisions here, particularly as facets may pertain to gender.

The Theravada *Cullavagga* portrays the Buddha to have reluctantly established a female monastic community only after being approached several times by disciples and his widowed aunt. He predicted that as a result of its creation, the *dharma* (here understood as Buddhist teachings) would last only five hundred instead of one thousand years. He also specified that nuns would be required to observe eight special rules mandating their subordination to all monks as a precondition for admittance. Thus, while the Buddha's initiation of a nuns' order confirms that women are capable of gaining the insights required for liberation, he also implicitly expressed or at least recognized endemic cultural prejudices concerning women's "materiality," inferior spiritual capacities, and their purported negative influence on men in the spiritual quest.

These views are confirmed in the ancient conviction that women were by their gender incapable of the full range of enlightenment experiences possible. There are five states of existence in the world for which a female's body renders her unqualified: she is barred from becoming a Buddha, a universal monarch (a person ready either to attain supreme temporal authority or Buddhahood), a Śakra-god (Indra, king of gods), Brahmā-god (creator and lord of the Brahmā worlds), or a *Māra* (lord of love and death, who tempts and destroys).[16] Both a Buddha and the universal monarch conform to the Great Man (*Mahāpuruṣa*) physique, among whose thirty-two characteristic marks is possession of a sheath-covered penis.[17]

Buddhist soteriological texts thus share certain similarities with Hindu works on gender. They also presume sex changes across multiple lifetimes, and male births are generally regarded as superior to female. Further, female imitation of "male" behavior is in a broad sense presumed to be necessary for success along the spiritual path, and, like Hinduism, Buddhist female renunciants are subject to different, stricter rules than males.

The *Therigatha*, "Songs of the Women Elders," includes numerous biographies and poems detailing nuns' efforts and expressions of attaining enlightenment. However, only several centuries after Buddha's death the monastic *sangha* or community became increasingly less open to both the laity and female renunciants. The Buddhist conviction that women could not gain enlightenment grew popular in India at the very time period as similar beliefs came to be accepted in Classical Hinduism. Though the nuns' order was transmitted to many places in South and Southeast Asia, for a variety of reasons, an order of fully ordained nuns did not survive in the Theravada countries. Gendered rules of initiation preclude women from being initiated by monks. Since Theravadins generally believe full monasticism to be necessary to gain the insight necessary for nirvāṇa, women cannot attain enlightenment in Theravada traditions while still embodied as women.[18]

Contemporaneous with and parallel to the rise of *bhakti* within Classical Hinduism, a new development emerged within Buddhism that like *bhakti* was less hierarchical and more universal in scope than the dominant tradition. Mahayana Buddhism deliberately emphasized the larger *sangha*, that is, the community composed of lay people of both sexes in addition to monks and nuns.

At the time of their split, there were many in both Theravada and Mahayana Buddhist camps who expressed negative attitudes towards women. However, "no one who strongly advocated women's positive qualities seems to have been in the camp of the more conservative, older forms of Buddhism."[19]

In Mahayana, "salvation" was possible even while living within the confines of ordinary society. The Theravada goal of personal enlightenment (*arhat*-ship) required complete renunciation of the world and entrance into the monastic *sangha*. Mahayana texts substituted the goal of *bodhisattva*-hood for *arhat*-ship. A *bodhisattva* develops both the proper insight into the true nature of things, as well as a correlative compassion for those still benighted. Having realized the interconnectedness of all things – and in later Mahayana, the ultimate emptiness of all phenomena – the *bodhisattva* thus vows to continue returning to states of embodiment to facilitate the enlightenment of all. Mahayanists thus assert a profoundly positive world view, even while maintaining its ultimate emptiness. Their claims about the value of the world are dramatically illustrated in allegorical texts which portray enlightened females and laypersons teaching hopelessly dull Theravada monks.

Mahayana thus both inherited and amended Theravada teachings on gender. Popular Buddhism in both divisions, like the popular Hinduisms of early Vedic ritual and later Bhakti, realizes that because of the difficulty of attaining enlightenment, most people will remain within the realm of *saṁsāra*. It thus incorporates rituals designed to ease and prolong life in the world, and a model of gradual spiritual progress which restructures bad karma to good, as it were, called the way of merit (*puṇya*). References to the misfortunes of female rebirth abound.[20] Since female birth is more painful and less meritorious than male birth, many rituals are designed to insure that future births be male, even though Mahayana affirms the possibility of women attaining enlightenment.

Likewise, in the Pure Land Mahayana tradition's *Land of Bliss Scripture* (*Sukhāvatīvyūha Sūtra*), the problem of female rebirth is solved by the great Buddha Amitabha by eliminating it entirely. With his great powers, he established a place for his followers to work on their salvation called the Western Paradise. This paradise is easily reached through devotion to him, and since the circumstances of unfortunate births are too difficult to overcome for most people, Amitabha ensured that his is a land where no unfortunate births of any kind will occur, including female births; not even the name of "woman" will be heard there. Pure Land's popularity led to the common practice in Japan of giving women practitioners male names during funeral ceremonies on the assumption that since there are no females in the next life in the Pure Land, at death they become male.[21] In the less well-known Eastern Paradise of the Buddha Akṣobhya, women are wonderfully beautiful, freed from the curse of menstruation, and – being a place devoid of sexual desire or jealousy – become pregnant without sexual intercourse. Thus, the problem of female rebirth can either be avoided in its entirety, or by removing its biological or physical constraints and incumbent sexual desires.[22]

Pure Land Buddhism thus depreciates the female human body to such an extent that rebirth as a man is expressly promised, or womanhood is shorn of supposedly negative female traits which cause suffering. Recall that the Buddha is believed to have predicted that the *dharma* would decline after a certain period. Pure Land Buddhism posits that the world itself is now in that predicted state of decline. All embodied creatures suffer under this entropy, and women more than men. In this theory of embodiment, the *dharma* cannot be fulfilled by people of unfortunate birth. Thus, the promise of a male-only or male-like paradise appealed to those who believed that embodiment in this world at this time in the female gender were three strikes that by definition meant losing one's place at bat. By escape to a pure world, in the future, in a fortunate birth, salvation could be assured.

The proscriptions of females from the five births whose characteristic marks included male physiology are continued in some Mahayana texts. While there are exceptions, most maintain that bodhisattvas in the final rebirths are always male, for instance, and those Mahayana *sūtra*s or sacred scriptures which do not hold emptiness as a major teaching, such as the *The Lotus of the True Law Scripture* (*Saddharmapuṇḍarīka Sūtra*), do seem to suggest that change of sex is necessary if a woman is to take the final step to Buddhahood.

Other texts rejected this view of gender and enlightenment. For those pursuing the way of perfected understanding (*prajñā*), gender is irrelevant, because from the point of view of ultimate truth, gender is like all such distinctions: an empty construct.[23] The only position consistent with today's standard Mahayana doctrine of the emptiness of all phenomena is that only the ignorant make distinctions between the religious aspirations and intellectual and spiritual capacities of men and women.[24]

In Mahayana texts positing fundamental emptiness, a striking illustration of this point is the magical and instantaneous "physical" sex change. These changes almost always involve females becoming males. Their transformations do not prove that women cannot attain enlightenment, however, or that bodhisattvas or buddhas cannot be female; rather, magical sex changes underscore the already realized state of the woman who changes herself which proves the irrelevance and falsity of gender distinctions. Females change their bodies only in response to challenges to their understanding, and transformations are only possible on the women first reaching the insight that no *dharmas* (constituents of reality) whatever are born, that none therefore has a fixed reality or anything to define, and that since *dharmas* are as fluid or as deceptive as illusion (*māyā*), they are fundamentally impossible to apprehend as distinct entities.[25] Thus, the women who adopt male bodies are demonstrably capable of enlightenment while embodied as women, as the very change is contingent on realization.

Changing the female body is a Buddhist narrative device which directly confronts earlier views of women's spiritual limitations. It challenges the notion that women's bodies are visible evidence that they have not reached a high level of spiritual maturity and cannot therefore be candidates for Buddhahood.

But in a sense, maleness is not merely physical in philosophical Mahayana Buddhism. Diana Paul has suggested that in many such works, it is not only one's female physique that must change, but also one's "woman's thoughts," that is, her woman's nature and mental attitude. A "male attitude" means being unattached to sexuality and responsible for one's actions, whereas being a female did not entail such detachment and responsibility.[26] In some Indian Buddhist texts, it is stated that female physiology and its concomitant sexual "power" result in a physiological weakness of will, such that to advance on the spiritual path one must not only seek rebirth in a male body, but a woman must also renounce and eradicate her sexual power, which ties her to sexual desire and therefore is seen as inferior and an obstacle. Once this power is removed, a male rebirth is possible, during which male sexual power can be destroyed and Buddhahood obtained. In Buddhahood, the male form is retained: the male body represents perfection of the mind. Transformation of sex thus represents a transition from the imperfection, impurity, and immorality of human beings, represented by the female body, to the mental perfection of bodhisattvas and buddhas, represented by the male body.[27] To a degree, the male is not truly embodied or even gendered; he is unmarked, beyond gender.

Thus, in both Hinduism and Buddhism, women and femininity symbolize the world or worldliness, and men and masculinity symbolize the "unmarked" or transcendence. Further, when one speaks of gender in both traditions, one must pay attention to more than just physical manifestation, since ways of thinking, action, and modes of perception have been understood in terms of gendered categories. Even in Buddhist texts stressing the emptiness of all things, or Hindu scriptures espousing the illusion or falsity of distinctions, the mode of ultimate being is still predicated on what the tradition has identified and valorized as the masculine.

On the whole, when phenomenal reality or the world is devalued, so is female embodiment. When phenomenal reality is valued or perceived as useful to religious quest, female embodiment is not an impediment to salvation. A key determinant in the perception of women's nature in the religious quest for both Hindu and Buddhist traditions is thus their understanding of the phenomenal world. A brief review of some of the traditions noted here illustrates this point. Popular Hindu devotional approaches which affirm the ability to be saved by deities during one's lifetime on earth have not only denied that being female is an obstacle, but some assert it may even be an advantage. Bhakti demands attachment and affection, both of which are identified as feminine – they are "women's thoughts," predispositions, or feelings. Similarly, those Mahayana philosophies which fused the realms of transmigration and enlightenment, and which also saw liberation within and through the world despite its ultimate unreality, deemed that being a woman was not necessarily an obstacle to enlightenment, and their magical sex changes demonstrate this insight. In contrast, in popular Buddhist devotional forms such as the Pure Land, in which detachment is seen as impossible for all while living in the current world, an alternate, gendered view emerges. Instead, one must pray to transcendental figures capable of assisting those living in the age of the decay of the *dharma* for rebirth in a pure place. In the two Pure Lands, one offers a direct gender change for females to male bodies, and the other allows for the transmutation of a woman's earthly, biological, and temperamental constraints due to her gender. Both claim to be better worlds; the first is an ideal single sex culture of males, and the other boasts a pseudo-androgyny where women become as men, that is, beautiful, non-menstruous, non-sexual, and able to create by their own power. Depending on their point of view of dichotomies, and, in particular, the phenomenal world, Hindu and Buddhist soteriological stances may allow for women to gain salvation as women, or they may assert the necessity of a female becoming male to experience the pinnacle of human destiny.

NOTES

1 W. Norman Brown, "Change of Sex as a Hindu Story Motif," in *Journal of the American Oriental Society*, vol. 47 (1927), p. 6.
2 For a careful study of the negotiated construction of a textualized view of women based on these rarified scriptures by Orientalists and Nationalists in the nineteenth century, see Uma Chakravarti, "Whatever Happened to the Vedic Dasi? Orientalism, Nationalism, and a Script for the Past," in Kumkum Sangari and Sudesh Vaid (eds), *Recasting Women: Essays in Indian Colonial History*, New Brunswick, N.J.: Rutgers University Press, 1989, pp. 27–87. In the same vein, Sumanta Banerjee traces nineteenth century Bengali urban elites of both genders whose actions stigmatized and suppressed popular women's traditions newly stylized as "lower class." Their elite artistic productions deliberately adopted Sanskritized views of women and culture. "Women's Popular Culture in Nineteenth Century Bengal," in *Recasting Women*, pp. 127–79.
3 Most of these trends have been well documented. I have drawn particularly on Katherine K. Young's "Hinduism", in Arvind Sharma (ed.), *Women in World Religions*, Albany: SUNY Press, 1987, pp. 59–103, and A. S. Altekar's succinct if not entirely correct review, *The Position of Women in Hindu Civilization: From Prehistoric Times to the Present Day*, Delhi: Motilal Banarsidass, 2nd edn, 1959, pp. 336–61. For ease of reading, I do not use diacritics or underline names of formal religious movements.
4 Robert P. Goldman, "Foreword," in Padmanabh S. Jaini, *Gender and Salvation*, Berkeley: University of California Press, 1991, p. xviii.
5 For instance, neophyte male ascetics should avoid contact with women because they would excite sexual desire and inhibit practice. Upon enlightenment, a male ascetic would not be affected improperly by women, hence he can interact with women once again without threat. Making discriminations between sexes is thus initially heuristic in thought and practice, but if kept, it would become an impediment to understanding the fundamental identity of all things.
6 Altekar, *Position*, p. 203.
7 Altekar, *Position*, pp. 345–6.
8 William Harman, *The Sacred Marriage of a Hindu Goddess*, Bloomington: Indiana University Press, 1989, p. 122.
9 Harman, *Sacred Marriage*, p. 127.
10 In recent years several excellent books have been published which explore the development of the *sati* tradition in India. See John S. Hawley (ed.), *Sati: The Blessing and the Curse*, New York: Oxford University Press, 1994; Sakuntala Narasimhan, *Sati: A Study of Widow Burning in India*, Delhi: Viking, 1990; and Arvind Sharma, *et al.*, *Sati: Historical and Phenomenological Essays*, Delhi: Motilal Banarsidass, 1988. See especially the revisionist essays by Lata Mani, for example,

"Contentious Traditions: The Debate on Sati in Colonial India," in Sangari and Vaid (eds), *Recasting Women*, pp. 88–126.

11 Brown, "Change of Sex," p. 23.

12 See Kathleen Erndl, for example, *Victory to the Mother: The Hindu Goddess of Northwest India in Myth, Ritual, and Symbol*, New York: Oxford University Press, 1993, pp. 114–34. A notable exception to women not adopting male deity's dress is some female devotees' impersonation of Krishna. This is perhaps done not so much in imitation of Krishna, however, as in imitation of the cowherd deity's preeminent *bhakta*: his lover, Radha. In myth and art, Radha is portrayed as having exchanged her clothing with Krishna, and "played" with gendered conventions of dominance and submission in their relationship.

13 A caveat might be introduced here. These five (called the *pañcamakāras* or "five m's" because each word begins with the consonant *m*) are replaced later by many adherents with symbolic substitutes, revealing the power of taboo and societal prohibition. Also, the gendered experience of Hindu Tantric women adherents in real-life situations may be little different than that experienced by women in other forms of Hinduism.

14 Lorna Rhodes AmaraSingham, "The Misery of the Embodied: Representations of Women in Sinhalese Myth," in Judith Hoch-Smith and Anita Spring (eds), *Women in Ritual and Symbolic Roles*, New York: Plenum Press, 1978, p. 104.

15 This does not fully acquit Tantra (both Hindu and Buddhist) from the evils of sexism. I recommend to all those interested in Tantra in general and Vajrayana in particular Miranda Shaw's *Passionate Enlightenment: Women in Tantric Buddhism*, Princeton, NJ: Princeton University Press, 1994. Rita M. Gross's study, *Buddhism After Patriarchy*, Albany: SUNY Press, 1993 has interesting theological insights on how Vajrayana practice might be redeemed so that it lives up to its egalitarian philosophy.

16 Nancy Schuster, "Changing the Female Body: Wise Women and the Bodhisattva Career in Some Mahāratnakūṭasūtras," in *Journal of the International Association of Buddhist Studies*, vol. 4 (1981), No. 1, p. 27.

17 Schuster, "Changing", p. 27.

18 Today, some Buddhist women in Asia advocate a revival of the nuns' *saṅgha* in places no longer retaining a lineage, but this is a controversial and disputed proposition. See Karma Lekshe Tsomo (ed.), *Sakyadhītā: Daughters of the Buddha*, Ithaca, NY: Snow Lion Publ., 1988, or Chatsumarn Kabilsingh, "The Future of the Bhikkunī Samgha in Thailand," in Diana L. Eck and Devaki Jain (eds), *Speaking of Faith: Global Perspectives on Women, Religion and Social Change*, Philadelphia: New Society Publishers, 1987, pp. 148–58.

19 Gross, *After Patriarchy*, p. 57.

20 Schuster, "Changing", p. 44.

21 Gross, *After Patriarchy*, pp. 65–6.

22 Gross, *After Patriarchy*, pp. 63–5.

23 Schuster, "Changing", p. 28.

24 Schuster, "Changing", p. 25. This more egalitarian position is very prevalent in Ch'an or Zen works, although in practice, Ch'an/Zen Buddhist nuns were often still discriminated against. See Kumiko Uchino, "The Status Elevation Process of Soto Sect Nuns in Modern Japan," in Eck and Jain (eds), *Speaking of Faith*, pp. 159–73.

25 Schuster, "Changing," pp. 50–1.

26 Diana Paul, *Women in Buddhism: Images of the Feminine in Mahayana Tradition*, Berkeley: Asian Humanities Press, 1979, pp. 186–7.

27 Paul, *Women in Buddhism*, pp. 171–5.

9

GENDER, POWER AND SPECTACLE IN LATE-IMPERIAL CHINESE THEATER

Sophie Volpp

In Chapter 36 of the late sixteenth-century novel *The Plum in the Golden Vase* (*Jin Ping Mei*), the wealthy merchant Ximen Qing hires an acting troupe to entertain a new first laureate of the civil service examinations.[1] Ximen Qing's personal servant in the study, Shutong, dresses as a woman and joins the actors of the troupe. The first laureate, mistaking Shutong for one of the actors, is much taken with him. He asks for a song from the play *The Jade Bracelet* (*Yu huan ji*).[2] Shutong sings the part of the chaste bride.

> Shutong poured the wine, and clapping his hands, sang:
>
>> From the time I was young to the time that I was ready to marry,
>> The grace of my mother and father was as profound and vast as
>>   the sky.
>> I am ashamed that there is nothing that I can do to repay them,
>> This is something that tugs at my heart.
>> my husband and I have deeply absorbed by parent's favor,
>> And I hope that my husband will be honored and distinguished.
>
> An, the first laureate, was originally from Hangzhou, and his preference leaned towards the "Southern Mode."[3] When he saw that Shutong sang well, he took his hand, and the two of them drank one after the other in turn .... Shutong was wearing a jade-colored jacket over a red skirt, and a gold band round his waist. Holding the jade cup high, he lifted his wine and sang again.[4]

When the chaste bride's words issue from Shutong's lips, the incongruities between Shutong's assumption of the feminine voice and his male body and between Shutong's promiscuity and the bride's chastity enhance Shutong's erotic allure. The lyric aids him in his self-dramatization as erotic spectacle, a spectacle for which the first laureate is the primary audience. In this performance, the boundaries between world and stage dissolve as the spectator becomes implicated in the spectacle.

That Shutong's self-dramatization as erotic spectacle has been successful becomes clear in the words of Ximen Qing's friend Ying Bojue, who exclaims, "The sound that issues from his throat is that of a flute. Why talk of those women of the bawdy houses ... we've heard all their songs. How could theirs be as luscious as his!"[5] Ying Bojue refers not merely to Shutong's lusciousness on-stage, but to his lusciousness off-stage, to his performance not just at the banquet, but in the bedroom, to the fact that he has a "flute" which plays different "songs" from those of a woman.[6] In Ying Bojue's words, we hear an implied competition between the courtesans of the bawdy houses and male actors, who, like courtesans, were considered sexually available.

One of the primary themes in late-imperial Chinese representations of the actor is the rivalry between actor and courtesan for the ground of femininity. Actors as a group were symbolically coded feminine; that feminization was a part of their professional identity in their off-stage interactions with patrons. We find anecdotes about male actors named "Elder Aunt" and "Sixth Sister," "Small Tenderness," and "Peach Blossom Rain," anecdotes about male actors who were acclaimed at public events as the "wives" of their literati lovers. The feminization of actors was an artifact not only of cross-dressing in performance, but of the sexual availability of actors to elite men.

As the appropriation of feminine names, feminine kinship terms, and allusions commonly used to describe courtesans implies, the discourse on male actors in late-imperial China is largely shaped by cultural icons of the feminine, and, in particular, the representation of courtesans. Yet representations of the male actor also resist the similarities implied by this appropriation, insisting instead upon the superiority of the male actor. Consider the following poem written in praise of three actors named Qinxiao, Yangzhi and Ziyun, who were owned by the literary luminary Mao Xiang (1611–93).

> Qinxiao sings and Yangzhi dances,
> Among them, Ziyun is particularly enticing.
> There are too many Little Hongs and Little Xues to count,
> And Peach Leaf and Peach Root are like muck and excrement.[7]

Little Hong and Little Xue are common appellations for prostitutes; Peach Leaf and Peach Root may have been prostitutes of Nanjing, where there was a Peach Leaf ford, or simply domestic servants. As we can see from this aggressive differentiation, it is partially the uniqueness of the male actor that makes him so enticing; the women are common in both senses of the term.

The most extended and complex seventeenth-century argument for the superior femininity of the cross-dressed actor is to be found in a drama entitled *The Male Queen (Nan wanghou)*. *The Male Queen* offers a unique opportunity to examine how the theater interprets such conventions of performance as the cross-dressing of male actors, for it is the only premodern play that takes a male who cross-dresses as a woman as its theme. The only surviving northern drama (*zaju*) written by the theorist of the theater Wang Jide (d. 1623),[8] *The Male Queen* tells the story of a young boy named Chen Zigao who seduces the King of Linchuan – the first Emperor of the Chen dynasty – with his feminine charms. The King, noting that Zigao is more seductive than any of the women in his harem, has the boy dress as a woman and crowns him Queen.

The boy's successful impersonation of a woman gives rise to an unusual comedy of errors. Soon not only the King, but the King's sister is after Zigao. Not knowing that Zigao is a boy, the sister, the Princess Yuhua, declares that this new Queen "has a seductiveness like nothing I have ever seen. Even I can't compare to her. Forget about my brother, a man, falling in love with her. I am a girl, and I wouldn't mind swallowing her down like a drink of cold water."[9] Her maid offers to find her a man, but the princess insists that no man could compare to Zigao. At this point, the princess's maid reveals to her that the object of her affections is, in fact, a boy. Armed with this knowledge, the princess forces Zigao to marry her secretly. But her maid, who herself has an interest in Zigao, reveals the marriage to the King. The King initially decides to behead both Zigao and the princess, but hesitates, unwilling to sacrifice his unique partner. Finally, he reasons that if he lets the couple formalize their marriage, both he and his sister can share the boy.[10]

Not only the plot, but the stage directions inscribe a series of gender crossings. Either a male or female actor trained to play the female lead could have acted the part of Chen Zigao in *The Male Queen*. For an actor to play the opposite sex in performance was quite ordinary. Most troupes were single-sex, and performers were trained from an early age to play a certain role type. Such role types included clowns, gentlemen, and leading ladies. Each role-type had a certain style of movement, vocal production, makeup and costume. What is extraordinary in this play is that Wang Jide's stage directions request that the actor who is trained to play the principal female role, the *dan*, play the role of a male character, Chen Zigao. This creates a nested set of gender crossings that would immediately force an audience – or reader – to view the gender of the actor's body in a different light. If a male actor played the role of the female lead, the audience would witness a male actor dressed as the female lead playing the part of a young boy who cross-dresses as a woman. If we were to imagine a set of Russian dolls, the Queen would be the outermost doll, the boy the next. Inside the boy we would find the female lead, and inside the female lead, the male actor. These nested gender crossings ensure that both genders are immanent in the body of the actor.

These layers of gender crossing create a parallel between the male actor, who cross-dresses as female lead, and the young boy, who cross-dresses to become queen. The play exploits this parallel between the cross-dressed actor and the cross-dressed character in that the erotic relationship between boy and king becomes a suggestive metaphor for the erotic relations between actor and patron.[11] The play also exploits the confusion between actor and character and, masculine and feminine that these layers of gender crossing create.[12]

The play opens with the boy's self-introduction, a playful poem in praise of himself. The poem becomes an advertisement of the actor's skill in approximating the feminine.

> Iridescent clouds of hair, black sleeves so graceful that I myself am surprised,
> I fear that you will not be able to tell when you cast your eyes.[13]

The actor's opening lines tease the spectator: can the spectator distinguish life from art? It is only if the spectator cannot that he will find pleasure in the spectacle. The spectator's pleasure lies in his being mastered, not in mastering.

The advertisement of the actor's mastery here is not just an advertisement of his ability to create the successful illusion of femininity, but of the actor's erotic charms. Zigao's self-introduction continues,

> Even though my body is that of a man, my features are like those of a woman .... If I were a woman, I would certainly make a match with a king .... I could be such a fox, I could bedazzle my man. Even if he were a man of iron, I could make half his body go so soft it couldn't move. It's a pity I was made a boy by mistake.[14]

Even as this speech introduces us to the conceit of the play, the erotic relationship between the boy and the King, it invites the audience to consider the actor as an erotic spectacle. Zigao's fantasy paradoxically suggests that the arousal of the spectator will paralyze him. Oddly enough, arousal leads to the spectator's feminization. To respond to the actor's eroticism is to become emasculated, paralyzed, and disempowered.

The boy Zigao is captured by soldiers, who take him to their king. The King asks, "What kind of abilities have you?" Zigao's reply advertises his flexibility, the range of positions he can assume.

> My charming figure is used to straddling a horse.
> My soft waist knows how to pull a bow of the most flexible wood.
> I can with great care hold your precious sword. ...
> When you are bored,
> I'll be the puppet you play with in your spare time.
>
> My King, I don't dare tell you that I will make you die of pleasure with this little treasure.[15]

As Zigao entices the King with this list of erotic positions, the actor advertises his own body before the audience, putting the audience in the position of the King. Zigao speaks of himself as a puppet, as an empty shell devoid of agency. The speech lures the King – and the audience – into believing in the fiction of the empowerment of the voyeur. And yet this puppet has the capacity to make the King die of pleasure. The empowerment of the voyeur is a pleasurable, but deadly, fiction.

Zigao adopts feminine speech both in response to the King's interest, and in an attempt to intensify that interest. But his feminine speech is exaggerated, theatrical, almost parodic. When the King asks him how old he is, Zigao rephrases the question using honorifics: "You ask how many fragrant years has this Blue Jade?"[16] This odd violation of usage underscores the transgression of gender boundaries, but it also reinforces the theatrical quality of the boy's positioning of himself as a woman.

Impressed with Zigao's quick wit, the King asks Zigao to enter his harem, saying that there are many women in his harem, but none with the charms of Zigao's figure. The King then orders the women of the palace to help Zigao dress as a woman. As the palace women dress him, at first he literally repeats their words. He mimics their speech and actions. But as his transformation proceeds, he declares himself independent of the "real women" on stage (who would likely have been played by men), independent of their tutelage and even of the rouge and powders which they have applied to his face. He explains, "You women just streak on a load of rouge in imitation of crabapples/If you don't make yourselves up, you're merely ordinary."[17] Zigao answers the implicit accusation that he is dressed in imitation of women by claiming that women are dependent on artifice. Not only are they dependent on artifice, but their femininity is itself imitative. Thus, he accuses the female sex of the very weakness that he is liable to.

Once Zigao has become symbolically identified as a woman, he begins to play games with that identification. He compares himself to such feminine icons of the cultural past as the archetypal *femme fatale*, the Tang consort Yang Guifei. If we are to believe the account of the poet Bai Juyi, the consort Yang became so powerful that families began to wish for girls instead of boys in hopes of duplicating her success.[18] In Bai Juyi's words, daughters became "the lintel of a family's gate," creating an inversion of the normal valuation of the sexes. Zigao promises to position a male body in Yang Guifei's place: "Who says that daughters are the lintel of a family's gate? I tell you, boys will ride the chariots of the inner palace!"[19] Now that a male body has taken the consort's position in the inner palace, families will wish for boys again. Zigao imagines himself to be, like the consort Yang Guifei, one whose rise to power creates a model of imitation, and a model of inversion. Oddly enough, according to his model, the boys of the future will become more valued than girls, but only because they occupy women's positions, riding the chariots of the inner palace. Zigao offers a model of inversion which supplants that of the consort Yang. He corrects the old model of inversion by adding a second layer of inversion. In doing so, he claims that it is better for boys to occupy the feminine position than for the female sex to do so, a variation on the claim that feminine charms are more charming in a male body.

Zigao gives another reason as to why a boy actor makes a better consort. He can fall back on masculinity.

> Think of those ladies who trail silk in the pepper chambers
> Stripped of their hairpins, having lost the King's favor.
> They still keep painting themselves like gourds.
> But if I were to change my clothes, and switch my tune,
> I would be a sturdy warrior in a helmet.[20]

The palace women paint themselves like gourds when they fall out of favor. All they can do is intensify their femininity in a vain attempt to attract the King. Zigao, by contrast, can employ gender strategically, choosing when to act a woman, and when to act a man. This strategic employment of gender is phrased in terms of changing clothes and switching tunes, drawing attention to the parallels between the character and the boy actor. Like the character, the boy actor can play masculine or feminine roles on-stage and off. It is through his self-mastery that he masters the king, and the spectator.

Once Zigao's ambitions to be crowned Queen have been realized, he changes his tune. "You have taken Song Yu, whom women peeped at over his eastern wall/ And guessed wrongly that I am the divine woman of Gaotang."[21] The goddess of Gaotang (the goddess of Chu) is a standard in the inventory of allusions typically used to describe courtesans and other women defined by their eroticism. Here Zigao resists an assimilation to that category, claiming that he is not the goddess, but the author who created the goddess. He is Song Yu, the author of the "Rhymeprose on Gaotang" and the "Rhymeprose on the Divine Woman," texts that launched the goddess in the literary tradition. Zigao accuses the king of mistaking the creator for his creation. He is not the deity, but rather the man who enabled others to visualize her. The audience has fallen for an illusion. Zigao divests the audience of the power to engender him with their eyes by making it clear that their desire has led them to be mistaken about his gender. Zigao exposes the rules of the game. Femininity has been created in order to be dismissed. The femininity of the female sex was always a foil for a more pressing concern, the femininity of the male actor.

Not only is Zigao not the goddess, he is the Song Yu whom "women peeped at over his eastern wall." In Song Yu's "Rhymeprose on Licentious Master Deng," the poet defends himself from the accusation that given his astounding good looks and persuasive wit, he cannot be trusted around the royal harem.[22] He argues that despite the fact that a comely neighbor has often peeped at him over the eastern wall of his garden, he has remained faithful to his ugly wife. In other words, Zigao argues that although he is an object of female desire as well as male desire, he can be trusted around the King's harem.

Ironically, it is at this point that Zigao succumbs to the desire of the princess, who robs Zigao of his power of self-improvisation and forces him to accept her redefinition of his gender. Zigao defined his gender in large part through the invocation of models from the cultural past. The princess also uses allusive reference to the models of the past to question the gender of the cross-dresser and press for redefinition.

The princess's desire for the new queen further complicates the question of the gender and sex of the cross-dresser. Unlike her brother, she falls in love with Zigao believing he is female. When her maid offers to find her "a husband like that," she replies scornfully, "Silly wench, she is a woman! How can a man compare to her? ... She is a goddess with pendants chiming in the mountains of Chu."[23] Zigao chastised the King for mistaking him for the goddess of Chu. Now the princess repeats the same mistake. Waking from her delusion, the spectator rebels, moving to take control of the play of gender and the play itself.

Unlike the King, once the princess realizes her mistake, she assumes the right of authorship of Zigao's gender. Once her maid tells her that Zigao is a boy, she immediately works to redefine him with an onslaught of literary allusion.

> You are not the female ghost of the Cui family, who gave a golden bowl,
> You are not Zheng Yingtao, the demon clothed in red robes.[24]
> You are not Zhu Yingtai, disguising her glamour,[25]
> You shouldn't copy the man of Lu,[26] who locked his vermilion doors.[27]

The princess shuts down the polymorphous play of crossed genders in which Zigao had engaged. Becasue she uses a process of negative definition, she does not define the gender of the cross-dresser concretely. The cross-dressed boy has been the object of the homoerotic desire of the King, and of the homoerotic and heteroerotic desire of the princess. Ultimately the intersection of these different types of desires leaves the gender of the boy indeterminate, unstable, and mutable, just as the gender of the actor is indeterminate, unstable, and mutable.

The gender of the actor's body is created by visual illusion and by speech acts. As such, it is not a stable entity, but constantly mutates as the actor works visually and vocally to establish symbolic identification as a woman, or a man, or as a feminine boy superior to a woman. But the gender of the actor is created not only by performance, but by the desiring eye of the spectator. The actor's gender is thus the result of a process of flirtation and negotiation between actor and audience.

The Male Queen shows us how the actor deflects the desiring eye of the spectator, frustrating the spectator's ability to feel confidence in what he sees. The actor observes the spectator falling for the illusion and taunts him about it. The site of the spectator's misrecognition is the gender of the body of the actor. It is in these senses that the gender of the actor's body is a theatrical construct. The gender of the actor's body is the product of the actor's performance and the spectator's reception of it, but it is also a product of the actor's recognition and manipulation of the spectator. The actor's insistence on the spectator's misrecognition is one enactment of this resistance to the identification of male actor with courtesan.

In the closing lyrics of the play, it becomes clear that the character Zigao views himself as an author as well as character, as the creator of the cultural icons of the future.

> Our karmic affinity should be recorded on red paper by the historian's brush.
> A new variation will pop out of the history books.
> A thousand years from now people will tell this amusing story as they trim their silver lamps.
> Who ever saw the exalted face of the Dowager Empress Bo on the misty terrace?
> Even though one ought to write literature in a spirit of jest,
> How could we merely have said whatever came to mind?[28]

One day Zigao himself will be the stuff of historical allusion, a new variation in the history books. But Zigao does not merely claim that he will be the mirror in which later ages will view themselves. He also challenges the verifiability of the historical models against which he himself will be measured. "Who ever saw the face of the Dowager Empress Bo?" If no one saw the face of the Dowager Empress Bo, how do we know that her existence was more real than that of this character in a play? Zigao moves to supplant the Dowager Empress by saying, "I'm as real as she was." These lines contextualize the present as represented on stage, making it the cultural past. *Inside* the world of the play, the cultural icons of the past were surpassed by Zigao, a fictional character of the present. *Outside* the world of the play, Zigao will become the cultural icon of the future.

The basic paradigm in the cross-dressed boy's relation to the female sex is an inversion of the normal relation between original and copy. The simulacrum becomes more highly valued than the original – in fact it becomes an original. In the closing lyrics of the play, we see the same paradigm taking shape in the boy's relation to history. Zigao asks how we know that the historical Empress Bo actually existed, and whether he, as a literary character, is not more real than she.

The closing lyrics of *The Male Queen* feature the actors as authors of their own literary destinies. We should not forget, however, that the figure of the male actor – and the femininity of the male actor – are projections of the fantasies of literati authors. The authors of such texts were themselves connoisseurs of male actors. The very rivalry that we have noted between male and female characters for the ground of femininity, then, is a construction of these authors. The author enables the actor to make a claim to a superior femininity by scripting the very words that the actor would recite as he made that claim. In this sense, a drama such as *The Male Queen* is not just a comment upon, but an aid to, the male actor's self-fashioning as an icon of femininity.

NOTES

1 The novel is considered one of the "Four Great Masterworks" of the Chinese narrative tradition. Both the authorship and dating of *The Golden Lotus* are unclear, but the research of Patrick Hanan and Wu Han suggests that the novel was completed sometime between 1582 and 1596.

2 Katherine Carlitz discusses the play's didacticism in *The Rhetoric of Chin P'ing Mei*, Bloomington: Indiana University Press, 1986, pp. 115–16.

3 "The Southern Mode" (*nan feng*) refers to homoerotic desire and activity. The term probably arises from a pun on the two words "Southern" and "male," both pronounced *nan*.

4 *Jin Ping Mei cihua*, ed. by Dai Hongsheng, Hong Kong: Joint Publishing Col, 1986, p. 454.

5 *Jin Ping Mei Cihua*, ed. Dai, p. 440.

6 Qu Youzhong, as quoted in *A Brief History of Yunlang* (*Yunlang xiaoshi*), ed. Mao Guangsheng and collected in *Historical Materials on the Pear Gardens of the Capital During the Qing Dynasty* (*Qingdai yandu liyuan shiliao*), ed. Zhang Zixi (reprint, Beijing: Zhongguo xiju chuban she, 1988), p. 962.

7 Wang Jide is remembered primarily as the author of the foundational treatise in dramatic scholarship, *The Rules of Drama Gulu*. (Preface by the author dated 1610, first published after 1623.)

8 Although we do not have a date for the composition of *The Male Queen*, it was likely written during the last decade of the sixteenth century or the first decade of the seventeenth. The play was anthologized in *Zaju Drama of the High Ming* (*Sheng Ming Zaju*), an anthology whose preface dates to 1629, six years after Wang's death. There is no record of any other edition. See Shen Tai, ed., *Sheng Ming Zaju*, vol. 1, *juan* 27 (two volumes). The only surviving edition is the illustrated edition by the *Song Fen* studio.
  Volume one was printed in 1918, volume two in 1925. Reprinted in a facsimile edition by Zhongguo xiju chuban she, 1958.

9 There are two narrative sources for *The Male Queen*. The first is a biography of a historical figure, the Chen dynasty general Han Zigao, which appears both in the *History of the Chen* (*Chen Shu*) and in the *History of the Southern Dynasties* (*Nan Shi*). See Yao Silian, *Chen Shu*, Beijing: Zhonghua Shuju, 1972, 20.269–275 and Li Yanshuo, *Nan Shi*, Beijing: Zhonghua Shuju, 1972. 68.1664.

10 Wang Jide, *Nan Wanghou*, 15a.

11 Even if an actor were to play the part of the young boy who cross-dresses, the interpretation of the play would still need to take this parallel into account.

12 No scholar has found mention of a performance of *The Male Queen*. We should keep in mind, however, that the late Ming conceptions of performance, audience and text were quite different from their modern Western counterparts. The text was not a "play" in the modern sense of the word in that it would have been more common for actors to sing excerpted lyrics than to have performed the play in its entirety. If the play were performed in this manner, the excerpted lyrics would be nearly indistinguishable formally from individual songs.

13 Wang, 1a.
14 Wang, 1b–2a.
15 Wang, 7a.
16 Wang, 15a. The phrase "Blue Jade" refers to a young virgin.
17 Wang, 9a.
18 *Bai Zhuyi ji jian jiao*, ed. Zhu Jincheng, 6 vols, Shanghai: Guji chuban she, 1988, 2: 656–659.
19 Wang, 7a.
20 Wang, 12b.
21 Wang, 11a.
22 Song Yu, "Rhymeprose on Licentious Master Deng," in Xiao Tong, compiler, *Wen Xuan* 19.892–895.
23 Wang, 16a.
24 Zheng Yingtao was the male lover of the Jin dynasty general Shi Jilong, also known as Shi Hu, who murdered both his wives in succession at Zheng's bidding. *The History of the Jin (Jin Shu)* vol. 168: 2761–2778.
25 According to popular legend, Zhu Yingtai was a girl who cross-dressed in order to pursue an education and fell in love with her schoolmate, Liang Shanbo. For more information on the permutations of this legend in poetry and drama, see Tseng Yung-yi, *On Popular Literature (Shuo su wenxu)*, Taipei: Lianjing chuban she, 1973, pp. 121–29.
26 The man of Lu refers to an anecdote about a man so concerned with propriety that he refused to allow a female neighbor to take shelter in his home when her home was destroyed.
27 Wang, 19b.
28 Wang, 29a.

10

EROTICISM, SEXUALITY, AND GENDER REVERSAL IN HUNGARIAN CULTURE

László Kürti

Traditional East European societies have been described in scholarly literature as patriarchal, homophobic, and male-biased. Often we have been
imagining men and women of former times as helpless, passive victims of
patriarchal institutions. In this chapter, I want to argue that however
patriarchal East European societies have been, men and women created
special occasions to undermine implicit assumptions about gender systems
and to contest the roles and rules assigned to them by the state, the Church,
and masculinized institutions. I am specifically interested in how these
practices – although few and far between – allow individuals to release pent-
up frustrations by enabling them to act out their desires, or misgivings, in a
socially sanctioned arena. While I am aware that the values and actions
described here may be considered by some to be "idiosyncratic" peasant
customs relegated only to annals of folklore collections, I maintain that these
unconventional practices have played important roles concerning the negotiation of gender identities as well as codified sexual relations.

In village communities throughout Eastern Europe, traditional roles
assigned to men and women were based on patriarchal rule and legitimized
by Church and upper-class ideology.[1] Throughout the second serfdom
(between the fifteenth and nineteenth centuries), extraordinary measures
were taken to curtail human rights, sexual practices, and family life. The
general subordination of women (and those classed as "others") to men was
concomitant with the solidification of a masculine gender model. Michel
Foucault's observation that the modern state attempts to regulate a specific
sexual discourse is applicable to rural producers and their masculine-centered
manorial and Church-supported states before the twentieth century as well,
where constraints were placed on fecundity and reproductive behavior.[2]
The conservative religious practices and behavior within the family and
marriage identified by Jack Goody in Eurasia I see as true also for Hungarian
rural societies which rely on patronyms, patrilineal descent, and patrilocal
residence (to which among others the equally powerful prefix "patri" may
be attached).[3] Such a patriarchal value system has determined sexuality
and eroticism strictly from the heterosexual male perspective.[4] A well-

documented seventeenth-century source proves this point; Miklós Zrinyi (1620–1664), Hungary's warring count, while constantly engaging in military missions against the Turks, offered a strictly male perspective on gender roles in his work *Török Áfium* (Turkish Medicine):

> The last thing we have to consider is what type of youth should we recruit into our military and whom should we reject. Fishermen, fowlers, bakers and weavers, and those engaged in feminine occupations, should be, in my mind, kept out of the military. On the contrary, blacksmiths, wheelwrights, butchers, deer and boarhunters should all be drafted.[5]

The majority of women, on the contrary, were confined to roles in the household, child rearing, gardening, and, in the case of the well-to-do, the arts.[6]

As these historical examples suggest, military and politics have always been legitimated as traditionally male domains (though not without the presence of women); yet this dominant mode of rationalization afforded men superordinate status in general.[7] Since Hungarian society was militarized from at least the fourteenth century well into the eighteenth, it is no coincidence that such (biased) perspectives determined gender relations. Passed from generation to generation, patriarchal ideology afforded men a superior status to be fighters, providers (*kenyérkeresók*) and "born" leaders. At the same time, women have been viewed largely in terms of their function in reproduction, as secondary to males, and even as "irrational" in their actions and thinking.[8]

Thus, for centuries, peasant communities have functioned by polarizing male/female and man/woman (*férfi/nó*) into two politicized clearly marked roles and identities.[9] Anything divergent from this classification has been considered a negative aberration. Even during the period known as "state socialism" gender identities were strictly divided along male/female lines, and homosexuals in Hungary and other East European states were forbidden to openly declare their orientations.[10] Homosexual behavior, for instance, has been shunned and practised outside the legitimate public domain for centuries. Homosexual individuals have been ostracized and ridiculed; terms assigned for them have been *buzi* or *csira* ("seed"), *meleg* ("warm"), *selyemfiú* ("silky-boy") and *homokos* (a derivative of "homosexual" but which could also mean "sandy"). Only after 1990, when Hungary elected a new parliament and a multiparty state was created out of the ashes of the former communist machinery, were differences in sexual orientation allowed to surface openly; for instance, the homosexual newspaper *Others* is a recent addition to the media revolution in Hungary since 1990. As will be seen in this study, however, there were some allowances made for "difference" in folklore, mythology, and ritualized gender roles.

GENDER TRANSFORMATIONS

In traditional patriarchy, as it has existed in East-Central Europe, there have been only a few ways to manage a multiplicity of gender identities. It has been even more difficult to challenge or renegotiate rules which appropriate status, power, and symbolic benefits to those monitoring and upholding them.[11] However, when role-reversals are taken as a way of breaking societal barriers and codes concerning gender roles and identities, the past experiences and folklore practices provide a wide array of examples. Therefore, those occasions which may enable participants to balance or neutralize such built-in inequalities, or even to contest and redefine them, are charged with powerful content and symbolism.

The historian Natalie Zemon Davis, in her influential article, "Women on Top," informs us that during carnival time men and women are allowed to reverse their assigned roles and gender identities.[12] As we know from Villon and Boccaccio, there were plenty of occasions in popular culture where even the lower classes were given carte blanche to parade in the mantle of their lords for the time being. Carnivals and popular culture, as the works of Mikhail Bakhtyn and Peter Burke describe so vividly, are, to be sure, times of rollicking licentiousness involving unbridled challenges to dominant modes of discourse and symbols.[13] These staged events limited in time and space enabled participants to relieve some of the frustrations associated with their conditions of servitude.[14] Men dressing as women, women as men, old as young, young as elderly, humans as animals, poor as rich – all these are traditional elements of carnivals, just as they represent the negation of social and class roles and the sanctioning of attitudes and norms otherwise strictly forbidden (the carnivals of Rio de Janeiro and Venice and the Halloween parade in New York City are well known for these).[15] As anthropologist Abner Cohen has said, "A cultural movement is *ipso facto* also a political movement. A carnival may ostensibly appear to be a pure cultural performance, but it is inevitably political from the start."[16]

In East-Central Europe, folk carnivals (*farsang* in Hungarian, *Fasching* in German, *saptamina nebulior* among the Romanians of Transylvania) are equally libertine events – that is, sexually explicit and eroticized differently from the heterosexual male's perspective – if only on a smaller scale. Among Hungarians, Romanians, and German Schwabs, the *mundus inversus* may be acted out in the "women's ball" or "women's carnival" (*asszonyfarsang*). This event is truly fascinating for it is organized by and for women without the presence of men, a fact which could have prompted the Church to forbid local communal carnivals of this nature. In fact, hired Gypsy musicians, all of whom are males, are needed but since they are considered "outsiders" (not "one of us") their presence is tolerated but their eyes may be covered; or, in some instances, they are asked to wear their hats pulled down over their faces. The reason for this gender-exclusivity is that on this occasion women dance with each other, sing bawdy songs, and drink heavily; they may dress as males, perform male dances, and parody manly sexual prowess. It is even noted by researchers that if males (some of whom are always said to be "spying" on their wives or loved ones) are caught, they instantly become the laughing stock of the gathering: for example, their pants are pulled down, they may be spanked, and sexually explicit verses may be yelled at them.[17]

Thus, the "women's ball", while allowing the participants to reverse temporarily patriarchal gender roles, is viewed by men as a small and relatively minor affair when compared to their own male-centered, erotic, and often abusive sexism, rampant in peasant communities.[18] Most songs, though not all, reflect a young man's (or woman's) preoccupation with obtaining a lover of the opposite sex; aside from the women's round dance (karikázó), most dances are strictly couples dances, with the more energetic, fleshy and impressive styles reserved for young bachelors (in fact some of these are simply called "bachelor dances" or "barn dances" legényes, csürdöngölő); moreover, ritual and everyday practices are divided according to strict heterosexual roles, constantly reminding the participants of their assigned and, at times burdensome, gender identities. Space does not permit me to enter detailed discussion of these; let me recall only dress codes, folk art, seating arrangements at home, school, and church, selection of linguistic codes, words and bodily gestures, and sexually divided labor in the house and on the fields.[19]

Similarly satirical – again in a light way – are staged plays and masked processions during carnival time, known all over East-Central Europe (of which the charivari or palio are well-known French and Italian counterparts respectively).

In southern Hungary, the sokác people of Mohács (Croats who settled since the seventeenth century) celebrate their carnival time through the ritual known as poklada. Cross-dressing is central to this carnival as young men disguise themselves as women and speak in high-pitched voices so as to imitate female style speech.[20]

Among Hungarians in Moha, a village in south-western Hungary, a similar ritual is the "chicken-kill" (tyúkverő or tikverő).[21] Having close parallels in Slovak and German cultures, the "chicken-kill" features young males disguised as women who proceed from house to house in search of food and good times; their clothes are large skirts, blouses, jackets, with ample ribbons and scarves; even toupées and facial hair, made of corn silk, horse-hair, and cloth, are utilized. The aim is to disguise oneself as much as possible so that the members of the household fail to uncover their real identities. During such visits these masked "women" are allowed a fairly great degree of debauchery in which male members of the household are especially targeted; but females are also caught up in the event, and a couple of dancing "women" and men may be laughed at for their mild implication of homosexuality.[22] Women too were allowed to dress as males at masked visitations at traditional pig-kills; the visible signs of their "masculinity" included a carrot or a cow-horn as an obvious penis-substitute.[23] Women dressed as "men" dance with women in a "heterosexual" context with an equal dosage of mild homosexual implications. In these rituals, women may take a humorous retaliation on men, express their pains and hardships and, in turn, brag about their power and wisdom in outwitting men.

Actually, the insinuation of such homosexual behavior appears only in rare instances in Hungarian folklore where such allusions are interpreted as negative and threatening by males. To illustrate I will cite two cases rarely interpreted by native scholars as possible confrontations with the over-arching heterosexual male world view. The first concerns homosexual insults that young males shout at one another during wedding rituals. I observed this practice in Hungarian communities in the Kalotaszeg region of Romania. When the groom's party arrives at the gate of the bride's family's house, a shouting match takes place between the defenders of the bride and the attackers. At this mock battle, as ritual leaders negotiate the terms of entrance, the rest of the party engage in verbal (less often mild physical) duels in which demeaning words are exchanged. The pornographic and sexual overtones are obvious from one such shout (*csujogatás*):

> Let us come inside
> And we'll take you from behind.
> (Eresszenek be bennünket,
> Hagy basszuk meg a seggüket.)[24]

The other instance is more subtle and less available for interpretation. During the early 1930s, the ethnographer Sándor Gönyey reported an interesting shepherds' dance from the Kiskunság region of central Hungary.[25] What distinguishes this particular dance form from other, more "traditional," shepherd dances is the close proximity of the dancers to each other, a style which may be interpreted either as threatening, or, which is the case here, as "sexual." Here two men engage in a solo performance facing each other and advancing and cajoling each other. At one point one man holds the other's arm and turns him, a movement quite common in male/female couples dances. However men touching each other in strictly male dances as such is quite rare, if not non-existent in Hungarian folk dances. In this version, the turning of one male dancer by the other reverses not only the standardized heterosexual dance code of ethic (males dance with females) but challenges taken-for-granted conceptions about roles taken by men. In couples' dances the male takes the lead, and by being the "active" partner, turns the female who, being the "passive", follows her partner's instructions and bodily commands.[26]

What makes the Kiskunság film rather unique is that here the two men execute the "active" and "passive" roles; the one who does the lead (the turner) is active, while his "partner" (the turned) is relegated to a more passive role. Traditional folkloric (heterosexual) interpretations concerning this "aberration" may claim that the men simply imitate the movements common in male/female couples' dances with similar music and footwork. Moreover this theory might suggest that, since the Kiskunság region was the center of animal husbandry, and because the dancers are herdsmen, the exclusion of women from the herding community living with the herd at the summer pasture is quite normal. Such closeness, thus, between two shepherds is not to be confused with gender reversals, or homosexuality, but is simply an expression of basic cameraderie.

To these, I might add, however, that the "imitation" of male/female couple dance theory suffers from an implied classism if not outright ethnocentrism on the part of native ethnographers. For it claims that the dancing men are just role-playing in a less serious performance and, moreover, that the dancers are simplistic in their attitude concerning this "fake" dance. As to the second part of the argument about the herding community's exclusion of women, and the way in which this reinforces a non-sexual, innocent and childish male bonding, it must be stated that *because* of the lack of women in the herding camp – although wives, lovers, and female prostitutes visited them at regular intervals – and *because* of the close working relationship between men of various ages, emotional bonding is even more likely to develop among them. Let us remember that the youngest herding-boy (known as *kisbojtár*) had to perform tasks which were strictly "feminine" (cooking, cleaning, and upkeep of the huts) to balance the over-masculinized profession of herding.[27]

I do not mean to suggest that these rare instances imply that there is a homosexual genre in Hungarian folklore, or that there might be a connection between latent homosexual desire in these utterances and a *technique du corps* of Hungarian males.[28] Instead, I will argue that these expressions are significant, if numerically infrequent, elements for balancing the extremist heterosexual male point of view. Moreover, in a curious way, such "feminin-ized" verbal and body discourse may serve to reinforce the extreme chauvin-istic heterosexual code of ethic. That this code exists is itself enough proof that traditional gender roles and identities are limited, if not overtly confined, and that in order to reinforce it, some "safety valves" are necessary.

Overt and implied eroticism from the male point of view is present everywhere: in joking relations, where double play on words occurs; and in wood carving, embroidery, songs, and dances where sexual symbolism abounds.[29] In places such as Kalotaszeg in Transylvania, even the Hungarian wedding cake (*perec*) of the best men is baked as a round cake, symbolic of the vagina, pierced by the arm of the men who are assigned to carry it.

As we have seen above, wedding calls (*csujogatás, rikótozás, hujjintás*), while they may be filled with magical incantations, are notorious mostly for their explicit pornographic content. This is especially true in the case of those which are shouted by young males at the bride's house the night before the wedding day.

Women, whether willing or not, are constantly tested as to their faith in this legitimated system of heterosexuality.[30] Even mothers, most of whom have experienced such ordeals themselves, encourage their daughters to live up to the expected level of sexual prowess and beauty. Dress codes are designed to mold young females into objects of heterosexual (male) gaze and desire. During my recent fieldwork among Hungarians in Kalotaszeg, Transylvania, one young bride constantly complained to me as well as to her mother about the wedding dress she had to endure during the day of her wedding (supposedly the "happiest day of her life"). Expressions such as "my shoes are too small," the vest and the waist-band of the petticoat "are too tight," the headdress too heavy, the boots are "too small," are constant utterances of submission and suffering. Needless to say, after young women become mothers – changing their attire to more comfortable pieces of clothes – they in turn purchase similarly uncomfortable clothes for their daughters. By so doing, they continue the same male-centered ideology of fashion, modernity, and aesthetics (*divatosság*).[31]

RITUALISTIC GENDER REVERSAL

While folklore and peasant customs tell a one-sided story of heterosexual world view, I maintain that there are enough challenges to allow a more balanced construction of gender relations and crossings of such standardized sexual boundaries. As we have witnessed above, dances and dance calls may, in fact, suggest a mild threat to such confines. However, the practice of naming, for example, is also imbued with an equal dose of semiotic double entendre. In Hungary, given names and family names are strictly separated according to male and female names. In a few instances, however, there may be an inversion: such as the coupling of "László" (strictly male first-name) with "Magda" (strictly female first-name) as "László Magda;" or, similarly, "Mihály Annus."[32] One general theory holds that forced army service under the Habsburg empire's strict military laws, predominant since the end of the seventeenth century, resulted in Hungarian peasants christening their sons with female names so as to enable them to avoid the fifteen years or lifelong draft. However, I tend to be more skeptical about such a utilitarian explanation and would favor a more inclusive understanding for such folkloric practices. A name with a dualistic (both male and female) meaning could represent the archaic practice of naming ritual specialists who are entrusted by the community with special duties, powers, and roles.

Such individuals with magical powers are: the witch (*boszorkány*) and the shaman (*táltos*). Both of these characters, heroes/heroines of endless legends, folktales and black magic (*babona*), are ambiguous as to their gender. The Ukrainian *Baba Yaga*, the Bulgarian *mora*, and the Romanian *iele* are all decidedly females.[33]

Although in most cases witches are female, represented generally as old

154

hags, there are plenty of male witches (or warlocks). At least in one instance, an eighteenth-century trial for witchcraft mentions one female witch who is accused of being dressed in man's clothes. The Hungarian shaman (*táltos*) may also be good or bad, but mostly they were males, often engaging in deadly fights with female witches. Interestingly, while in Hungarian folk belief one could change one's gender by passing under the rainbow – an equally impossible act in the eyes of the peasants – and while witches and shamans are able to change their human form into animal forms, none of these wielders of magical powers are able to change their gendered boundaries without great difficulties. Such supernatural specialists, however, as evidenced in witch trials, are mentioned with ambiguous names. One was Dániel Rózsa: where the latter part, "Rose," is reserved strictly for women. Another was titled Erzsébet Balási, the latter being a man's name, perhaps suggesting her sacred and ritual status.[34] There are other examples, such as the shepherd János Virág ("John Flower"), mentioned by the ethnographer László Timaffy, whose shamanistic personage reveals the combined man/woman social persona.[35]

The name "Canvas Paul" (*Vászon Pál*), while it may elicit smiles from contemporary observers, is also a curious one, for men with "feminine characteristics," lack of facial hair, were referred to by this name. An obvious reversal of the "bearded women" stories – a theme dating back to Pliny the Elder describing the story of the popular androgynous St. Uncumber who grew her beard in order to avoid an unwanted marriage foisted upon her by her family – this institutional characterization afforded such individuals special status and ritual powers.[36] That this may be another reference to Hungarian shamanism is further supported by the following saying: "He hides himself as Canvas Paul" (*elrejtette magát, mint Vászon Pál*). The verb *elrejtette* refers literally to "hiding," which was a term used to describe the sleep-like trance of Hungarian shamans.

Another shaman, Demeter Farkas (the last name means "wolf"), is mentioned in the trials at Tiszafüred in 1748, being advised by a seer to dress in woman's clothes for thirty-three days, if s/he wanted to be successful in finding hidden treasures.[37] Such a strong perseverance of gendered shamanistic behavior, however, is not unique to Hungary and, interestingly, the ambiguous shamanic persona is present elsewhere.

Several researchers have mentioned that shamans are sometimes recognized because they exhibit "feminine" characteristics (no facial hair, wear ragged clothes, drink milk, weak physical state, and so on).[38] Moreover, Hungarian shamans do not live in a marital relationship and do not live according to prescribed heterosexual regulations; they are, thus, described in the literature as lonesome wanderers or solitary individuals living on the margins of society. Their seemingly characteristic bodily weakness, or "sickness" as it is referred to, may, of course, be a part of their defense mechanism: who could hurt such a weak, fragile creature? However, what is extraordinary about these shamans is that despite all these "feminine" (or let us call them non-traditionally-masculine) characteristics, they may at will transform themselves into powerful *male* animals; more often than not, into stallions, bulls, or wolves. This makes the shaman superhuman, an individual of neither male, nor female gender who, by uniting the best characteristics of both in order to create something new, evolves into something more than either of those single-gendered selves.

Shamans are not alone in their superhuman capabilities, for female witches as a rule may also transform themselves into animals: into cats, dogs, frogs, horses, donkeys, and occasionally even roosters (obvious symbol of masculinity).[39] More often than not, their animal forms do not carry any gender-specific meaning. This way, however, they are able to step out of their previously defined (human and female) gender roles, leave behind all of their negative connotations, and become a neutral third, a ritual being, a non-gendered creature. (In a way, this is what happens in Greece with elderly women and widows, whose life-long second-class status is well documented by antropologists of Greece, and whose status is respect because of their magical qualities and supra-human knowledge in affairs of the beyond and hereafter.)

That witches and shamans, and other religious specialists and artists, could cross traditionally dichotomized gender boundaries may be illustrated by the examples of the North American Indian Zuni *berdache*, the *xanith* of Oman, the *mahi* of Tahiti, and the man/woman of Hindu mythology known presently in India as *hijra*.[40] These third-gender, androgynous categories may explain the existence of such ambiguities and diversity concerning alternative, transgendered roles, distinct from either male or female in Eurasian folklore and mythology as well.[41]

Not only ritual specialists but heroes of ballads and legends could also be assigned ambigous gender identities. Such heroes are generally accepted by the community because of their redeeming characteristics and features eliciting a positive role-model. However, this may even be the case with regard to heroes whose negative stereotypes and gender codes are pushing the limits of traditional roles.

For example, in two Hungarian folk ballads, "Joe the Hunter" ("Jáger Jóska") and "The Daughter of Bankó" ("Bankó Lánya"), we may witness interesting instances for gender inversions. These ballads belong to a larger category of world-wide ballads known as "changing of genders" (in Hungarian the *nemek cseréje*).[42] In the first case, the outlaw Joe the Hunter – of which Slovak and Polish parallels are found in the folk hero Janosik ballad cycle– surprises his victims dressed in woman's clothes.[43] This ballad, paralleling many early medieval European transvestite popular stories (often referred to as "quarrel over trousers," "the pregnant man," etc.), is constructed by folk wisdom so that the popular hero may outsmart the rich; and, in turn, it allows the poor to laugh and, at the same time, relax their strict codes and morals.

In the other ballad the daughter takes up the task of defending the family's honor in fighting against the intruders. Since there is no male descendant in the family, the daughter is encouraged to dress up as a warrior in order to fight against the marauding enemies (Turks in this instance). This type of ballad, known as the "woman warrior," with its feudal courtly gesture and warrior code of ethics, has many more variants in Western as well as Eastern Europe.[44] The similar theme appears in Balkan military history, especially in Serbian and Croatian folklore, where the heroic sister decides to enlist into the army to defend the honor of the brother killed by the enemy. Such courageous, and (un)timely, emancipated "amazon" women are less common in Hungary and those few (like Ilona Zrinyi or the women of Eger both fighting against Turkish invaders) are mythologized in nationalist historiography.

In more contemporary versions, the outlaws Pista Mari (another name with dual gender!) and Jóska Gesztény both commit their crimes in women's clothes. In the case of the former we are only told that the outlaw had a special dress made of "green silk;" while the latter is dressed in "crinolin," a special hoop skirt of the time.[45] In another version, the outlaw Jóska Gesztyén, dressed in female clothing, walks into a store and selects expensive "silk" material; the ballad ends with the outlaw leaving without paying. In order to make this a feasible story the singer commented on the beautiful "girl-like facial feature" of the hero.[46]

It is worth mentioning that such gender inversions are quite common in earlier (medieval) folk ballads as well as in the "Arabian Nights," Balkan fairy tales and Caucasian heroic legends.[47] Such ballads, despite the homophobic and heterosexual aversion concerning gender difference, exhibit the practice of cross-dressing as a positive step for reasons that are obviously morally justified: in the case of the "primitive rebels" the folk hero fights against the rich; and in the case of the "male-daughters," the family's honor and status is restored through the sacrifice of the "daughter-as-son."

CONCLUSION

I claimed in the beginning of this chapter that if we want to understand the relationship between "sexuality" and "society" we must find those mediating cultural elements and forms which enforce traditional behaviors by providing approved channels for temporary deviance from "normal" codes of behavior. I have, therefore, focused on practices which, however subtle and informalized they may be, involve actors whose presence and identities must be challenged and constantly renegotiated in the presence of others. In the heterosexual, male-dominated society, such as the Hungarian rural community, male and female, man and woman, masculine and feminine, are selves which are understood as "constants" and which, from time to time, undergo questioning and reinterpretations. This may be achieved by specific actions which either reinforce or deconstruct taken-for-granted ideas concerning gendered identities.[48]

Such transformations and gender reversals were sanctioned both by mores and by Church ideology, allowing the stage to serve as an open arena of playful gender inversion to challenge and renegotiate strict gender rules and roles. However, as Baudrillard argues, such cultural transvestism may be a product of political transformations as, for example, in Western culture where "the orgy" period of the sexual revolution of the 1960s, when gender roles were redefined, followed the McCarthy craze of the 1950s.[49]

What these examples reveal is how gender is constructed differently from culture to culture and how assumed gender identities may be a problematical experience for researchers and members of the community studied alike.[50] Whether contemporary or historic, urban or rural, the above examples suggest that one function of these gender plays is to allow the redefinition of gender-specific borders and actions, to (re)attach multiple meanings to sexual roles, and then to select and reuse them accordingly. Crossing "traditional" barriers, then, becomes essential in this process of challenge, for it shows categories to be limited, rigid, and impossible. Specialists, whether imagined or real, are asked to serve as mediators (interlocutors) to carry out these tasks and, in turn, their identities may be redefined as genderless or may be imbued with distinctive gendered meanings, often referred to as the "third sex."[51]

This is one of the fundamental reasons, I believe, why such folklore events as the "women's ball," ballads with cross-dressing theme, folklore genres with explicit as well as implied non-heterosexual identities, and magical practitioners who renounce their ascribed gender identities are allowed to exist, and may be looked upon with a certain trepidation and, therefore, respect by members of the community. For they reveal the possibility of diversion from the accepted and the expected by mirroring the limitation of norms and values based on singularity and dominance. To them, and to those of the believers – for it must be emphasized that belief in this is a *sine qua non* of such gender inversion – transgressing barriers and the all-too-often replayed scenarios illuminate tendencies in everyday thinking and actions, a practice necessary to renegotiate identities and boundaries in general. Such challenges to dominance and control also point to a fundamental flaw in human thinking and existence: that difference is dangerous, unacceptable and pernicious to the continuation of society; at the same time, it reassuringly discovers that such procedure (both transgressing the boundaries and creating difference) is essential, welcoming, and functional. It is also very human.

NOTES

1 For data on Hungarian women in traditional peasant society see: Judit Morvay, *Asszonyok a nagycsaládban* (*Women in the Extended Family*), Budapest: Szikra, 1956; and Edit Fél and Tamás Hofer, *Proper Peasants*, Chicago: Aldine, 1968.

Perhaps the best data may be elicited from published women's autobiographies, of which a few deserve to be mentioned here: Vankóné Juli Dudás, *Falum Galgamácsa* (*My Village Galgamácsa*), Budapest, 1988; Klára Győri, *Kiszáradt az én örömem zöld fája* (*The Tree of my Happiness has Dried Out*), Bucharest: Kriterion, 1975; and Berényi Andrásné, *Nagy Rozália a nevem* (*My Name is Rozália Nagy*), Budapest: Gondolat, 1975.

2 Michel Foucault, *The History of Sexuality*, New York: Vintage Books, 1980, pp. 33–4. The anthropologist Henrietta L. Moore, in her *Feminism and Anthropology*, Minneapolis: University of Minnesota Press, 1988, argues similarly, p. 129.

3 Jack Goody, *The Oriental, the Ancient, and the Primitive: Systems of Marriage and the Family in the Pre-Industrial Societies of Eurasia*, Cambridge: Cambridge University Press, 1990, pp. 465–6.

4 Tibor Szenti, "Genitalitás," in László Novák (ed.), *Hiedelem, Szokások az Alföldön*, Nagykőrös: Arany János Muzeum, 1992, pp. 573–92; and "Kurválkodás a Dél-Alföldön levéltári büntetőperek alapján, 1723–1843" ("Prostitution on the Southern Plains in court documents"), in ibid., pp. 247–66.

5 Such a dichotomization of professions into masculine and feminine styles is, of course, understandable from Zrinyi, a general himself, accupied with setting up a national army against the marauding Turks; see Miklós Zrinyi, "Török Áfium," in Márton Tarnóc (ed.), *Magyar Gondolkodók 17. század*, Budapest: Szépirodalmi, n.d., p. 258.

6 See, for example, the testimonies of upper-class women in the collection of life-histories by Sándor Takáts, *Magyar nagyasszonyok* (*Hungarian Noble Women*), Budapest: Genius, n.d.

7 Male midwifery, contradictory as it may seem at first, was an accepted village profession. In village communities local "male doctors" performing necessary tasks on males – mainly connected to genital deformations and venereal diseases – were referred to as "*kanbába*" (literally "male-midwife;" although in Hungarian *kan* also refers to male animals). See Sándor Szücs, "Javasok a Nagysárréten," in *Ethnographia*, vol. 52, No. 2 (1941), p. 266.

8 Even a university-educated colleague of mine argued recently that the reason why so many women drive trams and not buses in Budapest is because they are too emotional and irrational for bus traffic. For more on gender stereotypes and imbalances in contemporary Hungarian society, see: Judit H. Sas, *Nőies nők és férfias férfiak* (Feminine women and masculine men), Budapest: Akadémiai Kiadó, 1984; and Livia Mohás, *Férfiak mellett magányosan* (Lonely with men), Budapest: Minerva, 1990.

9 For materials from the Balkans see Andrei Simic, "Machismo and Crypto-matriarchy: Power, Affect and Authority in the Contemporary Yugoslav Family," *Ethos*, vol. 11, Nos. 1–2, Winter (1983): pp. 66–86.

10 For Hungarian state socialist gender relations, see: Eva Huseby-Darvas, "Introduction," in *East European Quarterly* vol. 23, No. 4, Fall, (1990): pp. 385–8; Susan Gal, "Peasant men can't get wives: Language change and sex roles in a bilingual community," in *Language and Society*, vol. 7, No. 2, Spring, (1978): pp. 1–16; László Kürti, "Red Csepel: Working youth in a socialist firm," in *East European Quarterly*, vol. 23, No. 4, Fall (1990): pp. 445–68; and "The wingless Eros of socialism: Nationalism and sexuality in Hungary," in H. G. DeSoto and D. G. Anderson (eds), *The Curtain Rises: Rethinking Culture, Ideology, and the State in Eastern Europe*, Atlantic Highlands: The Humanities Press, 1993, pp. 266–88.

11 Most of the Hungarian literature on eroticism and sexuality is from the heterosexual male perspective; see for example the articles in Mihály Hoppál and Erika Szepesi (eds), *Erosz a folklórban* (*Eros in Folklore*), Budapest: Gondolat,

1987. Quite different is the study written by Mária Vajda, *Hol a világ közepe: Parasztvallomások a szerelemről* (*Where is the center of the world: Peasant testimonies about love*) (Kecskemét: Forrás Könyvek, 1988).

12 See Barbara Babcock, A. (ed.), *The Reversable World. Symbolic Inversion in Art and Society*, Ithaca: Cornell University Press, 1978.

13 For a general view of the carnivalesque milieu in popular culture, see Mikhail Bakhtin, *Rabelais and His World*, Eng. trans., Cambridge: Cambridge University Press, 1968; and Peter Burke, *Popular Culture in Early Modern Europe*, London: Temple Smith, 1979.

14 For Hungarian popular tales describing such activities, see Olga Nagy, *Paraszt-dekameron*, Budapest: Magvető, 1977. An early sixteenth-century story, *Calandra*, written by Cardinal Bibbiena, depicts the adventures of identical twins, a boy and a girl, who mock the world in their transsexual frollicking.

15 See, for example, the recent anthropological treatment by Vern L. Bullough and Bonnie Bullough, *Cross Dressing, Sex and Gender*, Philadelphia: University of Pennsylvania Press, 1993; and the descriptions of Hungarian carnivalesque peasant traditions with men cross-dressing as women in Endre Makkai and Ödön Nagy (eds), *Adatok téli néphagyományok ismeretéhez* (*Data to Hungarian winter-customs*), Budapest: Magyar Tudományos Akadémia Néprajzi Intézete, 1993.

16 Abner Cohen, *Masquerade Politics: Explorations in the Structure of Urban Cultural Movements*, Berkeley: University of California Press, 1993, p. 154.

17 For a description, see Katalin Jávor, "Asszonyfarsang Mátraalmáson" ("Women's ball in Mátraalmás"), in *Népi Kultura – Népi társadalom* (Budapest) II–III: pp. 266–94; László Barabás, "Farsangtemetés a Sóvidéken," in *Kriza János Néprajzi Társaság Évkönyve* 1, Kolozsvár: Kriza János Társaság, 1990, pp. 104–5; and Zoltán Ujváry, "Asszonyfarsang," ("Women's ball"), in *Farsangi Népszokások* (*Carnival Customs*), Debrecen: Alföldi Nyomda, 1991, pp. 227–31.

18 See the testimonies of women despising men for their abusive and careless sexuality in Vajda, *Hol a világ*, especially pp. 90–1

19 See, for example, Károly Kós, "Szerelem és halál a Szilágysági népművészetben," ("Love and death in the folk art of the Szilágyság Region of Transylvania"), in *Népélet és Néphagyomány*, Bucharest: Kriterion, pp. 210–25; and László Novák, "Egy mángorló néprajzi és szemiotikai vizsgálata" ("Semiotic and ethnographic analysis of an implement," in *Művészet*, vol. 1(1976), pp. 39–42.

20 For a description of this ritual in German, see J. Ernyey, "Buso-Aufzüge und andere Faschingspiele," in *Anzeiger der Ethnographischen Abteilung des Ungarischen Nationalmuseums* VI (1914), pp. 137–67; and in Hungarian, J. Csalog, *Busójárás (poklada) a mohácsi sokácok tavasz-ünnepe*, Pécs: A Dunántúli Tudományos Intézet Kiadványai, n.d. These elements are also present in carnevalesque events in Germany, Switzerland and Romania; see, László Földes, "A Néprajzi Múzeum busómaszkjai," ("Masks in the Ethnographic Museum of the Sokác People"), in *Néprajzi Értesitő* (Budapest), vol. 60, No.2 (1958), p. 221.

21 László Lukács, "Farsangi alakoskodó népszokások Fejér megyében" ("Masked customs during carnival in Fejér county"), in László Novák (ed.), *Hiedelmek, Szokások a Nagyalföldön* (Nagykörös, 1992), pp. 481–98.

22 Interesting is the fact that squatting women (urination) are a sign of "obvious feminine" behavior on the part of men; see Lukács, *Farsangi*, vol. III, p. 60.

23 See Ibolya T. Bereczki, "Disznótori alakoskodás Jász-Nagykun-Szolnok megyében" ("Masked mummery during pig-kills in Jász-Nagykun-Szolnok county"), in L. Novák (ed.), *Hiedelmek, Szokások az Alföldön* (Nagykörös, 1992), p. 449.

24 This call is an obvious reference to anal intercourse which was referred to euphemistically as *"törökös élés"* (Turkish habit) in Hungary in the eighteenth century; see Szenti, *Kurválkodás*, p. 250.

25 Sándor Gönyey, "Kun táncok" (Dances of the Kun Region), in *Ethnographia*, vol. 47, Nos. 1–2(1936), pp. 214–18.

26 On sexual allusion in turning and rotating partners, see B. Bernáth, *A szerelem titkos kertjében*, Budapest: Gondolat, 1986, p. 28.

27 My data for Hungarian pastoralism in the Kiskunság region of the Hungarian Plains are culled from László Czirok Nagy, *Pászorélet a Kiskunságon (Herding life in the Kiskunság Region)*, Budapest: Gondolat, 1959; and István Tálasi, *Kiskunság*, Budapest: Akadémiai Kiadó, 1977.

28 The classic concept of *"les techniques du corps"* belongs, of course, to Marcel Mauss; see his "The techniques of the body," in *Economy and Society*, Vol. 2, No. 1, Spring (1973), pp. 70–88.

29 See, for example, Mihály Hoppál, *Tulipán és sziv – Szerelmi jelképek a magyar népművészetben (The Tulip and the Heart – Love Symbols in Hungarian Folk Art)*, Debrecen: Csokonai, 1990.

30 There is a specific song style, however, in which young women are allowed to joke and tease men *(legénycsúfolók)*, a genre having parallels in similar songs of males; see Zsuzsanna Tátrai, *Leányélet (Girls' Lives)*, Budapest: Crea-Print, 1994, pp. 184–93.

31 Other ethnographic accounts for the eccentric way of dressing village maidens in the Kalotaszeg region of Transylvania also confirm my observations; see J. Faragó, J. Nagy, and J. Szentimrei, *Kalotaszegi népművészet (Kalotaszeg Folk Art)*, Bukarest: Kriterion, 1978; Samu Vasas, *Virágzó Népművészet (Blossoming Folk Art)*, Bánffyhunyad: Kalotaszeg Kft, 1993, and *A Kalotaszegi gyermek (The Child in Kalotaszeg)*, Bánffyhunyad: Kráter-Colirom, 1993.

32 While I admit, however, that such names are quite rare in Hungarian culture, I was surprised to find many such names in the English language. Examples abound from Tracy, Ellen (Allen), to Chris, and Pat. I find it interesting as well that, while ancient Greek names are strictly divided accoring to male and female, Greek names since the Christian period have both male and female versions.

33 For recent analysis of Hungarian and other East European witch and shaman beliefs, see Gábor Klaniczay, *A civilizáció peremén (On the Margins of Civilization)*, Budapest:Magvető, 1990; and Éva Pócs, *Tündérek, démonok, boszorkányok (Fairies, Demons, Witches)*, Budapest: Akadémiai Kiadó, 1989.

34 See Mihály Hoppál, "Traces of Shamanism in Hungarian Folk Beliefs," in A.-L. Siikala and M. Hoppál (eds), *Studies on Shamanism*, Budapest: Akadémiai Kiadó, 1992, p. 164.

35 László Timaffy, "A honfoglaló magyarság hitvilágának maradványai a Kisalföldön" ("Remnants of archaic mythology of the Hungarians from the period of the Conquest in the region of the Kisalföld"), in *Arrabona* (Győr), vol. 6 (1974): pp. 309–32.

36 Bernáth, *A szerelem titkos nyelvén*, p. 33. That "Canvas Paul" was a historic figure and not simply a figment of the imagination is proven by Zoltán Trócsányi, *Régi világ, furcsa világ* (Old world, Strange world), Budapest: Bibliotheca, 1958, pp. 448–9.

37 Anikó Füvessy, "Tiszafüred környéki kincskereső történetek" ("Treasure finding stories from Tiszafüred"), in L. Novák (ed.), *Hiedelmek, Szokások az Alföldön* (Nagykörös, 1992), p. 310. Finding hidden treasures underground was a special trade-mark of Hungarian shamans. I have described the nature of shamanism and the heritage of Hungarian shamanism elsewhere in more detail; see "Language,

Symbol and Dance: An Analysis of Historicity in Movement and Meaning," in *Shaman: An International Journal of Shamanistic Research*, vol. 2, No. 1 (1994): pp. 3–60.

38 Sverov reports ethnohistorical cases of Koryak, Chukchi and Asiatic Eskimo transvestism where both men and women cross-dress, changing their hair-style and manners: "In such cases, men spoke the female dialect and woman the male dialect ... A transformed woman did not participate in male activities, but a 'soft,' womanlike man did woman's work;" See. S. Ia. Sverov, "Guardians and Spirit-Masters of Siberia," in W. W. Fitzhugh and A. Crowell (eds), *Crossroads of Continents: Cultures of Siberia and Alaska*, Washington, DC: Smithsonian, 1988, p. 249.

39 On Hungarian witches and their craft, see Sándor Solymossy, *A "Vasorrú bába" és mitikus rokonai* (*The "Iron-nosed" Hag and its Mythical Relatives*), Budapest: Akadémiai Kiadó, 1991.

40 See Will Roscoe, *The Zuni Man-Woman*, Albequerque: University of New Mexico Press, 1991; and Serena Nanda, *Neither Man Nor Woman: The Hijras of India*, Belmont: Wadsworth, 1990.

41 See Bernard Saladin d'Anglure, "Rethinking Inuit Shamanism through the Concept of 'Third Gender,'" in M. Hoppál and J. Pentikainen (eds), *Northern Religions and Shamanism*, Budapest-Helsinki: Akadémiai Kiadó and Finnish Literature Society, 1992, pp. 146–50; and R. Grambo, "Unmanliness and *seidr*: Problems Concerning the Change of Sex," in M. Hoppál and O. Sadovszky (eds), *Shamanism: Past and Present*, vol. 1, Budapest: Ethnographic Institute, 1989, pp. 103–14.

42 Actually both ballads have heroes/heroines with a play on their names. "Joe the Hunter" actually takes the names from the German, where *Jäger* means hunter; and in the other ballad "Bankó" also means money. This *double entendre* also indicates that these ballads have deeper symbolism attached to their characters than previously were believed by researchers.

43 For a treatment on the historical accuracy of the outlaw Jáger Jóska, see Sándor Dömötör, "A Jáger Jóska ballada történeti háttere," ("Historical Background to the Ballad of Jáger Jóska"), in *Ethnographia*, vol. 93, No. 4 (1982), pp. 560–9; and "Kegyetlen Betyárvilág és Jáger Jóska," in *Borsodi Levéltári Évkönyv IV*, 1981 (Miskolc), pp. 137–47.

44 Dianne Dugaw, *Warrior Women and Popular Balladry, 1650–1850*, Cambridge: Cambridge University Press, 1989.

45 For both ballads, see Imre Katona (ed.), *Szatmári gyűjtés – Gyűjtötte Móricz Zsigmond* (*The Folklore Collection of Zsigmond Móricz from the Region of Szatmár*), Budapest: Magyar Néprajzi Társaság, 1991, pp. 48, 52.

46 József Molnár, "Adatok a magyar balladák ismeretéhez" (Data Concerning Hungarian Folk Ballads), in *Ethnographia*, vol. 53 (1942), p. 52; and Sándor Dömötör, "Geszten Józsi Borsodban," in *Herman Ottó Múzeum Évkönyve*, vol. XVI (1977), pp. 239–67.

47 See, for example, M. Istvánovits, "Dissemination in the Caucasus of Tales Belonging to the 'Change of Sex'-type," in *Acta Ethnographica*, vol. 9, Nos. 3–4 (1960), pp. 227–50.

48 That these themes exist outside the folkloric realm of agricultural producers may be illustrated by numerous historic and contemporary examples from the arts including the theater stage, from historic "female" ballerinas impersonated by "male" dancers to cinematic role inversions. In a late 1970s Hungarian film, "Memories of Herkulesfürdő'," a similar gender transformation occurs depicting the story of a young Jewish hero trying to escape the Nazis by taking up a job as a nurse in a remote health resort. All is going well until one morning when, after

a night of escapade with his girlfriend with whom s/he fell in love, he forgets to shave. Naturally, his bearded face reveals his masculine identity and he is taken by the authorities. Elevation of similar folkloristic themes may be found in high-literature as well. In October 1992, the Attila József Theater, a prestigious down-town company in Budapest, staged a play based on the book of the well-known cosmopolitan author, Ferenc Molnár, the "Boys from Paul Street" (*Pál utcai fiúk*). Written just after the turn of this century, it is a heart-rending story of a group of boys playing tricks on one another ending in a tragedy of one of the heroes, Nemecsek. What makes this stage production rather unique is that all the roles – the "boys" – are played by *women*.

49 Jean Baudrillard, *The Transparency of Evil: Essays in Extreme Phenomena*, London: Verso, 1993.

50 On recent attempts to deal with sexuality and gender in an anthropological fashion, see Moore, *Feminism and Anthropology*; Micaela di Leonardo (eds), *Gender at the Crossroads of Knowledge: Feminist Anthropology in the Postmodern Era*, Berkeley and Los Angeles: University of California Press, 1991; and Margery Wolf, *A Thrice Told Tale: Feminism, Postmodernism, and Ethnographic Responsibility*, Stanford: Stanford University Press, 1992.

51 See the contributions in Gilbert Herdt (ed.), *Third Sex, Third Gender: Beyond Sexual Dimorphism*, New York: Zone Books, 1994.

11

SACRED GENDERS IN SIBERIA

Shamans, bear festivals, and androgyny

Marjorie Mandelstam Balzer

"Spirits when they please, can either sex assume, or both!"
John Milton *Paradise Lost* (New York: Seabury, 1983)

". . . each being contains many forms simultaneously, sometimes manifesting itself as one, sometimes as another"
Jill Furst and Peter Furst *North American Indian Art*
(New York: Rizzoli, 1982), p. 141, on Inuit soul beliefs

In the realm of the sacred, as well as in literature, gender distinctions appear and disappear, and are culturally constructed and deconstructed. Male and female forces can be used, balanced, adapted, and transformed by those who are skilled enough to handle their power. Within the cultural traditions of Siberia, some of the most diverse variations on the theme of gender flexibility are reflected in beliefs about shamans (spiritual healers), animal spirits, and power through manipulation of sexual energy. Gender transformations perceived according to some European standards as deviant become instead sacred.

Shamans, as the Sakha (Yakut) curer Vladimir Kondakov told me in 1992, should be able to balance and mediate energies within multiple levels of cosmological worlds.[1] To do so requires spiritual transformations into animals and the harnessing of both male and female sexual potential. For many, this means having male shamans accept female spirit helpers as guides, and vice versa, incorporating their power and even their gendered essence in trance and during séances. It can involve tapping the gendered spiritual force of a tree, for instance the female birch, to cure a male patient. And in a particularly dramatic form, the greatest shamans, even if they are males, are able to themselves give birth to spirit animals.[2]

The social and symbolically creative environment in which such events can be heralded is psychologically far from our own. Yet the mastery of a range of human potential inherent in Siberian shamanism is now being recognized as a system worth revitalizing in Siberia, and worth examining for clues to intertwined mental and physical health. Even before Soviet repression against shamans as medical charlatans and religious deceivers, esoteric knowledge of shamanic gender transformation was far from widely known or understood. It was manifest in different local and even individual ways, creating a challenge for modern Siberians rethinking their own traditions.

An historical story still told in the Sakha Republic (Yakutia) of Siberia in 1994 illustrates the degree to which thinking about gender is flexible, non-stereotypical and linked to spirit beliefs. During World War II, in a time of hardship and starvation, a Sakha man was left with his bawling baby, after his wife died in childbirth. Far from any human help, he prayed desperately to the spirits to be given milk in his poor male body. Suddenly, milk appeared in his breasts and the child was saved. According to several Sakha consultants, the man, though not a shaman, had tapped into the crucial life-forces of the opposite sex, as shamans do, using this syncretized, sometimes ambiguous, sexual power for salvation.[3]

At times, and in some Siberian cultures, the shamanic use of sexual power and symbolism meant that male shamans turned themselves into females, for particular shamanic seances, and, in some cases, more permanently. Among the Northeastern Chukchi, this transformation occasionally also went the other way, with female shamans taking on male identities. The turn-of-the-century Russian exile-ethnographer Waldemar Bogoras thus wrote of certain particularly revered and feared Chukchi shamans: "A man who has changed his sex" is termed "soft man," or "similar to a woman" (ne'uchica), and a woman in similar condition "similar to a man" (qa'chikicheca)."[4] Such transformations occurred on spirit (ke'let) orders, and were dreaded, at least at first, by young shamanic apprentices.

To probe the religious meanings and social significance of gender transformation, it is worth exploring not only the most explicit forms, manifest within shamanism, but also bawdy ritual transvestism in Siberian festivals honoring killed bears, and clues to gender identities in other Siberian practices and symbols. Issues of Soviet and post-Soviet change in Siberian spiritualism and identities can then be addressed.

SHAMANS IN MANY GUISES

In addition to some Native North American areas, Northeastern Siberia is the region where practices of transforming shamans are best documented, among the Chukchi, Koryak, Itelmen (Kamchadal), and Siberian Eskimo (Iupik), plus, less definitively, among the Northeastern Yukagir, and the Amur Region Nivkh (Gilyak) and Nanai (Gold).[5] Norwegian scholar Ronald Grambo argues that beliefs about the phenomenon are widespread and archaic, and correlates the Norse seidr and sorcery traditions with Siberian transformed shamans.[6]

Bogoras explained various degrees and stages of transformation among the

Chukchi shamans he met, beginning with the male personification of a woman "only in the manner of braiding and arranging the hair of the head."[7] Occasionally patients, as well as initiates, were asked (by spirits, via shamans) to do this for a cure. The second stage involved dressing as a woman, without a complete sex change:

> For instance, Kimiqui, who claimed for himself shamanic powers, wore woman's clothes, which he assumed in early youth. He was afflicted with a strange illness, which caused him to sleep in his inner room day after day, almost without interruption. At length a *ke'le* appeared to him in his sleep and ordered him to put on a woman's dress ... Notwithstanding this, Kimiqui had a wife and four children ... [and cheeks] covered with a stubby black beard, and there could be no misunderstanding about the sex to which he really belonged.[8]

Mere clothing change, however, was not considered decisive in conveying extraordinary powers. For this, an initiate "leaves off all pursuits and manners of his sex, and takes up those of a woman. He throws away the rifle and the lance, the lasso of the reindeer herdsman, and the harpoon of the seal-hunter, and takes to the needle and the skin-scraper." Spirits assist him in this, even to the point where his mode of speech changes "from the male to the female," and his body alters "in its faculties and forces." Thus, "he loses masculine strength, fleetness of foot ... endurance in wrestling, and acquires instead the helplessness of a woman." He has accompanying psychic changes, as he "loses his brute courage and fighting spirit, and becomes shy of strangers, even fond of small-talk and of nursing small children ... [Thus] the 'soft man' begins to feel like a woman."[9]

A true "soft man" enters into sexual competition with women for young men, and "succeeds easily with the aid of 'spirits.'" He chooses a lover and takes a husband. Bogoras added, "the marriage is performed with the usual rites, and I must say that it forms a quite solid union, which often lasts till the death of one of the parties. The couple live in much the same way as do other people." His open-mindedness, however, gave out when he explained: "They cohabit in a perverse way, *modo Socratis*, in which the transformed wife always plays the passive role ... some "soft men" are said to lose altogether the man's desire and in the end to even acquire the organs of a woman; while others are said to have mistresses of their own in secret and to produce children by them."[10]

Bogoras the voyeur (and all anthropologists have some of this in them) was so curious to "fully inspect" one "remarkable" young shaman named Tilu'wgi that he offered both the shaman and his/her husband a considerable bribe, after living with them for two days. Tilu'wgi declined, but the husband volunteered that, although Tilu'wgi was quite masculine in physique, they were hoping "he" would eventually "be able to equal the real 'soft men' of old, and to change the organs of his sex altogether."

Tilu'wgi's face, encircled with braids of thick hair arranged after the manner of Chukchee women, looked very different from masculine faces. It was something like a female tragic mask fitted to the body of a giantess of a race different from our own. All the ways of this strange creature were decidedly feminine. He was so "bashful," that whenever I asked a question of somewhat indiscreet character, you could see, under the layer of its usual dirt, a blush spread over his face, and he would cover his eyes with his sleeve, like a young beauty of sixteen. I heard him gossip with the female neighbors in a most feminine way, and even saw him hug small children with evident envy for the joys of motherhood.[11]

Gossip behind their backs was one of the aspects of gender transformation that both male and female shamans lived through. Bogoras only heard of, but was not able to meet, a woman who had been first called by the spirits to become a curer in the "usual" way, and then only later been ordered by them to become a man. She was a middle-aged widow with three children, and this may help to explain why circumstances as well as spirits could have led her to become a masculine hunter-shaman. "She cut her hair, donned the dress of a male, adopted the pronunciation of men, and even learned in a very short time to handle the spear and to shoot with a rifle. At last she wanted to marry and easily found a quite young girl who consented to be her wife."[12] Delicate matters of sex were taken care of by a "gastrocnemius from the leg of a reindeer, fastened to a broad leather belt . . . [used] in the way of masculine private parts." Child adoption was also accomplished in this case.[13]

The flip side of social stigmatization for being unusual was the extraordinary spirit power that the Chukchi believed accrued to both male and female transformed shamans. They excelled "in all branches of shamanism, including the ventriloquistic art."[14] Thus perhaps the widow used transformation to elevate herself, with the help of her spirits, to a new level of community respect that could also enhance her chances of survival without remarriage to an unwanted husband's brother. In both male and female cases, the supernatural protector spirits who guided transformations were believed to be particularly powerful, sometimes marrying their wards in sexual spirit-human unions that enabled gender identities to be traded. "Soft men," for example, were wedded to spirit as well as human males. "Because of their supernatural protectors . . . [transformed shamans were] dreaded even by untransformed shamans, who avoided having any contests with them, especially with the younger ones."[15] While meek and "bashful" in demeanor, "soft men" shamans were believed to have spirit protectors who could and would retaliate for slights. Threat of this both inside and outside of shamanic households made the shamans themselves doubly influential.

Explanations for gender transformations in shamanism, however, should not be reduced to quests for locally defined power and wealth. These aspects may have accompanied other, deeper issues of involuntary gender identity, for it is widely acknowledged that shamans underwent transformations, both into shamans and then (rarely) into an opposite gender, at great personal sacrifice. Cures of the transformed shamanic initiate included relief from, and control of, seemingly psychotic episodes, as well as resolution or balancing of personal gender ambiguity: taking a disadvantage and turning it into a strength.[16]

The scholar of Nivkh (Gilyak) shamanism Lev Shternberg was convinced that one key to the shamanic ability to be intercessors between their people and the spirits in times of trouble and sickness lay with their sexual relations with their main helper spirits.[17] In other words, he felt that the power of sex, and sexual transformation, lay at the heart of shamanism. Not surprisingly, this focus has not been well received by most subsequent researchers, including other Russian scholars of Amur peoples and the cross-cultural comparativist Mircea Eliade.[18]

The theme has been adapted by Canadian anthropologist Bernard Saladin d'Anglure, writing on gender change and transvestism in Inuit shamanism. D'Anglure explains that shamans made "use of helping spirits of the opposite sex," and also that "these spirits were often at the same time his/her eponyms." He elaborates: "an individual who was socialized in such a way as to straddle the gender boundary ought to be able to span all boundaries."[19] D'Anglure from this has developed a concept of "third gender" as potent in much archaic Northern shamanic tradition, and was able to test this theory quite productively among the Yukagir in the summer of 1993, much to the surprise of his Yukagir ethnographer host.[20]

Rather than resolving arguments over the antiquity, significance, or marginality of gender transformation and sex in shamanism, we can acknowledge that various degrees and kinds of gender-related symbolism have played a greater role than earlier thought in Siberian definitions of the sacred. Gender ambiguity or transformation is not encouraged or even condoned in every Siberian culture. The very diversity of cases and unevenness of data on sensitive topics has enabled many arguments to flourish.

Among Amur River peoples, Shternberg found some evidence of spirits demanding that a shaman change his sex. For example, one Nanai (Gold) man fell ill with a particularly horrible "shamanic sickness," during which he slept for days on end. Finally spirits told him, in his fitful sleeping state, that he must change his sex, even though he already had a wife and several children. Only after he became a transformed shaman was he relieved of his suffering.[21]

Occasionally "ordinary" people, outside the shamanic context, were of ambiguous or transformed gender among Amur peoples. Shternberg mentioned two Nivkh (Gilyak) cases, noting, "The attitude ... toward hermaphrodites is quite simple: they evidently view it merely as an anomaly and nothing to be abhorred at all." He specified that this was not to be confused with homosexuality, and described one couple that had been male hunting and fishing friends: "One day they went fishing and were forced to spend the night ... the hermaphrodite's secret was revealed. Thenceforth they began sleeping together and ended up by getting married – although people tried hard to talk the young man out of taking this step."[22] Since Shternberg only encountered this couple while traveling on Sakhalin, and did not know them well, it may be that he did not learn the full story of the alleged "hermaphrodite's" relations with the spirit world. Another reputed well-adjusted hermaphrodite from the Amur was said to have explained: "I have two chances, two happinesses."[23]

In the Sakha tradition, many shamans combined or balanced male and female spirit forces without full gender transformation. Those rare male shamans who were believed to give birth to animal spirits were said to be compensating for the creativity which human males lack in ordinary life. But Sakha shamanic practice included reinforcing more conventional sexual divisions, made clear by a little known "ritual for the enhancement of sexual power," reported in the 1920s by the Sakha ethnographer Gavril Ksenofontov.[24] This ritual aphrodisiac was for women, led by a vigorous male shaman with nine maidens and nine youths assisting him, dancing to his drumbeat. During the ritual, called "dzhalyn ylyyta," a small group of target women were captured by the shaman's frenzy, dancing with abandon and neighing like horses "inné-sasakh." "With their neighs they threw themselves on the shaman and performed various bodily movements," pushing him to the ground until men standing nearby took them off him. "The shaman, rising, whistled and made a circle with his drumstick. Then the women came to themselves, calmed down and sat [with blushing faces]." The procedure was repeated three times, and provoked an observer to remark that "the most respectable women simply did not come to such a ritual."[25] The roots of the ritual probably lie in both fertility and culturally defined eroticism.

The messages about gender within various shamanic rituals thus range from the enforcement of gender difference, to the encouragement of gender ambiguity, to the acceptance of gender transformation. One complex code through which some of these varied messages were manifest was transvestism. Thus, it is not surprising that numerous male shamans, including some Sakha, many Yukagir and Evenk and some Ob-Ugrians, wore cloaks fashioned in patterns of women's dress during their seances, even when they were far from being "soft men" in everyday life.[26]

BEAR CEREMONIALISM AND GENDER CODES

An additional realm where questions of gender identity can be explored is another famed Siberian religious complex, the bear ceremony. Bear ceremonialism, known throughout Siberia and much of Native North America, was most elaborately practised among the Ob-Ugrian peoples of West Siberia and the Amur River groups of the Far East.[27] In both regions, the skin and head of a ritually killed bear are placed on a sacred bier and fêted for multiple days, to assuage the potentially angered bear spirit and ensure the reincarnation of that spirit into another bear. On the Ob River, feasting, dancing, and partying builds into a climax of sacred epic song singing. Satirical plays are a main entertainment, both for humans and the bear spirit, during which the men take the women's parts in theatrics that sometimes become quite bawdy. While the roots of the festival may have involved male initiation, other aspects of its folk theater point to its possible inclusion in the ranks of carnivalesque "rituals of reversal."[28] Among the symbolic indications of rituals of reversal are not only male transvestism, but also male hunters saying the opposite of what they mean on the hunt and uncharacteristic female license.

Several kinds of social tensions are played out in Ob-Ugrian bear ceremony theater: male-female tensions, exogamous group tensions between two supra-lineages (called Mos, or people of the Hare, and Por, or people of the Bear); and inter-ethnic tensions (between Khanty and Mansi, Ugrians and Samodeic peoples, natives and Russians). Such tensions are not so much resolved as expressed, and in their expression, analysts can learn much about Ugrian cultural constructions of gender and change.

One satirical drama indicative of gender and inter-ethnic tensions was observed by the Russian empire official Nikolai Gondatti and later by Finnish ethnographer Kustaa Karjalainen.[29] In it a "Samoyed" (probably Nenets) comes as a guest to a married Khanty man who does not understand the Samoyed's language, but whose wife knows a little. Misunderstandings occur. The guest asks for a drink and his host gives him food. The guest compliments the wife, but her husband thinks he has complimented a reindeer and offers to sell it. Then the guest tries to convince the wife to run away with him. He tells her he is rich, will give her metal ornaments and a whole herd of her own reindeer. At first the wife demurs, but then agrees. To escape easily, she makes a concoction of brewed vodka and *mukhomor* (the hallucinatory mushroom *amanita muscaria*, which is bright red with white spots). She and the guest drink only a little, while her husband gets stone drunk. The guest then sets the wife on his sled and goads his reindeer to prance away. The Khanty host understands what is happening, but can do nothing: "his legs refuse to move, tongue to speak, hands to shoot."[30] He falls down in frustration and begins to snore.

This sad, realistic-in-detail tale produced squeals of laughter from Khanty audiences, perhaps because it is such a model of how not to behave that nearly everyone could feel secure in his or her own morality. The play sets the stage for understanding both on- and off-stage festival behavior. According to the Russian ethnographer Georgi Startsev, who saw festivals on the Vakh River, women, though barred from theatrical parts, become quite involved, to the point of behaving with frank masculine brazenness. They dance energetically and creatively, and are allowed to do things they are usually afraid to do. They mock their husbands with repartee and "curse, complain, race after each other, shout and call each other nicknames." During the dancing, "men come into ecstasy to the point where they take off each other's clothing and spit on the naked body. The women too are not quiet, but indulge in baiting the men – cursing, yelling, crawling into the melée."[31]

The release that this scene evokes is suggestive of rituals of reversal: rejection of ordinary life patterns, contorting of the sacred and the profane. Lest it be viewed as a post-revolutionary drunken degeneration (for Startsev worked in the 1920s), another play helps us see the link more explicitly between semi-controlled debauchery and the sacred spirit world. This is one of the dramas used toward the end of bear ceremonies throughout the nineteenth century and well into the twentieth. In Karjalainen's version, a huge masked forest spirit (*menk*) arrives from the edge of the village with his wife. They enter the room where the bear is lying resplendent amidst ribbons, scarves, coins and other symbolic offerings, and bow to the bear in respect. They then whistle, dance with scarves, yell, chant, and groan until they become exhausted and throw themselves on a sleeping pallet.[32] Gondatti's unexpurgated version of this play continues with the sexual advances of the husband *menk* to his wife.[33] At first "she" refuses, but then complies. Since *menk* are Por ancestors, the suggestion of the sex act is probably related (or once was) to sacred procreation of Por children. It is at the same time clowning, given that both actors are male.

Bear ceremony plays criticize the subject of marriage from various angles. A play seen by Karjalainen made fun of the very serious tradition of women needing to cover their faces in modesty before strangers and certain male relatives. In it a man is saved from marrying an ugly girl when Numi-Torum, the sky god, sends a gust of wind to blow the man's bride's scarf away from her face.[34] The tradition of face-covering stemmed from concepts of female "impurity" which were relinquished only very slowly in the Soviet period.[35] Other plays outlasted early Soviet prohibitions on the bear ceremonies. One involved the indecision of a groom in choosing among three brides. Another, influenced by Soviet propaganda, portrayed a senile old man trying to buy a wife, but she marries his son without payment.[36]

Even this snapshot of Ob-Ugrian bear ceremonialism hints at a dynamic of culture change that goes beyond maintenance of social and religious status quo. The dramas survived the intense pressures of Christianization and Sovietization in part because they were held in secret and were appropriate to the issues of the day. In the nineteenth century, Russian tax collectors were mocked. In the twentieth, Soviet brigade leaders took their place.

Gender tensions remained a theme throughout the documented history of bear festivals, but it may well be that the tensions became greater, and plays focused more on gender, as Soviet propagandists insisted on changing the way women worked, presented themselves and thought about themselves. Laughing over battles of the sexes was certainly an emotional release, particularly when women's parts were played by men. But the bear plays seem to have done more than provide a functional safety-valve through a "liminal" (mediating) period of ritual excess, as suggested by several scholars of rituals of reversal. According to such theories, sex role reversals in ritual tend to emphasize gender distinctions in parody and thus help to enforce the social status quo.[37] In this view, the pressures of Sovietization which undermined Siberian female subordination can be seen as an impetus for sharpening the traditional gender distinctions and roles through masquerade. This may be one aspect of the bear festival "carnival," but it puts undue stress on social equilibrium. Natalie Zemon Davis interprets French carnival more dynamically: "play with unruly women is partly a chance for temporary release from the traditional and stable hierarchy; but it is also part of the conflict over efforts to change the basic distribution of power within society."[38] Thus some aspects of gender reversals create the possibility of enactment of social change through conflict expression.

When I was in the Khanty region in 1976, people were very secretive about the continued existence of bear ceremonies, claiming they had been nearly eliminated or homogenized (made less sexy) by the Soviets. But when I returned in 1991, I learned of the emergence from underground, and the resurgence of both the seven-year periodic ceremony and the more impromptu bear festivals. Some of the more publicized festivals were sponsored by the newly formed Association for the Salvation of the Ugrian People. Several of the leaders in the revival movement were women, and several women had become hunters. But they still were not taking part in the most sacred of the epic song chants or in the plays, nor did they expect or want to. They regretted that social group imbalances had made strict observance of lineage marriage rules impractical, but rejoiced that the essential sacred reverence for the bear had weathered Soviet repression for most Khanty. In the many hours of videotaped bear ceremony that I studied, from a festival held in winter 1991 in the sacred Khanty village of Iuilsk, it was clear that both the spirit of raucous play and pious belief were still wedded in sacred revelry. Men took women's parts in a few plays, but the focus for revival, according to Khanty participants, was on the bear reincarnation itself and on teaching young boys sacred songs about Khanty ancestors.[39]

A brief comparative look at the Amur River bear ceremonies also reveals symbolic messages about gender relations and inter-group tensions, but they are couched in a different social context and in local understandings about the relation of humans to bears.[40] "Play with the bear" is usually the finale of memorials for specific dead relatives, in whose honor ceremonies lasting up to a month or more mark the return to "normal" social life, lifting prohibitions (including sexual and marital) surrounding death. Dog races, games, and dancing are more a focus of Amur festivities than satirical plays and temporary transvestism, although aspects of "carnival" are also present. Other social purposes of bear festivals include the merging of two lineages (whether previously enemies or friends), entertaining and solidarity-building among affines, adoption of an individual, the honoring of young boys, and the sending off of young girls in marriage.[41] The most striking difference between Ob-Ugrian and Amur festivals is that for many Amur ceremonies, live bears were raised, preferably as captured cubs sucking human women's milk, kept in cages, and then ritually killed. Raising live bears is prohibitively costly today, although several Amur River intellectuals have sponsored bear festivals in their home villages to revive and film the tradition.[42]

Nivkh ethnographer Chuner Taksami, who has participated in bear festivals held under Soviet conditions of restraint as well as in festivals revived recently, stresses the seasonal nature of many bear ceremonies, held mid-winter to mark the New Year and ensure human and animal prosperity and fertility. Bears, as "forest people" mediators with spirit masters of the earth, forest, and sky, are thus sacrificed after three or four years of being fed in a Nivkh village. Taksami reported a key moment in the festivities, when the bear was led from house to house for farewells. Skilled young male hunters, hoping to prove their mettle, acted as brazen "dare-devils:" "dressed in furs worn backward tied with a seal apron, *kosk*, [the daring] came up close to him [the bear], teased him, leapt on him, grabbing him from behind."[43] Some reports mention attempts to kiss the bear, with those pawed wearing the result as a badge of honor.[44] The paradoxical or reversal symbolism enacted here entails mixing gender-linked clothing and behavior, wearing seal skin associated with the water realm, and teasing an honored guest to danger-point. Ultimately, a key representative of the forest is nearly domesticated, only to be killed and returned again to the forest.

Gender coding occurs throughout the festival, with meticulous attention paid to the gender of the killed bear (which dictates the years a bear is raised, plus the number of times certain rituals are repeated), and to a human division of labor that partially runs counter to everyday patterns. Elaborately dressed women bang swinging larch log drums to set the tone for male games, fertility-associated dog races, and fast circular dances that end when centrifugal force breaks the line. While women do much of the cooking for enormous numbers of affinal guests, venerable elder men boil the bear meat, using pure melted snow water. They also distribute the meat according to social status, with attention to gender and host lineage prohibitions. Fur from a bear's genitals adorns the knife that cuts the bear carcass. Honored elderly women, not young women, participate in dancing to greet the bear carcass when it comes inside. Elders ensure that the bear carcass is brought into its host house through a smoke hole or window, to avoid being tainted by the impurities of menstruating women who have stepped over the threshold.[45] Elders past their sexual prime become important mediators of gendered and sacred space, making them analogous to male and female bears, called "[revered] old man" or "old woman," mediators of human and spiritual worlds.

On the Amur, shamanic seances are forbidden during the bear festival, although a shaman may indicate auspicious timing and shamans are involved in other rituals to escort dead human souls. Perhaps seances are forbidden because mediation with the spirit world, and purifications of both humans and animals, are believed to transpire during the bear festival through community-wide effort, without the need for special shamanic guidance. The festival may have earlier been a massive community therapy session, mourned today by Amur villagers threatened by ecological disasters and outsider encroachment on all sides.

CONCLUSION: (RE)DEFINING THE SACRED

Folklorists and scholars of religion have long been intrigued by boundary transcendence as one aspect of definitions of the sacred. The comparativist Joseph Campbell, analyzing Navaho mythology, explains, for example:

> And the brother heroes, though they are spoken of as masculine, are really both male and female; they are of both the male and female colors ... One thinks of the Chinese Yang and Yin. One thinks of the Hindu "Lord" and "Shakti." That final Void – or All – which is beyond all pairs of opposites cannot be male, cannot be female; is Both and Neither. But in the realms of manifestation the two are equally present. One may even conceive of the highest manifestation as androgynous, male-female.[46]

In Siberian contexts, British social anthropologist Maria Czaplicka came close to this kind of interpretation by describing shamans as neither males or females, but rather as belonging to a "third class," of shamans, who "may be sexless, or ascetic, or have inclinations of homosexualistic character, but ... may also be quite normal ... shamans have special taboos comprising both male and female characteristics."[47] Given the brief survey of Siberian data here, it is possible to expand understanding of the power of gender ambiguity and transference, without loading or prejudging normalcy or deviance, by encompassing male and female elders grown old and sacred in their communities, and by including temporary sacralization through transvestism and name changes in certain rituals.

Although it is important to carefully differentiate various Siberian traditions, for instance the Ob-Ugrian Khanty from the Amur River Nivkh and the Northeastern Chukchi from the Turkic Sakha, it is also worthwhile to make cross-cultural comparisons that can give us insights into theoretical linkages on such important identity issues as gender. Siberian cases reveal not only cross-cutting roots typical for peoples in historical contact with each other, but also cross-cutting experiences caused by Soviet repression and new chances for rich and varied cultural revival.[48]

Both bear ceremonies and shamanism have become symbols of cultural resurgence in many areas of Siberia, but it is misleading to presume the significance of gender reversals in the process. Instead, we can see varied gender transformations as one aspect of repeated and ancient attempts to harness, define, and redefine the power of sex by explorations of gender ambiguity and reversal in Siberian concepts of the sacred. Given that gender identifications are culturally as well as biologically constructed and that each generation remakes and redefines its own traditions, we should not be surprised that some cultures that once had "soft men" shamans seem to have lost them. Certainly none of the researchers who recently have been in the Chukotka, Kamchatka, or Amur regions have reported the revival of this particular tradition.[49]

Under strong Russifying influence, transformed men and women were doubly reviled in the Soviet period, just as they were doubly powerful before intense Russian contact. In the 1920s and 1930s, they were persecuted as both shamans and sexual deviants. Yet the possibility certainly remains for a reemergence of transformed shamans, given the renewed interest throughout Siberia in all forms of spiritual healing.

The dual concepts that a shaman can temporarily take on the identity of a spirit helper of the opposite sex, and that a shaman can have marital relations with such a spirit helper, are still part of the widespread lore of shamans in Eastern Siberia. These are intimate, esoteric identity secrets, rarely discussed with non-initiates, that form the foundation of a shaman's perceived ability to cure. One Sakha shaman (oiuun) explained that he uses opposite sex spirit helpers and that sometimes it is helpful for male shamans to cure female patients and vice versa. In other interviews with Sakha shamans, I have been lucky to learn of their animal helper spirits, such as the horse or the raven, but have never had personal relations with the spirits revealed. One female shaman (udagan) claims she manifests her powers by becoming a white stallion. A key to the acceptance of such claims is belief in shamanic ability to manipulate, bridge, and change cultural boundaries and symbols.

Shamans traditionally could adopt the name of their helper spirits, at least among the Chukchi, Koryak, and Eskimo, as well as incorporate their essence if needed during seances. For instance, Bogoras reported that one shaman was named She Walrus; and another was Scratching Woman, a shaman who sometimes turned himself into a bear to cure particularly ill patients. Bogoras also noted that even for ordinary people, "female names are given to men, and visa versa," in order to confuse the spirits.[50] Some "cover name" practices continued through the Soviet period throughout much of Siberia.

Spirit name adoptions, "cover names," and some beliefs about possible reincarnation into different genders give us clues to the creative and flexible use of cross-gender referencing in some Siberian cultures. Gender definitions in terms of balances or tensions between sexual opposites could be mitigated by wary reverence for people with characteristics of both sexes. More precisely, those people who were perceived to be able to utilize the energies of both sexes were often sacralized. In the bear festival, this happened temporarily when men took women's parts. The bear festival itself, as a community-wide spiritual healing, growing, and socializing drama, was an occasion for both reinforcement of human-spirit relations and social critique. Usually on a smaller scale, shamanic seances also enabled adaptations or manipulation of gendered power relations for intertwined psychological and physiological cures. Gender transformation of shamans was a matter of degree, ranging from temporary adoption of hair-style or dress for seances, to the full gender reversal of male and female shamans.

Gender ambiguity is not the same as full transformation, and neither is congruent with ritual reversals. Yet I argue that these are related phenomena, variations on themes that can help us understand more completely the full range of symbolic, socially constructed meanings for human sexual diversity. In European fiction and fantasy, reversals have long held fascination. Barbara Babcock cites the seventeenth-century Jesuit novelist Balthasar Gracian as saying "The things of this world can be truly perceived only by looking at them backwards."[51] The novelist Ursula LeGuin, daughter of two anthropologists, wrote about a fantasy society where people could change their gender at will, depending on the social context.[52] It is time to better understand the data already gathered on sexual practices and gender meanings, and to collect more with open-mindedness. Instead of seeing gender reversals as deviant, we may see a mirror image: anomaly turned into sacred power. The study of gender reversals can help us reverse assumptions about the sacred and the "civilized."[53]

Among the postmodern, post-Soviet Sakha, many of the most talented artists, musicians, poets, and actors are those who are exploring themes of gender tensions and ambiguity. Some are people who are not afraid to be slightly effeminate males and masculine females. In 1992, I was given a recently made drum embellished with old Sakha motifs: a dancing shaman wore female dress, through which was a clearly drawn penis. In the *fin-de-*Soviet 1990s, the Sakha and other Siberians are looking to their spiritual past for their cultural future.

NOTES

1 I am grateful to Vladimir Kondakov, head of the Association of Folk Medicine, and widely reputed *oiuun* (shaman) for conversations in 1991, 1992, and 1993. For a literature review, see Marjorie Mandelstam Balzer, *Shamanism: Soviet Studies of Traditional Religion in Siberia and Central Asia*, Armonk, NY: M. E. Sharpe, 1990 and Anna-Leena Siikala and Mihály Hoppál, *Studies on Shamanism*, Budapest: Akadémiai Kiadó; Helsinki: Finnish Anthropological Society, 1992. This chapter is based on a literature survey, discussions with colleagues, and fieldwork in two main areas of Siberia: the Ob-Ugrian region of Western Siberia (1976, 1991) and the Sakha Republic (Yakutia) of Eastern Siberia (1986, periodically 1991–5). I am grateful for fieldwork and research support from the International Research and Exchanges Board, the Social Science Research Council, Harvard's Russian Research Center, Columbia's Harriman Institute, and the Kennan Institute of the Wilson Center. For fieldwork assistance, thanks are due to the Sakha Republic Ministry of Culture, the Museum of Music and Folklore,

the Khomus Museum, Yakutsk University, the Institute for the Problems of Northern Minorities, and the Institute of Languages, Literature and History of the Academy of Sciences.

2 The part-Sakha ethnographer Alexander A. Popov, "Poluchenie 'shamanskogo dara' u Viliuiskikh Iakutov" *Trudy instituta Etnografii*, vol. 2, 1947, p. 292, explained that a great shaman's spiritual initiation, usually around age thirteen, entailed first giving birth, deep in the forest and alone, to a raven or loon, which would instantly fly away. In the second year of initiatory pain and trial, the shaman gave birth to a pike that quickly swam into water. And in the final year, a truly great shaman could give birth to a bear or wolf. These three events eventually ensured that the most revered Sakha shamans could mediate three worlds (celestial, earthly, and underground) and could be reincarnated three times. In other contexts, fertility and shamanism are not compatible.

3 I am grateful to the historian Egor Spiridonovich Shishigin for this story, considered plausible by many of my Sakha friends. See also my "Two Urban Shamans: Unmasking Leadership in Fin-de-Soviet Siberia," in George Marcus (ed.), *Perilous States: Conversations on Culture, Politics and Nation*, Chicago: University of Chicago Press, 1993, pp. 131–64; and my "Dilemmas of the Spirit: Religion and Atheism in the Yakut-Sakha Republic," in *Religious Policy in the Soviet Union*, edited by Sabrina Petra Ramet, Cambridge: Cambridge University Press, 1993, pp. 231–51.

4 Waldemar Bogoras, *The Chukchee*, New York: Memoirs of the American Museum of Natural History, vol. 11, 1909, p. 449. Compare Waldemar [Vladimir I.] Jochelson, *The Koryak*, New York: Memoirs of the American Museum of Natural History, vol. 10, 1908, p. 53. Both authors were part of the Jesup North Pacific Expedition.

5 As with the Siberian cases, a very diverse range of gender concepts and practices exists in North America. The social practice of *berdache*, as exemplified by the Plains groups, is the most direct correlate to the Chukchi "soft man," with comparable traditions among the Navaho, Hopi and some Algonquin groups. See Walter L. Williams, *The Spirit and The Flesh: Sexual Diversity in American Indian Culture*, Boston: Beacon Press, 1992, 2nd edn; Weston La Barre, *The Ghost Dance: Origins of Religion*, London, New York: Dell, 1972, pp. 138–40, 156–7, 179–81; Alice Beck Kehoe, *North American Indians: A Comprehensive Account*, Englewood Cliffs, NJ: Prentice-Hall, 1992, p. 344 figure; and Sabine Lang's chapter in this book.

6 Ronald Grambo, "Unmanliness and Seidr: Problems Concerning the Change of Sex" in *Shamanism Past and Present*, edited by Mihály Hoppál and Otto von Sadovszky, Budapest: Hungarian Academy of Sciences, 1989, pp. 103–13. His argument is mostly convincing, though over-generalized when he states (p. 107–8) that Yakut "black shamans" "tended to behave like women, since it is from women shamans that they derive their origin." See also Vladimir N. Basilov "Vestiges of Transvestism in Central-Asian Shamanism," in *Shamanism in Siberia*, edited by Vilmos Diószegi and Mihály Hoppál, Budapest: Akademiai Kiado, 1978, pp. 281–90; and his *Shamanstvo u narodov Srednei Azii i Kazakstana*, Moscow: Nauka, 1992.

7 Bogoras, *Chukchee*, p. 450–1.

8 Ibid., pp. 450–1. Another degree involves gender transformation only during seance, especially to personify a main helping spirit. This provides an interesting parallel with the female shamans of Korea, who "manifest" male authority figures during curing rituals. See Laurel Kendall, *Shamans, Housewives and Other Restless Spirits: Women in Korean Ritual Life*, Honolulu: University of Hawaii Press, 1985, pp. 138–43.

9 All quotes in this paragraph are from Bogoras, *Chukchee*, pp. 450–1.

10 Ibid., p. 451.

11 Ibid, pp. 453–4. Writing on "transformed persons" among the Eskimo of Indian Point, Chukotka, Bogoras also reports Russian empire official and amateur ethnographer Nikolai Gondatti, "Naselenie Anadyrskogo Okruga," *Zapiski Priamurskogo Otdela Imperatorskogo Russkogo Geograficheskogo Obshchestva*, vol. 2, pt. 1, 1896, as condemning the practice and actively campaigning for the demise of "soft men." But the tradition was carried on to a small degree into the twentieth century, according to Jane Murphy, "Psychotherapeutic Aspects of Shamanism on St Lawrence Alaska," in *Magic, Faith and Healing*, edited by Ari Kiev, New York: Free Press, 1969, pp. 74–5. Jane Murphy was told in 1940 that a transformed shaman from Siberia believed himself to be pregnant, and then tragically ended his life "by having himself abandoned on another island, and the story goes that the following year the corpses of an adult and a child were found where he had been left." Precise timing is unclear.

12 Bogoras, *Chukchee*, p. 455.

13 Bogoras, *Chukchee*, p. 455–6, explains: "After some time the transformed husband, desiring to have children by her young wife, entered into a bond of mutual marriage with a young neighbor, and in three years two sons were really born in her family ... They were considered her own lawful children. Thus this person could have had in her youth children of her own body, and in later life other children from a wedded wife of hers."

14 Ibid., p. 453.

15 Ibid., p. 453. On spirit-human unions, compare Leo [Lev], Sternberg [Shternberg], "Divine Election in Primitive Religion," in *Congrès International des Américanistes, compte-rendu de la XXIe session Deuxième Partie tenue à Goteborg en 1924*, 1925, Part 2, pp. 472–512.

16 Compare Balzer, *Shamanism*, p. ix.

17 Leo Sternberg, "Divine Election," p. 476–80. See also Lev [Leo] Shternberg [Sternberg], "Gilyaki," *Etnograficheskoe Obozrenie*, No. 2 (March–April 1904), pp. 19–55; Leo Sternberg, "Die Religion der Giljaken," *Archiv für Religionswissenschaft* vol. 8, 1905, pp. 244–74; and *Pervobytnaia religiia v svete etnografiia*, Leningrad: Nauka, 1936. For sensitive treatment of the issue, see Roberte Hamayon, *La chasse à l'ame: Esquisse d'une théorie du chamanisme siberien*, Nanterre: Société d'etnologie, 1990, pp. 448–53.

18 Mircea Eliade, *Shamanism: Archaic Techniques of Ecstacy*, Princeton: Princeton University Press, 1972, p. 73. Compare E. A. Kreinovich "Ocherk kosmogenicheskikh predstavlenii giliakov," *Etnografiia*, vol. 7, No. 1, 1929, pp. 78–102; Kreinovich, "Rozhdenie i smert cheloveka po vozzreniam giliakov," *Etnografiia*, vol. 9, Nos 1–2, 1930, p. 89–113; Anna V. Smoliak "Novye dannye po animizmu i shamanizmu u nanaitsev", in *Sovetskaia Etnografiia*, No. 2 (March–April 1974), pp. 111–13. Basilov, *Shamanstvo*, pp. 126–8 reviews the argument, which he sees as focused on whether shaman–spirit helper "intimate ties" were the most prior, archaic form, rather than whether they existed at all. Certainly Anna Smoliak, *Shaman: lichnost, funktsii, mirovozzrenie (narody Nizhnego Amura)*, Moscow: Nauka, 1991, p. 227, and many others, give evidence that some shamans did have marriages with their main spirit helpers. Unresolved is how crucial these ties were, whether some involved gender transformation, and how spirit marriages influenced cures.

19 Bernard Saladin d'Anglure, "Shamanism and Transvestism among the Inuit of Canada," in *Shamanizm kak religiia*, edited by Anatoly I. Gogolev, *et al.*, Yakutsk: Yakutsk University, 1992, p. 18; d'Anglure, "Rethinking Inuit Shamanism through the concept of the 'Third Gender,'" in *Northern Religions and Shaman-*

ism, edited by Mihály Hoppál and Juha Pentikainen, Budapest: Akademiai Kiado; Helsinki: Finnish Literature Society, 1992, p. 147; d'Anglure, "Sila, the Ordering Principle of the Inuit Cosmology" in *Shamans and Cultures*, edited by Mihály Hoppál and Keith Howard, Budapest: Akademiai Kiado, 1993, pp. 160–8. D'Anglure's data are similar to flexible Inuit soul beliefs described by Peter and Jill Furst, *North American Art*, p. 173. However, Dutch scholar Jarik Oosten, "Theoretical Problems in the study of Inuit Shamanism," in *Shamanism Past and Present*, edited by Mihály Hoppál and Otto von Sadovszky, Budapest: Hungarian Academy of Sciences, 1989, p. 334, does not feel d'Anglure's "notion of a third sex" is warranted.

20 I am grateful to Bernard Saladin d'Anglure and to colleagues in the Sakha Republic for discussion of these issues. The literal term for "soft man" in the tundra dialect of Yukagir (of the Sakha Republic) would be "pukol'an kejp," but the Russian ethnographer Vladimir Jochelson, *The Yukagir and the Yukagirized Tungus*, New York: Memoirs of the American Museum of Natural History, vol. 12, 1910, p. 112 noted, "I found no indications of such an institution among the Yukagir, except in the dress of the shamans, which includes articles of female attire." If we see the "institution" as a matter of degree, views of Jochelson and d'Anglure can both be accommodated.

21 Shternberg, "Divine Election," p. 473–80; Grambo, "Unmanliness," p. 108. Compare Leopold von Shrenk [Schrenk], *Ob Inorodsakh Amurskogo Krai*, St. Petersburg: Imperial Academy of Sciences, 1903, vol. 3, p. 121–5; and Eveline Lot-Falk, "Eroticism and Shamanism," *Sexology*, vol. 22, No. 1 (January 1956), pp. 378–83.

22 Chester Chard, "Sternberg's Materials on the Sexual life of the Gilyak", *Anthropological Papers of the University of Alaska*, vol. 10, No.1 (1961), pp.21–2. See original: Shternberg, Lev, "Sotsial'naia Organizatsiia Giliakov," in *Giliaki, Orochi, Gol'dy, Negidal'tsy, Ainu*, Khabarovsk: Dal'giz, 1933, p. 256–7.

23 Chard, "Sternberg's Materials," p. 22. Lydia Black, *Nivkhi*, p. 66, is skeptical of Shternberg's "hermaphrodite" designation, considering one case homosexuality and the other transvestism. Following Shternberg, she discusses these cases under the category of "sexual perversion." See also Gisela Bleibtreu-Ehrenberg, "Homosexualität und Transvestition im Schamanismus," *Anthropos*, vol. 65, No. 1/2 (1970), pp. 189–228, who discusses a range of shamanic transvestism cases, only some of which involve homosexuality; and Stepan Krasheninnikov, *Opisanie zemli Kamchatki*, St. Petersburg: 1819, vol. 2, p. 158 on the Itelmen (Kamchadal) "soft men" who were houseworkers called "koiekchuch," and kept as concubines.

24 Gavril V. Ksenofontov, *Shamanizm: izbrannye trudy (publikatsii 1928–1929)*, Yakutsk: Sever-Iug, 1992, p. 203–5.

25 Ksenofontov, *Shamanizm*, p. 204. Ksenofontov did not see this ritual, but reported the observations of Mikhail Govorov, recorded in 1924.

26 British anthropologist Maria Czaplicka contrasted "change of sex" as a "Paleo-Asiatic" institution with the use of "female garments" in shamanic dress, associating female dress with "Neo-Siberians" (plus the Yukagir), in *Aboriginal Siberia*, London: Oxford University Press, 1914, p. 252. She noted (p. 253) that many "costumes" combine male and female features. Compare Bleibtreu-Ehrenberg, "Homosexualität und Transvestition," pp. 190–5, 203; Yekaterina D. Prokof'yeva, *Shamanskie kostiumy narodov Sibiri*, Leningrad: Sbornik Muzeiia antropologii i etnografii, vol. 17, 1971. Valerie Chaussonnet ("Needles and Animals: Women's Magic," in *Cross-roads of Continents: Cultures of Siberia and Alaska*, Washington, DC: Smithsonian, 1988, p. 225) reminds us, on the basis of Bogoras' materials, that some Chukchi patients wore women's earrings and boots on order of a shaman as "a ploy to hide and protect the person from evil spirits."

27 A. Irving Hallowell, "Bear Ceremonialism in the Northern Hemisphere," in *American Anthropologist*, vol. 28, No. 1 (January–March 1926), pp. 1–175; Boris Chichlo, "L'Ours Shamane," *Etudes Mongoles*, vol. 12, 1981, pp. 35–112; Eva Schmidt, "Bear Cult and Mythology of the Northern Ob-Ugrians," in *Uralic Mythology and Folklore*, edited by Mihály Hoppál and Juha Pentikainen, Budapest: Hungarian Academy of Sciences; Helsinki: Finnish Literature Society, 1989, pp. 187–232. Eva Schmidt's work, based on recent and continuing fieldwork, is especially valuable, and shows the diverse range of concepts about the bear, even within Ob-Ugrian culture.

28 The male initiation theory is Valerii N. Chernetsov's ("Fratrial'noe ustroistvo ob-ugorskogo obshchestva," *Sovetskaia etnografiia*, 1939, vyp. 2, pp. 20–41; "Period-icheskie obriady i tseremonnye u obskikh ugrov sviazannye s medvedem," in *Congressus secundus internationalis Fenno-Ugristarium*, Part II, Acta Etnologica, Helsinki: Societas Fenno-Ugrica, 1968, pp. 102–11). On rituals of reversal see Barbara Babcock, *The Reversible World: Symbolic Inversion in Art and Society*, Ithaca: Cornell University Press, 1978, pp. 13–36. The theory of "carnival" was most famously developed in the 1920s by Russian folklorist Mikhail M. Baktin, e.g. *Rabelais and his World*, trans. Helen Iswolsky, Cambridge: MIT Press, 1965. See also Olga M. Freidenburg, "Proiskhozhdenie parodii," in *Trudy po znakovym sistemam*, vol. 6, vyp. 308, Tartu: Tartu State University, 1973, pp. 490–512.

29 Nikolai L. Gondatti, "Kul't medvedia u Zapadnoi-Sibirskoi inorodtsev," in *Trudy obshchestva estestveni nauk antropologii i etnografii*, vol. 8, 1887, p. 83; Kustaa F. Karjalainen, *Die Religion der Jugra-Völker*, Porvoo: Finnish Academy of Sciences, 1927, vol. 3, p. 218.

30 Gondatti *Kul't medvediia*, p. 83, with seeming authority(?), explained the effects of the vodka–mushroom brew: "One does not just get drunk. One loses all sense of where one is: one walks into a river or lake, throws oneself into a fire, falls out of trees, and in general does things for which it is necessary to pay later."

31 Georgi Startsev, *Ostiaki: Sotsial'no-Etnograficheskii ocherk*, Leningrad: Priboi, 1928, pp. 107–8.

32 Karjalainen, *Die Religion*, p. 219.

33 Gondatti, *Kul't medvediia*, p. 85.

34 Karjalainen, *Die Religion*, p. 218.

35 For background on beliefs about "female impurity" and the importance of women "growing old and sacred" among the Khanty after menstruation, see Marjorie Mandelstam Balzer, "Rituals of Gender Identity: Markers of Siberian Khanty Ethnicity, Status and Belief," *American Anthropologist*, vol. 83, 1981, pp. 850–67. See also Thomas Buckley and Alma Gottlieb (eds), *Blood Magic: The Anthropology of Menstruation*, Berkeley: University of California Press, 1988.

36 Ethnographer Zoia P. Sokolova, *Strana Ugrov*, Moskva: Msyl, 1976, p. 65, saw these bear festival plays in the 1960s and 1970s.

37 Edward Norbeck, "The Anthropological Study of Human Play," *Rice University Studies*, vol. 60, No. 3 (Summer 1974), p. 6, for instance, states, "Many of the institutionalized customs of play, notably including wit and humor and rites of reversal . . . may readily be seen to serve in various ways as sanctions for standards of behavior that apply at other times." See also Victor Turner, *The Ritual Process: Structure and Anti-Structure*, Ithaca: Cornell University, 1977, pp. 183–5.

38 Natalie Zemon Davis, *Society and Culture in Early Modern France*, Stanford: Stanford University Press, 1975, pp. 130–1; Baktin, *Rabelais and His World*, whose work on dialogics and "carnival" is relevant for its combination of status quo and adaptation-change orientation. See also theorist of sexuality and gender as expressions of power relations Michel Foucault, *Histoire de la Sexualité: La Volonte de Savoir*, Paris: Gallimard, 1976.

39 During the festival, reindeer were also sacrificed to the main Kazym Khanty ancestress. Folklorist of the Eastern Khanty, Olga Balalaeva (personal communication, April 1994) warns that evidence for male initiatory aspects of the festival is slim and that Valerii Chernetsov may have been straining for universals when he stressed male initiation in the bear ceremonials. Olga Balalaeva has seen recent bear festival plays with males taking women's parts, and considers this a temporary "not real" transvestism done primarily for the sake of clowning and buffoonery. Active participant-ethnographer Eva Schmidt, "Bear cult," p. 201, 228–9, provides numerous Khanty and Mansi explanations for the origin of the bear ceremonies, concluding that some symbolize subconscious projections, especially those regarding the marriage of a human woman with a bear. She too refutes aspects of Chernetsov's bear phratry (Por) origins theories (p. 203).

40 The bear among the Nivkh (Gilyak) and Olchi, for example, is often seen as a more direct relative of humans. On bear ("forest people") ancestry from the union of a human female with a bear, however, some Ob-Ugrian legends about the origin of the Por people and an Amur River Olchi legend are remarkably similar. These legends explain the origin of bear ceremonialism through instructions given by a human female transformed into a bear. But other Ugrian legends take different form, for example having the original bear be a transformed human boy-hero or supernatural "son of God." See Chernetsov, "Periodicheskii obriady," pp. 102–11; Schmidt, "Bear Cult," pp. 187–232; and Alexander M. Zolotarev, "The Bear Festival of the Olcha," *American Anthropologist* vol. 39, 1937, pp. 123–4.

41 Chuner Taksami, *Nivkhi*, Leningrad: Nauka, 1967, pp. 217–22; *Osnovnye problemy etnografii i istorii Nivkhov*, Leningrad: Nauka, 1975, pp. 163–73; Lydia Black, "The Nivkh (Gilyak) of Sakhalin and the Lower Amur," in *Arctic Anthropology*, vol. 10, 1973, No. 1, p. 94; Shternberg, "Gilyaki," p. 34; and Shrenk, *Ob inorodtsakh Amurskogo Kraia*, pp. 64–103. Alaskan Indian potlatch-like elements were also present. See Zolotarev, "The Bear Festival," pp. 116, 121, 129.

42 This includes Evdokiia Gayer, Nanai ethnographer and former parliament deputy, and Chuner Taksami, head of the Siberian section of the Petersburg Institute of Ethnography and Anthropology. I am grateful to both for informative discussions. Evdokiia Gayer, in Fall 1991, explained that she had tried to fund the raising of a bear cub for several years, but villagers gave up after two and held a festival prematurely.

43 Taksami *Osnovnye problemy*, p. 165.

44 Lydia Black comments that the bear's mark was "sort of a laying on of hands [paws?] in reverse" in "The Nivkh," p. 95. See also Shternberg, "Gilyaki," p. 34.

45 Many of these details are from Taksami, *Osnovnye problemy*, pp. 163–73; Shrenk, *Ob inorodtsakh Amurskogo Kraia*, pp. 64–103; and Black, "The Nivkh," p. 94–102. On concepts of female pollution, see Balzer, "Rituals of Gender Identity," pp. 850–67.

46 Joseph Campbell, *Where the Two Came to Their Father: A Navaho War Ceremonial given by Jeff King*, Princeton: Princeton University Press Mythos Series, 1991, p. 78. Campbell, as well as some Jungians and New Age shamanists, is working on a level of universals that is not attempted here. Some trance journeys of Americans and Europeans do, however, appropriate and syncretize very widespread symbols and concepts. One participant in a trance workshop of Felicitas Goodman recalled: "The left side of my body was female, the right side male. I became a white female horse, and I shook off my male side." See Felicitas Goodman, *Where the Spirits Ride the Wind: Trance Journeys and Other Ecstatic Experiences*, Bloomington: Indiana University Press, 1990, p. 209; Michael Harner, *The Way of the Shaman: A Guide to Power and Healing*, New York: Bantam, 1982.

47 Czaplicka, *Aboriginal Siberia*, p.253. Compare Bernard Saladin d'Anglure, "Rethinking Inuit Shamanism," p. 149.

48 Chances for revivals are themselves locally varied, and linked to demographics. But a spirit of Siberian solidarity was evident on the Lena River during a 1992 conference on shamanism. See Marjorie Mandelstam Balzer, "Shamanism and the Politics of Culture: An Anthropological View of the 1992 International Conference on Shamanism, Yakutsk, the Sakha Republic", *Shaman*, vol. 1, No.2, 1993, pp. 71–96.

49 Such scholars include Tatiana Bulkakova, Boris Chichlo, Evdokiya Gayer, Bruce Grant, Mihály Hoppál, Anna Kerttula, David Koester, Igor Krupnik, Juha Pentikainen, Debra Schindler, and Chuner Taksami.

50 Bogaras, *The Chukchee*, pp. 467,503. Bogoras mentions, however, that usually transformed shamans kept their original male names. This reinforces the androgynous, not fully transformed nature of many "soft men." In contrast, in the Inuit tradition, names are not necessarily gendered at all, according to Oosten, "Theoretical Problems," p. 334. Very different levels of identity are expressed in naming related to reincarnation beliefs, versus temporary naming or dressing to fool spirits.

51 Babcock, *The Reversible World*, p. 13.

52 Ursula LeGuin, *The Left Hand of Darkness*, New York: Ace, 1969. One of the best lines in the novel is "the king was pregnant." Note also Lola Romanucci-Ross, "The Impassioned Cognito: Shaman and Anthropologist" in *Shamanism Past and Present*, edited by Mihály Hoppál and Otto von Sadovszky, Budapest: Hungarian Academy of Sciences, 1989, p. 37, for her comparison of shamans and anthropologists as mediators, whose "art is to be inside but also outside everything."

53 My interpretation can be seen as an adaptation of Margaret Mead's basic points in *Sex and Temperament in Three Primitive Societies*, New York: Mentor, 1950, pp. 215–7, concerning expansion of our understanding of the cultural construction of gender. But Mead still sees Native American *berdache* behavior in a context of biological deviance, whereas I would place it on a continuum of culturally and psychologically interactive responses to a range of sexuality that some societies widen and others narrow. See also Micaela de Leonardo (ed.), *Gender at the Crossroads of Knowledge: Feminist Anthropology in the Postmodern Era*, Berkeley: University of California Press, 1991; and Carol MacCormack and Marilyn Strathern (eds), *Nature, Culture and Gender*, Cambridge: Cambridge University Press, 1980.

12

THERE IS MORE THAN JUST WOMEN AND MEN
Gender variance in North American Indian cultures

Sabine Lang

When the Spanish *conquistadores* came to Central and South America, they made acquaintance with a New World in the truest sense of the word. Many of the religious customs, manners of interpersonal behavior, but also ways of expressing sexuality that they saw among American Indian cultures seemed completely alien to the Spaniards' own perceptions of culture and "civilization," and some elements of New World cultures they found positively shocking. From the early 1500s, for example, Spanish chroniclers frequently mentioned the custom of males donning women's clothes, doing women's work, and entering sexual relationships with other males.[1] Some of these womanly males even officiated as religious specialists, and all of them apparently were treated with acceptance, sometimes even with reverence, by the other members of their communities in Central and South America.[2] The Spaniards, seeing only the sexual component of this institution – which oftentimes involved the womanly males and their male sexual partners – equated it with sodomy and prostitution. Sodomy was considered to be a severe crime in sixteenth-century Spain, ranking third only after heresy and crimes against the person of the king.[3] The Spaniards in the New World acted accordingly, the most drastic example being Nuñez de Balboa who, when encountering a number of womanly males at a chief's court in Panama, ordered them to be thrown before his dogs, and torn into pieces.[4]

When Spanish expeditions were sent out from New Spain to explore what is now the southern part of the US, they found men living like women there, too, Cabeza de Vaca's account – based on observations he made in the 1520s among the Coahuiltecans living in what today are Coahuila, Mexico, and Texas – being the earliest description:

"I saw a devilry," he writes, "which is, a man married to another man, and those are some effeminate and impotent men. They go dressed like women, and they do women's work, and they shoot the bow and carry heavy loads ... And they are larger than other men, and taller: They are able to carry very heavy burdens."[5]

The "effeminate men" (*hombres amarionados*) described by Cabeza de Vaca express a trait evidenced in the roles of womanly males in a number of North American Indian cultures: rather than adopting the culturally defined women's role completely, they combine, to varying degrees, elements of both the man's and the woman's roles, and rather than becoming "women" they are seen as a separate gender, combining masculine and feminine elements. Carrying burdens in Native American cultures, for example, generally is a component of the woman's domain within the division of labor between the sexes, whereas archery in hunting and in warfare is done by the men, with some exceptions.

Since the publication of the first Spanish accounts, dating from the first half of the sixteenth century, the custom of males partially or completely adopting the role of a woman as defined by their respective culture has been reported from most American Indian cultures, and even though in many cases it has disappeared temporarily or completely due to the massive influence of Western culture, it is still alive in a number of Indian communities on and off the reservations today.[6] Compared to the literature describing and discussing males living like women, sources relating to females who take up the occupations and ways of men more or less completely are not nearly as numerous.[7]

The cultural institution of special roles and gender statuses for males preferring women's work and exhibiting non-masculine personality traits, as well as for females interested in doing men's work activities, has come to be referred to as the *berdache* in anthropology, a term originally deriving from the Arab *bardaj*, meaning a male prostitute, or catamite.[8] Because of this original meaning, the term *berdache* has come to be rejected both by Native Americans and by an increasing number of anthropologists doing research in the area of gender variance in American Indian cultures. Apart from being offensive to womanly males, the term *berdache* also becomes downright grotesque when applied to females living in a man's role. A number of contemporary Native Americans who self-identify as either gay or lesbian, or as being of a gender different from both woman and man, have come to refer to themselves, and to those formerly called "*berdaches*" in anthropological literature, as "two-spirit people."

To avoid any terminology that might prove inappropriate in a historical context, in the following the descriptive term *woman-man* will be used to refer to males who partially or completely adopt the woman's role as defined by their respective culture, and who are classified as being of a gender of their own by their respective culture, and the term *man-woman* will refer to females taking up the occupations of men, also being classified as being of a gender different from both "woman" and "man."[9] These terms also come closest to the translation of words referring to such individuals in many Native American languages.

In anthropological literature the traditions of males living like women and females living the lives of men in American Indian cultures have, for a long time, been interpreted as a means by which "homosexual" individuals could be integrated into those cultures.[10] The fact that quite a number of women-men do enter sexual relationships or even marriages with women – and men-women, with men – was generally overlooked, as was the possibility that, instead of just accommodating "deviant" individuals, Native American cultures may have constructions of gender and sexual behavior that differ from our own.

More recent anthropological research has shown that exactly this is the case. The earliest sign that a person will turn out to be a woman-man or a man-woman is not an interest in sexual relationships with members of the same sex, but a marked interest in work activities belonging to the role of the "other" sex. This will be noticed by other members of the individual's community, and it will result in a reclassification of that individual in terms of gender; this reclassification, however, is not just a "gender reversal" from man to woman or vice versa. Instead, a woman-man or a man-woman will be classified as being of a gender different from both man and woman. In most North American Indian cultures, there exist not only two genders, woman and man, but three or four: women, men, men-women and women-men. This cultural construction of more than just two genders, the "cultural expressions of multiple genders (that is, more than two) and the opportunity for individuals to change gender roles and identities over the course of their lifetimes,"[11] is referred to as *gender variance*. Gender variance is a feature not only of Indian cultures of the Americas, but can also be found, for example, in India, Polynesia, Siberia, Africa, and Asia.[12] In the following, gender variance in North American Indian cultures will be discussed within its diverse cultural contexts and within Native American constructions of gender and sexual behavior as well as Native American world views.

BINARY VS MULTIPLE: CULTURAL CONSTRUCTIONS OF SEX AND GENDER

Cultures differ widely in the ways they recognize and value ambiguity in terms of sex and/or gender as expressed, for example, by intersexed individuals, some of them being born with both male and female external genitalia, or by *gender blenders* who exhibit "a complex mixture of characteristics from each of the two standard gender roles."[13] Jacobs and Cromwell quote the example of the East African Pokot where parents are expected to kill intersexed children immediately; if intersexed children are not killed, they are socialized to fulfill either a man's or a woman's culturally defined roles for their families. Still, due to their dual sexual nature, they are excluded from certain activities open to any Pokot individual who is not intersexed.[14] Western culture likewise values the existence of two sexes only, even though – as in Pokot culture – the existence of another category (or more than just one other category) is recognized. In Western culture and in Pokot culture, gender and gender roles are primarily determined by "the physical characteristics of the external genitalia".[15] If an intersexed child is born in Western culture, the usual procedure is to perform surgery in order to remove that child's sexual ambivalence, which is considered to be an anomaly rather than part of the natural order of things. The child will be classified as either a girl or a boy by his/her parents and by physicians, and be raised to fulfill the gender roles culturally assigned to his or her surgically created, now unambiguous, sex.

It is within this binary system of sex and gender that transsexual or transgender[16] identities have to be viewed; as was stated by a female-to-male transsexual interviewed by Kessler and McKenna, "There're only two alternatives in society. You're either a man or a woman. If I don't feel like a woman then it's got to be the other way."[17] There are no culturally defined gender categories to fit individuals who feel ambivalent in terms of gender and who basically would feel comfortable blending aspects of the masculine and the feminine instead of being "a man" or "a woman", even though this is exactly what some people do, regardless of the lack of multiple gender categories in our culture.[18] It cannot be overlooked that gender roles in Western society have become flexible to some degree, making a considerable amount of variation and experimentation possible for the individual. Yet most people will feel extremely uncomfortable when confronted with an individual who is very ambiguous in terms of sex and/or gender, or who even identifies as belonging to a third sex. Even transgendered individuals who decide not to have surgery, and who may blend genders comfortably, such as some of the female-to-males interviewed by Jason Cromwell,[19] will usually say that they are men or women, not something in between, and not something different from both women and men.

Other cultures hold different views of sex and gender, creating multiple genders and making gender-mixing statuses available to individuals who do not behave according to the gender ascribed to them when they were born, or who are born intersexed.[20] There are varying numbers of genders in those cultures around the world that not only recognize more than two genders, but also institutionalize gender variance, valuing the fact that nature does not necessarily lay out things in binary, opposing systems. The Chukchi of Siberia recognize as many as seven gender categories apart from man and woman.[21] Many if not most North American Indian cultures, as mentioned above, traditionally recognized, and in some cases still recognize, three or four genders: woman, man, woman-man, and man-woman.[22]

Why cultures differ so much in the ways they view ambivalence in terms of sex and/or gender is a question still waiting for an answer. Part of it, however, certainly has to do with the religion and world view of a given culture. In the Judaeo-Christian origin story (Genesis), the world is declared completed after the seventh day by the Creator, and humans are created man and woman. In Native American religions, Earth is usually not left in a perfect state after the act of creation. Most often, the world remains in a state of transformation for a long time, the transformations resulting through the deeds of supernatural beings, such as the so-called trickster or various culture heroes. Also, everything that exists on Earth does not come in neat, unambiguous categories. Transformation and what we may perceive of as ambiguity are recurrent themes in Native American stories. Beings who resemble humans yet manifest non-human characteristics are transformed into animals, plants, and natural features. Beings are animals and humans at the same time and yet none of both. What we may think to be inanimate objects, such as rocks, are endowed with life, thought, and the ability to act. Tricksters/culture heroes themselves are masters of transformation and disguise, the best example being Coyote.

Within world views where things can not be taken at face value, and where anything within the realms of the worldly and the supernatural may manifest itself in two or more forms at the same time, the thought of a person combining the masculine and the feminine becomes just another aspect of a sense of ambiguity and transformation that is a central part of Native American religions. Humans who manifest a combination of gender (or sexual) characteristics will be accepted and not seldom welcomed as individuals who, in one way or another, have been touched by the supernatural. In some Native American cultures, there are even supernatural precedents of or role models for women-men and men-women.[23]

GENDER VARIANCE IN NORTH AMERICAN INDIAN CULTURES

When discussing gender variance in North American Indian cultures, it has to be kept in mind that these cultures are widely diverse, ranging, for example, from the hunter-gatherers of the Arctic to the sedentary farmers living in the pueblos of the Southwest, and from the city-states of the Mississipean cultures of the Southeast to the tiny tribes of California. It seems, however, that one generalizing statement that can be rightfully made is that most of those widely different cultures at least traditionally recognized more than two genders, even though other generalizations pertaining to gender variance can certainly be made as far as regions or culture areas are concerned where there are more or less close cultural similarities between neighboring tribes.

Another generalization that can be made is that becoming a woman-man or a man-woman is not a matter of sexual orientation but of occupational preferences and personality traits. As has been mentioned above, gender variance has long been interpreted as institutionalized homosexuality. Native American informants, however, when asked how they recognize a child that is not a boy or a girl, but of a different gender, will usually reply that such children, from an early age, show a marked interest in work activities of the "other" sex.[24] Even though women-men and men-women often, but by no means always, eventually enter into sexual relationships with or marriages to persons of the same physical sex (i.e. persons with the same genitals and set of chromosomes as the woman-man or the man-woman), there still remains the question of whether these relationships can be termed "homosexual." Within a system of multiple genders, a same-sex relationship is not necessarily, at the same time, a same-gender relationship.

In defining sexual relationships, Native American cultures emphasize gender instead of (physical) sex. Thus, in Native American cultures concepts of homosexuality do exist, but they differ from the Western definition, and, due to the fact that women-men/men-women and their same-sex partners are of the same physical sex yet not of the same gender, their relationships do not fall into Native American categories of homosexuality. A homosexual relationship, within those categories, would be a relationship between two women-men or two men-women, or, for example, a relationship between two men or two women.[25] Since anthropologists generally equated gender variance with homosexuality, little is known about the existence of homosexual relationships as defined in Western culture – between two individuals of both the same sex and the same gender, between two women or two men – in traditional Native American cultures.[26]

WOMEN-MEN

Expressions of gender variance vary as widely as do the Native American cultures where they are found. In some cases, a woman-man or man-woman would take up the gender role culturally assigned to the "other" sex completely, such as traditionally among the Navajo:

> The traditional *nádleehé* is a person who is the true *nádleehé*, but I think only very few exist . . . A true [male, S.L.] *nádleehé* or traditional *nádleehé* is somebody who is one hundred percent a woman, [who] was born a man but is a woman in Navajo society – not in their sexual preferences or sexual persuasion, but as an occupational [preference].[27]

In other cases, women-men and men-women will combine elements of both the man's and the woman's gender role to varying degrees, as did the Coahuiltecan women-men described by Cabeza de Vaca. Women-men sometimes apparently participated in raids, warfare being part of the men's domain; this, however, is not contradictory to the women-men's non-masculine gender since especially in the Plains women would occasionally accompany the men on raids, too.[28] Some women-men lived kind of "double lives", such as an Osage warrior who, due to a vision, started to dress and speak as a woman in his everyday life, even though he married and had children. Every once in a while he would still go to war, and he continued to be successful as a warrior, yet whenever he went on a raid "he discarded his women's clothing and dressed himself as a man."[29] Among some tribes of California, women-men adopted the culturally defined women's role yet continued to spend time in the sweat lodge, which was a place where the men spent their days together and where women often were permitted only during ceremonies.[30] Hidatsa women-men – called *miati* – regularly joined the Holy Women Society, a religious society restricted to women; still, in certain rites where women were barred from participation, the *miati*, due to their "mixed" gender status, acted as representatives of the female members of the Holy Women Society.[31]

Cross-dressing is frequently mentioned as part of women-men's expression of their gender status, even though it is not indispensable, especially in situations of forced culture change when they may choose to wear men's clothes in order to escape the attention of white government agents or missionaries (and, probably, anthropologists!). In some cases, women-men also combine masculine and feminine garb.[32]

Whereas some sources just tersely state that women-men did or do "women's work", others are more specific. In California, women-men joined the women to collect seeds, and their domestic duties included cooking, grinding acorns, and weaving baskets; they sewed, carried firewood, and participated in educating the girls.[33] Among the tribes of the Plateau region, women-men and women collected berries and roots, wove baskets and mats, and did the cooking.[34] In the Northeast, women's work done by women-men includes cultivating corn, providing firewood, spinning, and weaving blankets as well as items for personal adornment using opossum hair and buffalo wool. They did all kinds of domestic work and raised children within their extended families.[35] Plains women-men likewise did the domestic chores that were part of the woman's role; the sources also describe them as excelling in beadwork and quillwork. They collected wild turnips and wild potatoes, processed the game brought in by the men, and did the cooking.[36] Especially among the Plains tribes, women-men not seldom are said to do all kinds of women's work and women's crafts better than the women themselves, which is seen as a manifestation of special powers bestowed upon them by those female supernatural beings who, usually by means of a vision, cause them to take up the manners and occupations of a gender separate from man and woman.[37]

Apart from doing women's work, women-men in quite a number of tribes are said to "act like women" or to "behave like members of the opposite sex," meaning that they also adopted manners, gestures, and ways of moving or sitting exhibited by the women of their culture, but not by the men; for example, they will talk in a voice that is closer to a woman's than to a man's. Where there are specific figures of speech only used by men in a tribe's language and others only used by women, women-men will adopt the ways of talking appropriate for women.[38] Where men and women wear different hair-styles, women-men will wear their hair as do the women. In some tribes where especially women or girls at least traditionally got tattooed at a certain point in their lives, women-men apparently got tattooed the same way. And among the Mohave of California, *alyha* (women-men) even imitated menstruation and pregnancy.[39]

In a number of tribes, women-men are medicine people of one kind or another. In some tribes, they will be viewed as being eligible for such a position because of their special gender status; in others, especially in tribes where it is predominantly women who are healers or "shamans," they apparently take up the role of a medicine person or "shaman" as another element of their feminine role.[40] There are also other areas in which women-men specialize or where they have special roles. Among some Californian tribes, they had special functions during funerals. Among some other tribes of California, the Southeast, and the Plains, women-men accompanied the warriors on raids in order to take care of the wounded. In several Plains tribes, there were special tasks for women-men associated with the Sun Dance. Sometimes it was considered good luck to be given a name by a woman-man. Due to their dual nature, women-men were also often asked to be go-betweens for lovers or couples.[41]

There are various ways for males to take up the gender and role of a woman-man. In some cases, a family will decide to raise a boy like a girl, such as among the Aleuts, the Kaniagmiut, the Californian Juaneño and Luiseño, the Yuma, and in the pueblo of Zuni.[42] In other tribes women-men are said to be usually members of certain families or larger kinship groups. Especially in the Plains, boys or men enter a gender apart from "man" and "woman," and take up feminine dress, manners, and pursuits, because of a vision which is usually sent by some female supernatural being.[43] Among several tribes of California and Arizona, it is not visions but supernaturally sent dreams that tell a boy to take up the ways of a woman-man.[44] In some cases there were also special "tests" or rituals a womanly youth had to undergo in order to establish and legitimize his/her status.[45] Oftentimes, taking up the role and status of a woman-man was also just based on the individual's own choice, and he/she would be accepted for who he/she was.

Wherever multiple genders are constructed in Native American cultures, there are terms referring to men, women, women-men, and men-women. The terms referring to women-men and men-women usually translate in a way that points to the combination of masculinity and femininity manifested by such individuals. Even if a woman-man, for example, takes up the culturally defined woman's role more or less completely, he/she does not become a woman, he/she is classified as a *winkte*, a *lhamana*, *heemaneh*, an *elxa*, or whatever his/her tribe's gender term is for someone who was born male but chose to live a woman's life partially or completely.

MEN-WOMEN

There are considerably less sources on men-women than on women-men, and it is difficult to determine whether males in a woman's role actually were much more common or whether anthropologists and other chroniclers of North American Indian cultures just have not paid much attention to females taking up the ways of men. On the other hand, however, there are examples of women from quite a number of tribes who transcended the boundaries of the culturally defined women's role and who combined women's and men's work without being reclassified in terms of gender. Due to the scope of this contribution, only men-women classified as belonging to a separate gender category will be discussed below.[46]

A culturally defined separate gender for females adopting men's work, garb, and manners existed – and, in some instances, still exists – in tribes mostly in the western part of North America, such as California, western Arizona, the Plateau and Great Basin areas, and the western arctic and subarctic. Usually such females would be referred to by a term different from the terms "man," "woman," and "woman-man." The Mohave, for example, called women-men *alyha*, men-women were called *hwame*; among the Californian Yukli, women-men are referred to as *i-wa-musp*, "man-woman," or *iwap-naip*, "man-girl," whereas the word for man-woman is *musp-iwap-naip*, "woman man-girl." Sometimes men-women and women-men would be referred to by the same term, such as *tw!inna 'ek* among the Klamath or *tainna wa'ippe* among the Shoshone.

Like some women-men, men-women – for example, among the Atsugewi and Shasta of California – would sometimes not cross-dress, and combined women's and men's work rather than adopt the man's role completely.[47] In many instances, however, they apparently took up masculine pursuits more or less completely. Whereas women-men often not only did women's work but also exhibited feminine manners of speech, gestures, and so on, men-women are said to act or behave like men. Like their male counterparts, they exhibit characteristics of a special gender while still very young, preferring to play and hunt with the boys and refusing to learn the work tasks culturally attributed to the woman's role. As adults, they would traditionally hunt like the men and, wherever raiding was practiced, join the men on raids. If there were different hair-styles worn by women and men in their tribe, men-women would wear their hair men's style. Sometimes they would be healers, mostly in cultures where this profession was chosen by both women and men, so it is difficult to say whether they became healers or "shamans" because of their special gender status or because of those vocations' association with the man's role.

While women-men, in rare instances, imitated female physiological functions like menstruation, men-women sometimes would deny those functions – it was said of some men-women that they never menstruated, that they had small or nonexistent breasts, or that they were muscular like men.[48] Men-women would usually enter into relationships or marriages with women. Some of them, however, are said to have remained single (which does not mean, of course, that they may not have had lovers of either sex), and some were married to men.

Among the Ingalik in Alaska, men-women would join the men in the *Kashim* or men's house. Cocopa *warrhameh* had their septum pierced, as did boys in puberty, whereas girls got tattoos on their chin. Mohave *hwame* were said to be excellent providers, and whenever their wives were menstruating or pregnant, *hwame* would follow certain taboos appropriate for the husband of a menstruating or pregnant wife.[49]

There are some references to females who were attributed a special status in tribes that otherwise did not recognize a female gender variance category. When a Kutenai woman, Ququnak patke, early in the last century returned to her tribe after having spent a year with a white husband who worked as a fur trader for the Northwest company, she claimed that she had been transformed into a man. This was a kind of behavior alien to the Kutenai, at least as far as females are concerned, and people in Ququnak patke's community, rather than accepting her as a man-woman, thought she had lost her mind. Since she later on led a man's life successfully, being a warrior, a courier for white explorers and traders, a shaman, and a prophet, her tribe finally came to accept her, yet her life story was apparently considered so unusual that it was passed on for generations.[50] The same holds true for Running Eagle among the Piegan and Woman Chief among the Crow, two women who were granted status and privileges otherwise reserved to men in their tribes. In both tribes, as among the Kutenai, there existed genders relating to women-men, but not to men-women. Both Running Eagle and Woman Chief were granted special status first of all because they showed extreme prowess in war. Woman Chief's war deeds are said to have been so daring that the men asked her to join them in the council. Running Eagle's participation in her first raid was so successful that she was given a man's name, being the only female in the history of her tribe who was ever honored that way. Both these females, like Ququnak patke, are not "men-women" within institutionalized female gender variance categories, but individuals unique to their tribes.[51]

As in the case of women-men, dreams and visions sometimes prompted and legitimized men-women's choice to adopt the occupations and manners of a man. Thus, most men-women took up a masculine role because it was their own wish to do so or because they were instructed to do so by some supernatural being. In some tribes, however, parents would sometimes raise one of their daughters like a boy. This usually happened in regions where subsistence largely relied on hunting, which is part of the men's domain within the sexual/gendered division of labor. If no boys were born into a family, or if all boys in a family had died, there was a need to socialize a girl to be a hunter, and to fulfill the role of a boy or man within the family in other respects, too. Examples of this have been reported from the Canadian Ojibwa, the Kaska of Alaska, and the Inuit or Eskimo.[52]

CONCLUSIONS

Within the majority of North American Indian tribes, there existed – and, in a number of instances, still exists – a cultural construction of more than just two genders, allowing individuals to either take up the gender role of the "other" sex completely, or to mix the culturally defined men's and women's roles to varying degrees. Such individuals are not seen as "men" or "women," but as belonging to genders different from both "man" and "woman," characterized by a combination of the masculine and the feminine. This combination can be expressed by an individual who is intersexed, combining male and female physical characteristics; it can be expressed by an individual who was born male but who, usually from an early age, adopts the work activities, manners, speech patterns, and so on, culturally associated with women and not with men. It can be expressed likewise by a person born female who takes up the ways and occupations associated with the man's role within his/her respective culture. It can also be expressed by someone who was born either male or female and who combines elements of both the culturally defined woman's and man's roles. Since more than two genders are culturally recognized and defined, the adoption of manners and work activities of the other sex can not properly be termed a "gender reversal," which implies exchanging one gender for the other within a two-gender system. Moreover, in many cases individuals grow up as members of a gender that is neither "man" nor "woman" from a very early age, which means that they never really "shift" from one gender to another.[53] Due to the cultural construction of more than two genders, Western concepts such as "transsexual" or "homosexual" can also not be applied to Native American women-men and men-women: a sexual relationship, for example, between two individuals of the same sex, yet not of the same gender, is not necessarily considered homosexual, and within a gender system that provides four or more genders to accommodate individuals who do not feel comfortable with the gender and gender role assigned to them by birth, the concept of transsexualism, which was developed in a culture that only recognizes and values two genders and two sexes, is not applicable.

NOTES

1 For references see Francisco Guerra, *The Pre-Columbian Mind*, London-New York: Seminar Press, 1971, *passim*.

2 Ibid., *passim*.

3 Ibid., p. 221.

4 Theodor De Bry, *Collectiones peregrinatorium in Indiam Occidentalem. America*, German edition, Frankfurt a.M.: Bry, 1590–1634, p. XXII.

5 Alvar Nuñez Cabeza de Vaca, *La relacion y comentarios del gouernador Aluar Nuñez Cabeca de vaca, de lo acaescido en las dos jornadas que hizo a las Indias*, Valladolid, 1555, p. 36.

6 Walter L. Williams, *The Spirit and the Flesh: Sexual Diversity in American Indian*

Culture, Boston: Beacon Press, 1986, pp. 201 ff; Sabine Lang, "Masculine Women, Feminine Men: Gender Variance and the Creation of Gay Identities Among Contemporary North American Indians," paper presented at the conference "The 'North American Berdache' Revisited Empirically and Theoretically," sponsored by the Wenner-Gren Foundation for Anthropological Research, Washington, DC, 17 November 1993.

7 Evelyn Blackwood, "Sexuality and Gender in Certain Native American Tribes: The Case of Cross-Gender Females," in *Signs*, vol. 10, No. 1 (Autumn 1984), pp. 1–42; Charles Callender and Lee M. Kochems, "The North American Berdache", in *Current Anthropology*, vol. 24, No. 4 (August–October 1983), pp. 443–70; Beatrice Medicine, "'Warrior Women:' Sex-Role Alternatives for Plains Indian Women," in Patricia Albers and Beatrice Medicine (eds), *The Hidden Half: Studies of Plains Indian Women*, Washington: University Press of America, 1983, pp. 267–80; Walter L. Williams, *The Spirit and the Flesh*, pp. 233–51; Sabine Lang, *Männer als Frauen – Frauen als Männer: Geschlechtsrollenwechsel bei den Indianern Nordamerikas*, Hamburg: Wayasbah-Verlag, 1990, pp. 310–63; Harriet Whitehead, "The Bow and the Burden-Strap: A New Look at Institutionalized Homosexuality in Native America," in Sherry Ortner and Harriet Whitehead (eds), *Sexual Meanings: The Cultural Construction of Gender and Sexuality*, London: Cambridge University Press, 1981, pp. 80–115; Will Roscoe (ed.), *Living The Spirit: A Gay American Indian Anthology*, New York: St. Martin's Press, 1988, *passim*.

8 Henry Angelino and Charles L. Shedd, "A Note on Berdache," in *American Anthropologist*, vol. 57, No. 1, Part I (February 1955), p. 121.

9 Terminology relating to Native American gender variance was one of the issues discussed at two conferences titled "The 'North American Berdache' Revisited Empirically and Theoretically," recently sponsored by the Wenner-Gren Foundation for Anthropological Research, and organized by Sue-Ellen Jacobs, Wesley Thomas, and the author. Consensus was reached among the Native and non-Native participants to replace the term "berdache," for the time being, with the term "two-spirit," defined as "a term in current use by a number of self-identified alternative sex and gendered Natives as a contested compromise to move forward the debate in eliminating the culturally inappropriate usage of 'berdache' [*sic*]." The descriptive terms woman-man and man-woman were given preference in this contribution, however, in order to avoid both the inappropriate term "berdache" and pitfalls potentially inherent in the term "two-spirit", which was coined by urban gay and lesbian Native Americans in the 1980s.

10 For references and discussion see Lang, *Männer als Frauen*, pp. 31–4 and chapter 3.3, *passim*; Williams, *The Spirit and the Flesh*, pp. 65 ff.

11 Sue-Ellen Jacobs and Jason Cromwell, "Visions and Revisions of Reality: Reflections on Sex, Sexuality, Gender and Gender Variance", in *Journal of Homosexuality*, vol. 23, No. 4 (Summer 1992), p. 63.

12 Vern Bullough, *Sexual Variance in Society and History*, New York: Wiley, 1976; David Greenberg, *The Construction of Homosexuality*, Chicago and London, University of Chicago Press, 1988; Serena Nanda, *Neither Man Nor Woman: The Hijras of India*, Belmont: Wadsworth, 1990; Williams, *The Spirit and the Flesh*, pp. 252–69.

13 Holly Devor, *Gender Blending: Confronting the Limits of Duality*, Bloomington and Indianapolis: Indiana University Press, 1989, p. vii.

14 Jacobs and Cromwell, "Visions and Revisions," p. 49.

15 Ibid., p. 50.

16 Jason Cromwell, *"Fearful Others: The Construction of Female Gender Variance,"* unpublished paper, 1992, submitted to *Signs*.

17 Suzanne J. Kessler and Wendy McKenna, *Gender: An Ethnomethodological Approach*, New York: Wiley, 1977, p. 112.

18 Devor, *Gender Blending*, is dealing with females who "blend" genders without questioning their identity as women.

19 Jason Cromwell, "Not Female Berdache, Not Amazons, Not Cross-Gender Females, Not Manlike Women: Locating Female-to-Male Transgendered People Within Discourses on the Berdache Tradition," paper presented at the conference "The 'North American Berdache' Revisited Empirically and Theoretically," sponsored by the Wenner-Gren Foundation for Anthropological Research, Washington, DC, 17 November 1993.

20 For discussion and examples see Jacobs and Cromwell, "Visions and Revisions."

21 Ibid., p. 50 ff.

22 Callender and Kochems, "The North American Berdache;" Williams, *The Spirit and the Flesh*; Lang, *Männer als Frauen*; Lang, "Masculine Women, Feminine Men"; Wesley Thomas, "A Traditional Navajo's Perspective on The Navajo Cultural Construction of Gender," paper presented at the conference "The 'North American Berdache' Revisited Empirically and Theoretically", sponsored by the Wenner-Gren Foundation for Anthropological Research, Washington, DC, November 17, 1993.

23 Sabine Lang, "Hermaphrodite Twins, Androgynous Gods: Reflections of Gender Variance in North American Indian Stories," paper presented at the 93rd annual convention of the American Anthropological Association, Atlanta, Ga., 30 November–4 December 1994.

24 Lang, *Männer als Frauen*, pp. 154 ff. (Data on all aspects of gender variance have been compiled systematically by the author in her dissertation, *Männer als Frauen – Frauen als Männer*; in the following – not in order to strengthen the author's ego, but in order to avoid a notes section that is as long as the chapter itself - rather than listing all the numerous bibliographical references whenever a certain aspect of gender variance is found in a number of Native American cultures, reference will be made to the author's dissertation instead of primary sources used in that dissertation.)

25 Williams, *The Spirit and the Flesh*, pp. 65 ff., pp. 110 ff; Lang, *Männer als Frauen*, pp. 241 ff. *et passim*; Lang, "Masculine Women, Feminine Men," pp. 4 ff; Wesley Thomas, "A Traditional Navajo's Perspectives on the Cultural Construction of Gender in the Navajo World," taped lecture, Frankfurt, Germany, September 1993.

26 On lesbians in traditional Native American cultures, see Paula Gunn Allen, "Lesbians in American Indian Culture," in *Conditions*, vol. 7 (1981), pp. 67–87; for examples of male and female homosexual relationships in the ethnographic records, see Lang, *Männer als Frauen*, pp. 375–83.

27 Wesley Thomas, taped conversation with Sabine Lang, 25 April 1992.

28 Medicine, "Warrior Women."

29 Alice Fletcher and Francis La Flesche, *The Omaha Tribe*, Washington: 27th Annual Report, Bureau of American Ethnology, 1911, p. 133.

30 Lang, *Männer als Frauen*, pp. 92–5.

31 Alfred Bowers, *Hidatsa Social and Ceremonial Organization* (Bulletin 194, Bureau of American Ethnology, 1965), pp. 324, 326, 330.

32 Williams, *The Spirit and the Flesh*, pp. 71 ff; Lang, *Männer als Frauen*, pp. 123 ff.

33 Lang, *Männer als Frauen*, pp. 101–2.

34 Ibid., p. 102.

35 Ibid., pp. 104–7.

36 Ibid., pp. 108 ff.

37 Williams, *The Spirit and the Flesh*, pp. 31–42; Lang, *Männer als Frauen*, pp. 289–96.

38 Lang, *Männer als Frauen*, pp. 146–51.
39 George Devereux, "Homosexuality Among the Mohave Indians," in *Human Biology*, vol. 9 (1937), pp. 498–527.
40 Lang, *Männer als Frauen*, pp. 173–97.
41 Ibid., pp. 197–217.
42 Ibid., pp. 261–6.
43 Ibid., pp. 266–77; Williams, *The Spirit and the Flesh*, pp. 31–43.
44 Lang, *Männer als Frauen*, pp. 276–7.
45 Ibid., pp. 282–7.
46 For females taking up masculine activities without being reclassified as "non-women," see, e.g., Medicine, "Warrior Women;" Ruth Landes, "The Ojibwa of Canada," in Margaret Mead (ed.), *Cooperation and Competition among Primitive People*, New York: McGraw-Hill, 1937, pp. 87–126; Lang, *Männer als Frauen*, pp. 317–22, 331–4; see also Oscar Lewis, "Manly-Hearted Women among the Northern Piegan," in *American Anthropologist*, vol. 43 (1941), pp. 173–87.
47 Lang, *Männer als Frauen*, p. 315; for females taking up the culturally defined man's role more or less completely, see ibid., pp. 322–56.
48 Ibid., pp. 335–6.
49 Devereux, "Homosexuality," p. 515.
50 Claude E. Schaeffer, "The Kutenai Female Berdache," in *Ethnohistory*, vol. 12, No. 3 (Summer 1965), pp. 193–236.
51 Ibid., pp. 213 f, 227 ff.
52 Lang, *Männer als Frauen*, pp. 329–35.
53 For a discussion of terminology relating to gender variance see Kath Weston, "Lesbian/Gay Studies in the House of Anthropology," in *Annual Review of Anthropology*, vol. 22, 1993, pp. 339–67.

13

THE PROCREATIVE AND RITUAL CONSTITUTION OF FEMALE, MALE, AND OTHER

Androgynous beings in the cultural imagination of the Bimin-Kuskusmin of Papua New Guinea

Fitz John Porter Poole

"I am truly one of 'Afek's double-gendered daughters' (*afek'aan maag'maak migiim mun*), ... and also walk on the ritual path of the cassowaries ... But the hidden secret of 'androgyny' (*maag'maak migiim'aan*) is always inside 'the living center of the life-force' (*mutuuk kwan kuur finiik*) of many things ... connected to the ancestral underworld ... "

Gooraniin, paramount female elder of the Watiianmin clan

This chapter is an ethnographic exploration of some key images of androgyny in the cultural imagination of the Bimin-Kuskusmin of the West Sepik hinterland of Papua New Guinea.[1] It represents, however, only a sketch of certain features of a cultural map of a complex terrain of variously gendered phenomena. The analytic focus of the endeavor is the articulation of some central contours of androgynous images on a more general landscape of constructions or representations of gender among Bimin-Kuskusmin. Indeed, notions of the androgynous form a powerful, yet often tacit foundation of Bimin-Kuskusmin understandings of the very possibilities of being gendered. Images of androgyny are often an epistemological puzzle for societies in which a cultural dichotomy of male and female seems altogether "natural" and anchored to the very foundations of human "reality" in which a duality of gender is firmly inscribed in culture, nature, and society. The prominent cultural marking of images of androgyny among Bimin-Kuskusmin, therefore, is of particular interest in a community that otherwise often draws rather sharp, pervasive, and powerful dichotomous boundaries between female and male in myriad sociocultural contexts, and infuses those

197

boundaries with considerable ideological significance and sociopolitical force. Yet, *afek'aan maag'maak migüm men* ("Afek's double-gendered children") – androgynous images both human and non-human – are culturally elaborated in a number of social contexts and are most significantly embedded in the Bimin-Kuskusmin cultural imagination focused on notions of procreation and maturation and in contexts of myth and ritual in which gender is formed and transformed.

The analytical ambitions of this chapter are founded upon a particular theoretical framing of certain puzzles of gender. Gender, whether dual, androgynous, or otherwise, invariably inflects fundamental senses of personhood,[2] which pervade any "culturally constituted behavioral environment" and the diverse contexts of social action, experience, and orientation that such an environment encompasses.[3] Any particular image of gender implicates only some facets of an always complex and often subtle repertoire of cultural ideas arranged and rearranged in contextually instantiated representations or schemas, embedded in social "force fields" of varying ideological composition, and manifested in discursive configurations that are held together in tension not only with other and intertwined dimensions of identity,[4] but also with other recognized possibilities of gender enabled in different cultural arrangements and social crystallizations.[5] Gender is indeed a *combinatoire* of profound, multifaceted, polysemic, and often elusive complexity – neither monolithic, nor fixed, nor stable, and immutable.[6] Thus, constructs of gender, constituted through cultural representations or schemas in their social instantiations, are complex, polyvalent signifiers without a singular, inevitable, and essential link to a fixed referent. Particular gender constructions become momentarily crystallized in their contexts of social embeddedness, only to be disarticulated and rearticulated in kaleidoscopic patterns as they are refracted through the lenses of new discursive figurations of different cultural images under other social circumstances. They are constantly and intricately reworked, sometimes subtly and at other times dramatically, as they are culturally enunciated in fluid social fields of multiple and changing meanings, in arrangements that tacitly exhibit variability in kinds and degrees of connection, and in shifting contexts in which they are variously being put into social play, tentatively or forcefully, in community life.

Certain configurations of gender, however, may be privileged in the senses that they come to be constituted through, articulated with, legitimating of, and encased in dominant ideologies; enshrined in prominent, powerful, and pervasive stereotypes; and deployed in centrally institutionalized or otherwise significantly marked arenas of social action. Yet, these ideologically, stereotypically, and institutionally marked models of gender, although often deeply embedded and strongly sanctioned in many realms of social life, are sometimes personally oppressive and problematic, admit imaginable cultural alternatives, and, thus, are not always beyond debate and challenge. However the resources and constraints of gender categories may be negotiated through the contestations and resistances of turbulent historical moments of socio-cultural conflict, none the less, they are also – and always – negotiated in the more quiescent ebb and flow of everyday social life as persons navigate the courses of their ever-gendered lives in the currents of their community experiences. The multifaceted, open-textured characters of gender con-structs and their discursive or imaginative possibilities, articulated through cultural frameworks within cultural horizons and, thus, imaginatively con-strained within any sociocultural world, are constantly in play, tenuously qualifying, inflecting, or displacing (or, occasionally, more radically revi-sioning) the momentarily (or, sometimes, more stably and enduring) ordained forms of gender imagery through the recognition of divergent, discordant images of gender.

At the forefront of these dominant ideologies, stereotypes, and arenas, however, there is often some central epistemological assumption that the very foundations of gender difference involve a "natural" dual classification of male and female, although the organization of that duality may vary con-siderably in terms of its foci and contours, its boundaries and encompass-ments, and its trajectories of significant contrast and connection. This dichotomous framework tends to give shape not only to local, but also to analytical, understandings of gender. Indeed, the problems of the preeminence of dichotomies pervade theories of gender in two interrelated ways. On the one hand, it is generally recognized that cultural concepts of gender are variably articulated with some cultural reckoning of "biological" sex di-morphism as their "natural" foundation,[7] and an elaborate edifice of other "natural" gender differences – moral, psychological, or social – is culturally built upon, or inferred from, that foundation. Gender images that deviate from that foundational "logic" are often deemed anomalous or pathological or are experientially distanced as a genre of self-conscious cultural fantasy, illusion, or trope. On the other hand, it is often implied that this first and foundational "natural" binary contrast renders sensible a theoretical program of analytic dichotomies which are more or less assumed to be entailed by and, thus, to follow from the form of the first contrast: natural/cultural; domes-tic/public; reproductive/productive; and subordinate/superordinate; as well as distinctions between women's and men's modes of consciousness and feeling and motivation, moralities, relationships, selves, spaces, styles, values, and so on.[8] Yet, the posited rigidities and stabilities of such dichotomies of gender, both local and theoretical, have often proved to rest on unwarranted, simplistic assumptions, and have repeatedly failed to illuminate many of the differently or, indeed, less structured complexities of the sociocultural forms, foci, and forces of gender.[9]

In the backgrounds and at the margins of these privileged ideologies, stereotypes, and arenas are, nevertheless, other figurations of gender, often submerged, tacit, cast in metaphoric discourse, and manifested in such specially bracketed contexts as myth and ritual, which bring into relief,

199

illuminate, transform, permute, transcend, blur, blend, bend, bridge, unite, or otherwise qualify, render ambiguous, challenge, defy, or subvert prevailing models of gender through inversions, reversals, fusions, and confusions of the ordinary and the ordained. The contours of the usual maps of the territories and technologies of gender are disrupted, decentered, destabilized, disfigured, disarticulated, diluted, and then redrawn. This imaginative cultural "work" reveals other images, shapes, spaces, trajectories, articulations, and lines of sociocultural force reconfiguring the centers, peripheries, and semantic fields of the normal, normative, and ideologically privileged portraits of gender that ordinarily prevail.

As Francette Pacteau maintains, gender implicates an unstable, fluid "amalgam of signifiers," and androgyny is often a particularly complex semiotic configuration.[10] Images of androgyne, androgyny, and androgynous present a dilemma for the development of theories of gender, for they often seem to confound normal, normative, and privileged dualities of female and male that infuse much of community life in most societies.[11] Yet, mythic, ritual, and other images of androgynous phenomena – including images embodied in community members and informing their experiences of themselves – abound in diverse sociocultural settings.[12] In a Western classical tradition extending at least from Ovid and Plato, the androgyne appears as a figure of primordial unity, created out of an integration of opposed forms and forces, that has served artists and philosophers as a means of representing a transcendental ideal or, in Jacques Derrida's phrase, a "transcendental signifier."[13] Indeed, in Euripides' *The Bacchae*, the always ambiguous, ever refigured persona of Dionysus – the embodiment of vitality – appears as both woman-in-man or man-in-woman.[14]

Androgyny is an especially privileged trope of the romantic period, a metaphoric vehicle of German idealist philosophies for envisioning the union of subject and object and of material and spiritual realms.[15] Like the *schöne Seele*, a dominant theme in eighteenth- and nineteenth-century literature, the androgyne often functions as a figure of privileged language in which sign is transparent to idea.[16] More recently in this century, images of androgyny have become especially elaborated in various genres of women's fiction.[17] Indeed, the androgynous imagery of women's literature, the promotion of androgyny as a social ideal by Carolyn G. Heilbrun,[18] and the research by Sandra L. Bem on the psychological and cultural significance of androgyny and gender,[19] have brought feminist interests to bear on the promises, problems, and limitations of androgyny in understanding the cultural imagination and social experience of gender.[20]

In this chapter, the idea of androgyny enfolds a variety of symbolic mosaics constructed from varied local understandings of sex, gender, and sexuality and their interrelationships, reconfiguring dimensions of gender categories ordinarily anchored and framed in female–male dichotomies. Thus, androgyny encompasses various dimensions of culturally constituted embodiment usually segregated in dichotomous gender reckonings, cultural constructions of maleness and femaleness beyond bodily imagery, and cultural visions of the erotic, of desire, and of heterosexual, homosexual, bisexual, or asexual orientations. The notion of androgyny refers to myriad and variably constituted cultural images of woman-in-man (female-in-male, feminine-in-masculine), man-in-woman (male-in-female, masculine-in-feminine), and other, more fluid, double-gendered arrangements, and yet referentially it often remains anomalous, ambiguous, or even opaque. The fluidity of androgynous images, nonetheless, enables them to provide diverse and illuminating cultural mirrors in reflecting otherwise often unseen, tacit, unacknowledged, or obscured aspects of more usual gender configurations. In androgynous imagery, maleness (masculinity) and femaleness (femininity) are disassembled, transmuted, and reinscribed in imaginative ways that interweave, outreach, undercut, and sometimes overturn their ordinary prescriptions of boundedness and distinctiveness, with various entailments and consequences for the cultural reimagination of gender and its reinfusion in varied social contexts and cultural experiences.

The notion of androgyny evokes a relaxation of the rigidities of gender stereotypes, an opening of gender boundaries, a fusion or reconnection of gender attributes, and, thus, an enablement of some genre of appropriation by one gender of an "other." Yet, particular cultural portraits of the androgynous may reveal symmetry or asymmetry, balance or imbalance, harmonious or tensive integration, or other structural characteristics which suggest that such images commonly enfold and are shaped by more ordinary distinctions of male (masculine) and female (feminine) variously recombined or juxtaposed. Indeed, there is perhaps always some appropriation of the androgynous by the dichotomous forms of ideologically marked and also everyday gender reckoning, and, thus, images of androgyny often exhibit a veiled dualistic cultural geometry of gender, a masked bifurcation of gender difference recast and encased in tensive, fluid, or ambiguous singularity.[21] Those enduring vestiges of duality, nevertheless, are commonly perpetuated in the androgynous through bodily symbolism, which otherwise tends to secure most fundamentally gender differentiation as "natural." Thus, androgyny is marked by a cultural obscuring of the very contrasts and asymmetries that it ostensibly seems intended to decenter, deflect, suppress, or overcome, creating a chiaroscuro of foregrounded and backgrounded imagery. The consequent tension and ambiguity of the androgynous, often met with ambivalence, nonetheless renders uncertain the referentiality of such images vis-à-vis dual gender categories and opens an imaginative path toward transcending such duality. In evoking a sense of some transcendence of sociocultural encompassment and imprisonment by gendered dualities, images of androgyny commonly imply some extraordinary power unleashed in that transcendence – a power sometimes manifested in their prominence as religious symbols.

Fusions and confusions of everyday gender categories, therefore, may be focused through the cultural imagination on a marked confounding of the usual verities of ethnobiological understanding, sexual orientation, political ideology, social action, or personal experience. Such imagery may articulate cultural significata from dispersed loci on continua from the genderless and asexual to the double-gendered and bisexual, whether marked as embodied or disembodied, human or non-human, or real or illusory. Thus, androgyny is often a precarious cultural construct which is simultaneously seen as marginal, liminal, abnormal, and fantastical, and yet also as a reflection of the normal and normative lineaments of gender articulations, boundaries, or contrastive alignments mirrored back upon themselves but refracted through a lens that disarticulates, unbounds, and disaligns their constitutive elements in illuminating and provocative ways.

In consequence, androgynous images are not merely mediations of dichotomous gender contrasts, for they are commonly bound up with some form of cultural commentary on the inversions, reversals, inconsistencies, contradictions, blurrings, and ambiguities that are perhaps always tacit dimensions of the cultural imagination of the foci, contours, boundaries, and possibilities of more ordinary representations of gender. By rendering the tacit explicit, such imagery brings to the cultural foreground a wider and richer range of gender possibilities than is ordinarily available for exploration and contemplation. Narratives of the androgynous become cultural vehicles for the imaginative construction of extraordinary connections of gender attributes composed of disconnections and reconnections assembled from dissections of the ordinary, ostensibly yielding new and differently gendered phenomena. Indeed, the very idea of androgyny admits of myriad possibilities of degendering, regendering, and double-gendering persons or instantiations of personhood – some emphasizing images of wholeness, transcendence, and undifferentiated being, and others illuminating recombinations of elements of dual gender difference.

The multi-faceted, polysemic character of gender constructions, including the androgynous, precludes its analytic capture by attending to only one set of narratives, schemas, or instantiations, although ideological elevations of particular images of gender do indeed often center on marked and privileged genres of representations in certain contexts. In various myths, rituals, and narrations of notions of procreation and maturation, Bimin-Kuskusmin images of androgyny are central and highly elaborated, although often articulated in bounded, esoteric contexts and forms of ritual knowledge and language in their richest elaborations. Nevertheless, androgynous imagery, albeit less elaborated, is infused in more ordinary, everyday contexts and experiences of Bimin-Kuskusmin community life. At birth and at death, in sickness and in health, throughout the rites of passage that punctuate the social life-cycle, in myths that portray an enfolding sense of enduring "tradition" (*khaankharaak'khaan*), and in the course of everyday life, diverse but often interconnected threads of cultural imaginations of androgyny are woven into a fabric that ultimately envelops most Bimin-Kuskusmin understandings of the esoteric "sacred meanings" (*aiyem'khaa*), fundamental "kernel meanings" (*dop aiyem*), or everyday "underlying meanings" (*miit maagamiin*) which illuminate the full cultural spectrum of the possibilities of being gendered.

Among Bimin-Kuskusmin, androgynous imagery, variably constituted in sociocultural form and force, gives shape and significance to a broad range of phenomena – rendering some as feminized but male or masculinized but female, others as double-gendered without inflection, and yet others as altogether ambiguous and unstable. Although many flora, fauna, geological and meteorological phenomena, astronomical bodies, and spiritual forms are seen to be variously androgynous, the dominant referents of the very idea of "androgyny" (*maag'maak migiim'aan*) are two paramount ancestral figures – Afek, with masculine attributes embodied in female form, and Yomnok, with feminine qualities embedded in male substance – and the "totemic" creatures with which they are most commonly associated – the cassowary and the echidna or *yom'saaganiim* fruit bat – and their primordial and singular parent, Gowpnuuk, often represented as a great monitor lizard.[22]

All phenomena identified as androgynous are marked as being not only animate and sentient, but also significantly endowed with personhood or the quality of *finiik* "spirit or life-force" and, thus, with judgmental capacity, agential power, mystical potency, moral responsibility, and social accountability. They are generally imagined to provide sacred linkages, portrayed in myth and harnessed in ritual, with both the "ancestral underworld" (*kusem am*) and the "time of the primordial ancestors" (*anaak khyrkhymin*), in which the now "unseen images" (*takhaak kiin'ba*) of androgyny could then be "understood" (*khaim'khraak'khaanamin*) more clearly and completely. In the "time-places" (*anaak aneng*) of the primordial era and of the ancestral underworld, all phenomena are powerfully androgynous. Only with the coming of mortality and the retreat of the first ancestors to the ancestral underworld did the gendered differentiation of the realm of mortal humans and non-human phenomena begin to take place, weakening human efficacy in many realms. Vestiges of this androgynous legacy, however, still permeate the "center place" (*abiip mutuuk*) of all Bimin-Kuskusmin and are embedded especially in ritual and myth as the foundation of "sacred" (*aiyem*) power.

The mysterious Gowpnuuk, the primordial monitor lizard, emerged from the roar and flash of thunder (male) and lightning (female) in the great storm that created the sky, earth, and underworld and began to sculpt the landscape with her/his gigantic tail. When the terrain was finally bounded by its great rivers, Gowpnuuk retired to an enormous, deep cavern where he/she impregnated herself/himself by thrusting her/his tail into two vaginas – one in each buttock – cut open by flinging herself/himself on sharp stalagmites. Then, he/she gave birth through a mysterious kind of fission in which her/his bodily substances dissolved and flowed together, congealing in two androgynous shapes. From the left buttock emerged the "stone ancestral spirits" (*anuung kusem tuum*), which retain the androgynous qualities of Gowpnuuk and are represented by fossilized giant trilobites still found in deep caves and enshrined in clan cult houses. From the right buttock appeared Afek, embodied as a great cassowary, who was female but also endowed with male anatomical attributes and mystical powers. She was to become the great ancestress of all Bimin-Kuskusmin.

When Gowpnuuk had given birth, he/she emerged from the cave and drew lightning to herself/himself, disappearing in flames and smoke, which was borne by the winds to the east across the great Strickland Gorge. Then Afek too left the cavern where she was formed and traveled throughout the land giving parthenogenetic birth to significant fauna and flora and creating new contours of the terrain. Once the center-place of Bimin-Kuskusmin territory had taken shape, she ejaculated semen which she combined with her menstrual blood to create Yomnok, embodied as a giant echidna or *yom'saaganiim* fruit bat, who is identified as being at once her brother, son, and consort. Yomnok was male but also endowed with female anatomical characteristics and mystical capacities. Afek and Yomnok incestuously mated, and Afek then gave birth to the immortal human founders and totemic ancestors, both eventually female and male but at first androgynous, of all original patriclans of the Bimin-Kuskusmin. Afek then taught the human ancestors both ordinary and esoteric secrets enabling the proper conduct of life, both domestically and ritually, in the domain that she had created for them. With the advent of a primordial dispute and the coming of mortality, however, Afek and Yomnok began to differentiate the phenomena of the center-place into female and male categories, leaving at first only a few androgynous forms as their sacred legacy. They then departed for the ancestral underworld, but vowed eventually to return their still androgynous lastborn to the center-place to reveal ritual secrets then withheld from now mortal humans.[23] She then left some additional androgynous phenomena in the center-place, however, to enhance the efficacy of ritual until that return.

The mythic and ritual invocations of Afek and Yomnok, narrated in the sacred corpus of "afek myths" (*afek sang aiyem*) and sometimes accompanied by ritualized hunting and sacrifices of cassowaries and echidnas or *yom'saaganiim* fruit bats, evoke many powerful images of androgynous forms. Such forms are revealed not only in the narrative portraits of myth and the iconography of ritual displays, but also in esoteric genres of spirit possession and trance associated with Afek and Yomnok and often focused on their androgynous qualities.[24] In these dissociated states, vivid "images" (*takhaak*) of androgynous forms are commonly experienced and later recounted.[25] Such images frequently become the focus of special ritual divinations and mythic interpretations to decipher their hidden realms of significance.[26] Such significance is usually believed to be bound up with the fertility or fecundity of not only humans, but also a variety of domestically and ritually important fauna and flora. Indeed, numerous rites of fertility or fecundity ordinarily focus elaborately on androgynous imagery – portrayed in myth, chant, and prayer; evoked in ritually induced states of spirit possession or trance; enacted by ritual performers as transvestites; embodied in human androgynes; and encased in ritual icons of the androgynous.

Threaded through these myths, rituals, spirit possessions, trances, and other vehicles of representations of androgyny, there are certain prominent images that appear repeatedly and both constitute and enfold conceptualizations of androgynous being. Among fauna, the cassowary and echidna or *yom'saaganiim* fruit bat predominate as the most complex and powerful images of the androgynous.[27] Beyond these dominant symbols of androgyny, however, are other semiotic configurations of androgynous significance. Images of crystals, sheet lightning, rainbows, waterfalls, spirit paths, spider webs, and phosphorus, all invoke the diffuse androgyny of the primordial past, the ritualized present, and the enduring ancestral underworld, and cast or capture reflections and shadows of androgynous images within themselves or from beyond. The joining of sun (male) and moon (female) when an image of the moon appears before sundown or in a solar eclipse, and of thunder (male) and lightning (female) during storms, constitute the androgynous in omens.[28] The totemic qualities of the "wild red-mottled boar" (*samiin imok'maakhaan waam'aan*),[29] the *diriim* and *duboor* marsupials as siblings incestuously mating,[30] the venomous "androgynous centipede" (*maag'maak migiim'uur inaabuk*) associated with Afek,[31] the *maag'kuurdaak* larva,[32] the giant *anung'amkyaak* python,[33] the wild and never eaten ancestral *taam'maaginop* taro (male) and *kiir'maagubiik* sweet potato (female),[34] and the wild *kusem'am kandaak seaiir* pandanus,[35] all are representations of powerful forms of androgyny both in mythic narrations and in ritual performances and in the ancestral underworld. Although they are sometimes objects of important sacrifices, they are ordinarily considered taboo *vis-à-vis* any form of mundane human contact. Certain birds, portrayed as spirit messengers from the ancestral underworld, are often believed to undergo transformations from male to female as a sign of ancestral powers still unfolding.[36] The *firaak, karoom, kasiim, kiirang, kraang'en,* and *toyook* birds of paradise,[37] the *fuungen'en* bowerbird,[38] and the *a'on kuuririip miiririip ataan'bey* night birds,[39] are all among the most prominent exemplars of such gender transformations. As transient inhabitants of the "sky world" (*abiir am*), an androgynous realm mirroring aspects of the ancestral underworld, these birds are constantly being reinvested with androgynous power as they soar above the forests of the center-place.

These diverse androgynous images, portraying different facets of androgyny, are particularly evident in two prominent genres of rituals – rites of divination and curing at the occurrence of certain kinds of illnesses, and rites of passage that punctuate the social life-cycle from birth to death. Within these ritual performances and the mythic narrations that they encompass are vivid images of the androgynous portraying many of the phenomena noted above, either framed in the special genres of mythic discourse, or assembled in the distinctive iconographies of ritual displays, or manifested in both. Mythic narrative portrayals of the androgynous often seem to evoke the iconographic imagery of androgyny through non-iconic discursive signs and, thus, to press against the limits of language. Thus, ritual representations of the androgynous commonly interweave the iconography of artifactual ritual displays and the semiotic assemblages of mythic narrations, orchestrating a complex cross-referentiality of both representational forms in synchronizing image and word in the distinctive tropes of ritual speech. Indeed, image and sound envelop these rituals, which are ordinarily staged at dawn or dusk and during storms when there is a conjunction of the androgynous imagery of thunder and lightning – the voice and torch of Afek – and sun and moon – the twins of Gowpnuuk.

These two kinds of ritual are intricately interwoven with ideas about the procreative formation and maturational transformation of bodily substances and processes that enfold capacities to think, feel, judge, be motivated, and act. Bimin-Kuskusmin ideas of procreation and maturation are remarkably elaborate.[40] In brief, any female or male body is marked by male and female anatomical elements. Female elements are deemed soft and external, connected to bodily apertures of ingestion and excretion, prone to the weakening effects of illness, and first to decompose at death. Male dimensions of anatomy are said to be hard and internal, connected to bodily passages of the senses and of sexual fluids, prone to the strengthening effects of ritual action, and last to decay at death.[41] Each "anatomy" has different strengths and vulnerabilities. Located within the female anatomy is the *khaapkhabuurien* "spirit or life-force," which represents the more idiosyncratic self, takes the imprint of all life experiences, and dissolves at death. Centered in the heart of the male anatomy is the *finiik* "spirit or life-force," which is portrayed as the more social person and site of significant cognitive-emotional and agential capacities, absorbs ordained experiences of ritual socialization, and is transformed into an "ancestral spirit" (*kiir'kusem*) at death. In being transformed into a *kiir'kusem*, the *finiik* becomes highly androgynous and remains so when, reappearing as a *finiik*, it enters a woman's womb through a man's semen to animate a foetus at the moment of conception and then acquires varying gendered forms and attachments from prenatal through post-natal development until it is again transformed at death into an image of the androgynous. At birth, during prenatal development, in illness, in dreams and trances and spirit possessions, and at death, when the *finiik* is unstable in or dislodged from its corporeal abode, it becomes variously but profoundly androgynous; yet it also retains varying vestiges of this androgyny when it is properly embodied. The states of a person, ever reconfigured through "natural" and ritual maturation, are complexly bound up with varying balances and imbalances of *khaapkhabuurien* and *finiik*, with their implications for the embodied constitution of the female, male, and androgynous in any person.

Those illnesses known as *maag'uuraniin maafagaarinuuk* are distinguished by their tendency to weaken or transform male or female anatomical structures or processes and, thus, to create an imbalance in bodily constitution and in the always delicate relation between *finiik* and *khaapkabuurien*. The etiology of this class of illnesses is usually attributed to some breach of either food taboos or other ritual prohibitions that are intended to ensure the gendered stability of bodily substances and their interrelationships. Persons believed to be afflicted by such illnesses are subjected to rites of divination and curing that are intended to fathom and remedy some improper alignment of a distinctively male or female and nonetheless simultaneously androgynous state of being. Divinations attend to both "reflections" (*fom takhaak*) and "shadows" (*ataan takhaak*) of the person, for it is within such images that the androgynous constitution of a person is revealed in subtle signs. Curing involves a variety of bodily intrusions in the forms of ritually prescribed substances to be ingested and sometimes of ritual surgery. Because male and female illnesses of this genre affect both correspondingly and differently gendered anatomical sites, their ritual remedy requires both male and female and also androgynous diviner-curers, who supplicate ancestral spirits of androgynous identity. Among these illnesses, the most dramatic instance of androgynous imbalance is that of male suicide.[42] Indeed, suicide marks a gender reversal in which the subordinate gender of one's asymmetrically double-gendered being comes to overwhelm the normally dominant gender, with fatal consequences as the *khaapkhabuurien* "spirit or life-force" becomes dangerously ascendant. Men, more essentially formed by their gendered particularity as male, are more prone to the most dire consequences of this reversal.

Rites of passage mark significant sociocultural transitions throughout the life-cycle, and each maturational transition ritually marked represents a realignment of the shifting balances of male and female substances in the bodies of both females and males. From conception to birth, the androgynous foetus constantly oscillates between female and male shapes until it comes to rest at the moment of birth near one gendered pole. Birth is marked by elaborate rites of couvade in which mothers and fathers take on opposite gender attributes to ensure safe passage of their still androgynous child.[43] When unnatural twins are born and the "non-human" twin is divined and strangled, the surviving human twin is said to be forever marked androgynously by the gender of the deceased twin, who is assumed to have been either of opposite gender or itself androgynous. From early infancy to the eve of middle childhood, girls and boys, seen as female- or male-inflected androgynes, undergo together rites of passage to strengthen their *finiik*, ensure against the ravages of high infant mortality, and prepare them for incorporation into community life as proper and, eventually, as distinctively gendered actors.[44] Thereafter, the rites of males and females diverge in their emphases on contrastively gendered being and in the gender-segregated realms in which those rites occur, and androgynous characteristics become increasingly veiled and manifested only through divination in the inner recesses of body and spirit. For most women, female rites culminate in "female initiation" (*waneng men'faagumiin*) in late adolescence at first menses, enabling fertility, menstruation, and reproduction, and legitimating marriage-ability. For all males, the *am yaoor* cycle of male initiation begins at nine to twelve years of age, consists of ten stages, and continues for a decade. For the first nine stages, beginning with the initial *ais am* rite, the ritual emphasis is on expunging female and enhancing male attributes of the initiates through myriad intense and ordeal-ridden experiences.[45]

In the final *en am* stage of initiation, however, an unanticipated revelation of enduring androgyny unfolds to initiates who have experienced almost a decade of apparently becoming ever more male and masculine. In this last rite of initiation, they suddenly encounter a profound sense of powerful and persisting androgynous inner being within their otherwise elaborately masculinized bodies. Through myriad articulations of female (feminine) and male (masculine) in mythic narratives and ritual displays, in complementary acts of male and female initiators, and in their own acts of rubbing menstrual blood from the residues of menstrual huts and semen from ritual masturba-tion on their bodies, of consuming female and male substances, of adorning themselves in dress and bodily decoration with transvestite imagery, of inhabiting special huts for menstrual and birth seclusion, and of simulating both female and male acts of copulation, the initiates are forced to engage experientially the androgyny encased in the bodies of male warriors – their own. Myths of Afek and Yomnok and their androgynous characteristics are richly interwoven throughout this ritual performance. Personal narratives and dream reports, however, reveal a profoundly subjective sense, often marked by high ambivalence and some anxiety, in the initiates of being androgynous.

During these experiences of the androgynous, the ritual structure of the *en am* itself comes to be called the "men's womb" (*men am kunum*), and each of the initiates is ultimately enclosed in a large *baatbat aiyem* ritual netbag in a foetal position, to be ritually reborn as a masculinized androgyne known as *kunum maag'maak migiim imok* ("man male double-gendered"). Indeed, various cultural arrangements of netbag as womb are distributed throughout rites of passage, divination, and curing and always significantly mark the androgynous qualities of whatever is encompassed by them.[46] Thus, in the rites of death, when the *finiik* of the deceased ascends to karst holes at the summits of mountains to become transformed into an ancestral *kiir'kusem* and descend into the ancestral underworld, the corpse is enclosed in a sacred netbag on the burial platform in the high forest; and the bones are later carried to clan cult houses and ossuary caves in other ritual netbags. In dying and in

death, the transition to androgyny, already prefigured in procreative substance, maturation, myth, ritual, and embodiment from conception to rebirth,
is symbolized in the image of a womb – male substance encased in a female
body, made fertile by female and male substances, animated by androgynous
ancestral spirits who will reclaim its issue at death, and cosmologically
represented as Afek's mantle, which is portrayed as an enormous netbag
enveloping and shaping sky world, center-place, and underworld.

In the background or foreground of rites of divination, curing, and passage
that are bound up with the significant androgynous balances of persons are
two living ritual figures of special importance – the "paramount female ritual
elder" (*waneng aiyem ser*) and the "male pseudo-hermaphrodite" (*yomnok'min aiyem*).[47] Both are distinctively androgynous and are identified as
the living descendants of Afek and Yomnok, respectively. Paramount female
ritual elders are old, post-menopausal women, two of whom are selected to
undergo a special rite of installation as ritual elders of their clan. In this rite,
their androgyny is marked by a ritual veiling of their marriages and children,
ritual scarification usually associated with male initiation, and ritual prest-
ations of taro (male) and sweet potato (female) gardens, bows (male) and
digging sticks (female), male and female bones in female and male netbags,
and other assemblages of androgynous imagery. In ritual arenas, they are
commonly adorned either as transvestites or in a non-gendered fashion,
obscuring what lies embodied beneath as the gendered anatomical surface of
their ultimately androgynous identity remains visible as a cloak over their
hidden androgyny. When the imagery of the androgynous comes to the
foreground in diverse rituals, they become key ritual actors, enabled in their
very being to constitute and to manipulate efficaciously various extraordinary
and inherently dangerous linkages of female and male substances.

In turn, the *yomnok'min aiyem* are actually male pseudo-hermaphrodites,
who are seen to be born with labial folds, reared as girls, and then recognized
as being descendants of Yomnok when distinctive but diminutive male
genitalia descend into view on the eve of puberty.[48] In this remarkable event,
it is believed that normal prenatal oscillations of foetal gender have mysteri-
ously persisted well into post-natal development as a sacred mark of special
and auspicious ancestral destiny. Once recognized, the *yomnok'min aiyem* is
deemed a powerful ritual repository of fertility, is specially initiated, is never
allowed to marry or engage in sexual intercourse, and is adorned with special
ritual markings distinctive of his status.[49] The *yomnok'min aiyem* becomes a
celibate and solitary embodiment of androgyny. He wears both male and
female adornment in dress and body pigment, bears some of the ritual scars
of both female and male initiation, and is denied the phallocrypt that all men
wear at the inception of male initiation. Instead, his genitalia are covered only
with a flap of bark cloth in everyday activities and are exposed and encircled
by red parrot feathers during ritual performances. Unlike the defective
monorchid male strangled at birth, the *yomnok'min aiyem* becomes a revered

ritual figure and exemplar and embodiment of androgynous power. Together, the *waneng aiyem ser* and the *yomnok'min aiyem*, adorned with cassowary plumes and echidna quills or dried fruit bat penises and embodying the images of Afek and Yomnok, respectively, become ritual encasements of androgynous fertility or fecundity and central participants in male and female rites of divination, curing, and passage whenever articulations of both female and male phenomena are the focus of ritual. Often abroad in the public arenas of community life, they are also the living, embodied representations of androgyny as a visible, tangible, and experiential reality for most Bimin-Kuskusmin.[50] Their own subjective experiences of their culturally marked androgynous status in a community in which a duality of gender shapes most realms of social life, however, are often fraught with deep ambivalence and uncertain senses of "shame" (*fiitom*).

Also in the background of such rites are other androgynous figures that are seen either to erode or to enhance ritual efficacy. At the negative pole are *tamam* witches, *anengmotiir* forest spirits, and the male *gabruurian* and female *kamdaak waneng* trickster figures. The ferocious *tamam* witch is a perversely masculinized and exaggeratedly feminized figure who constantly exudes polluting menstrual blood, copulates incessantly but is barren, and voraciously destroys male substance in both women and men.[51] The *anengmotiir* forest spirits are truly double-gendered and attack both the rituals and the substances that serve to enhance the dominant gender of any persons, causing their illness or death. The *gabruurian* and *kamdaak waneng* tricksters are both complexly androgynous and possessed of exaggerated male and female genitalia, respectively.[52] In myth, their penises and clitorides are often subjected to various forms of castration and regeneration, for they are portrayed as surviving terrible genital mutilations only to emerge as differently double-gendered. They disrupt rituals and contaminate persons through promiscuous dispersal of their polluting and infertile sexual fluids on and in the bodies of persons of either gender, while draining fertile sexual fluids from the bodies of persons opposite in gender to their dominant gender. As wanderers, they are constantly gathering, incorporating, and transforming various gendered phenomena into their ever more complex androgynous constitution. Witches, forest spirits, and tricksters are all fiercely cannibalistic, devouring the gendered substance of the dominant gender of any person, thereby weakening or destroying them.[53] Among these figures, anuses, mouths, vaginas, penile apertures, and ritually formed openings may become orifices at once for ingestion, excretion, and sexual intercourse.

At the positive pole are *biis* and *kiimon* sorcerers, *kuutang utaang* forest spirits, and *kiir'kusem* ancestral spirits. The *biis* and *kiimon* sorcerers are often male or female ritual elders who powerfully harness the ritual capacities of the opposite gender to guard against intrusions of persons or spirits disruptive of particular gender configurations into ritual arenas focused on dichotomous gender alignments, and also to ensure the efficacy of male or female rituals by enhancing the power of androgynous images. The *kuutang utaang* forest spirits are profoundly androgynous and inhabit ritual displays of androgynous character, infusing "androgynous spirit substance" (*diim kwan maag'maak migiim'utaang*) into such ritual assemblages and enhancing their efficacy. The *kiir'kusem* ancestral spirits, representing the dead, unborn, and primordial in androgynous form, are summoned through sacrifices to dwell in human and other skulls during ritual performances in order to guide the performance, enhance its efficacy, and protect the sanctity of its artifacts, discourses, acts, and participants. Through their powerful androgynous character, they are able to ensure not only that ancestral embodiments of androgyny become harnessed as an integral part of rituals, but also, in part, that ordinarily polluting contact between male and female substances does not erode the efficacy of ritual performances.

An exploration of the forms and contexts of the androgynous enables some understanding of the circumstances in which social and personal access to this elaborated focus of the Bimin-Kuskusmin cultural imagination is activated and anchored in various realms of community life. This brief ethnographic sketch has only touched upon the cultural complexity and subtlety of Bimin-Kuskusmin ideas of androgyny. Indeed, the Bimin-Kuskusmin cultural imagination of the androgynous is rich, varied, and variably infused in varying phenomena and realms of social life. Although the most elaborated visions of androgyny are constituted as esoteric knowledge and in ritual contexts largely restricted to aged elders, androgynous images of variable construction, elaboration, and intensity are also diffused throughout the personal trajectories of experiences of the social life-cycle enclosed within the cultural horizons of the center-place of the Bimin-Kuskusmin world. From early childhood to the threshold of death, androgyny is marked not only as an everpresent feature of community life and a counterpoint to pervasive gender contrasts, but also as a part of one's experience of being a person and a self that is etched into one's body and consciousness through procreation, maturation, and ritual. Beyond those calendrically regular but nonetheless occasional ritual moments when the cultural significance of the androgynous is brought into the social foreground, however, the notion and image of the androgynous remains a more or less constant background presence, appearing in illuminated form now and again, fleetingly, and ambiguously, to alter suddenly one's sense of the forms, hues, and textures of gender, and then recedes once more – leaving the landscape as before but imaginatively remapped with memories of possibilities of gendered difference. As enculturation proceeds, the recognition becomes enlivened and then enriched in sensing that beneath, behind, or within the appearances of the duality of gender so embellished in the discourse of the dominant ideologies giving powerful shape to the contexts of everyday life, there is another, different, but also powerful, gendered reality embedded in the cultural idea, social

211

instantiation, mythic and ritual signification, and personal experience of *maag'maak migiim'aan* ("androgyny").

In the swirling imagery of Bimin-Kuskusmin androgyny, there is an oscillation not only between singularity and duality of gender, but also among embodied reality, iconic artifact, discursive construction, and cultural fantasy. Androgynous images may be organized as fragile, tensive integrations of male and female that nonetheless seem to remain forever partially segregated internal to the images themselves. A centripetal momentum toward androgynous union is often somewhat countered by a centrifugal return to duality. Gender boundaries tend to emerge at the margins of narrative efforts to suppress or transcend them and to reappear in the wake of narrative action, sometimes deflecting narrative images back into their dualistic folds until renewed discursive momentum regains ground and again, but only momentarily, moves beyond them – only to be recaptured once again. Dual gendered "reality" seems always threatening to close around androgynous figures. The bounded indivisibility of Apollonian androgyny is rigid, removed, and alien to Bimin-Kuskusmin imagery, in contrast to the fluid, oscillatory, or transformative possibilities of a more Dionysian image of the androgynous.

Among Bimin-Kuskusmin, the androgynous can be only partially (re)presented in a singular image, but neither arrested nor captured therein. Its implicit fluidity overflows its particular overt images, transforming its shapes beyond the pace and possibility of articulations of its representational forms. Thus, most Bimin-Kuskusmin representations of androgyny are neither complete nor autonomous, but interconnected and embedded in complex symbolic mosaics of differently constituted and inflected images of both the androgynous and the dual-gendered. In momentary isolation, therefore, the androgynous seems to require a veiling that enhances ambiguity, for an unveiling often brings some reversion toward either male or female poles of gender dualism. In mosaics of images, however, the multifaceted character of androgyny is better illuminated in an unfolding representational process loosely interconnecting arrays of images in flux and without a stable center or, perhaps, even a clear distinction between reality and illusion. As some Bimin-Kuskusmin elders note, androgyny is only dimly seen at the nexus of myriad reflections and refractions of a ritual crystal, in diverse images fleetingly "matted together" (*duunduun*). The facets of androgyny presented in this chapter are interwoven in mosaics in this way. In Bimin-Kuskusmin experience, nonetheless, one begins and ends in androgynous states, being formed from and then transformed into androgynous *kiir'kusem*, yet androgyny inflects one's femaleness or maleness throughout the intervening course of the life-cycle. After all, Bimin-Kuskusmin still view themselves as the descendants of Afek and Yomnok, who inhabit the center-place of their mountainous fastness at the elevated hub of central New Guinea, and that vision deeply marks their sense of who they are in that remote realm of montane valleys. As some myths and rituals claim, they must be sensitive to the forest tracks of the cassowary, of the presence of Afek in their domain. In their cultural imaginations, social institutions, and personal experiences, the complex imagery of androgyny becomes a powerful, constant, and enduring inflection of the more apparent but illusory dualities of gender ordinarily inscribed in bodies, persons, and selves.

NOTES

1 The data presented here are drawn from field research among Bimin-Kuskusmin between 1971 and 1973, and with the generous support of the National Institutes of Health, the Cornell University/Ford Foundation Humanities and Social Sciences Program, and the Center for South Pacific Studies of the University of California, Santa Cruz.

2 As Elspeth Probyn notes for selfhood, personhood is always gendered. See Elspeth Probyn, *Sexing the Self: Gendered Positions in Cultural Studies*, London: Routledge, 1993, p. 2. On the concept of social "personhood," see Grace G. Harris, "Concepts of Individual, Self, and Person in Description and Analysis," in *American Anthropologist*, vol. 91, No. 3 (September 1989), pp. 602–9.

3 On the idea of a "culturally constituted behavioral environment," see A. Irving Hallowell, *Culture and Experience*, Philadelphia: University of Pennsylvania Press, 1955, pp. 86–91.

4 A proper appreciation of the *processes* of the varied cultural constitutions of gender must avoid a reification of gender difference or similarity as encased in bounded, closed structures to the exclusion of other, interwoven facets of other schemas of identity with which gender configurations interact and intersect (e.g. age, class, ethnicity, race, sexuality, and so on).

5 In turn, it must not be assumed that cultural constructions of gender are inevitably framed or shaped by a singular, dichotomous "logic" of mutual exclusivity which contrastively structures dual categories of female (feminine) and male (masculine), relegating all images not unambiguously subsumed by these categories to be peripheral, superficial, fictional, fantastical, or otherwise non-essential aspects of gender reckoning.

6 By analogy, gender constructions may be imagined as multiple layers of variably etched transparencies aligned in particular situations so as to reveal multi-dimensional patterns of lines and shapes that constitute culturally particular, socially contextualized figurations of gendered possibilities articulated with other dimensions of situated identities, inscribing shifting patterns in fluid, open-textured sets of potential gender arrangements. On the notion of "open-textured," see Friedrich Waismann, *How I See Philosophy*, edited by Rom Harré, Garden City: Anchor Books, 1968, p. 199.

7 As Judith Butler suggests, the apparent facticity of sex difference, as it enters into the cultural construction of gender categories as their "natural" foundation, may itself be culturally constituted in significant ways. Biological sex dimorphism, however it may constrain the cultural variability of gender categories, is not simply mirrored in cultural configurations of sex difference, and, thus, sex and gender become difficult to distinguish at some levels of analysis. See Judith Butler, *Gender Trouble: Feminism and the Subversion of Identity*, London: Routledge, 1990, pp. 7–9.

8 As Suzanne J. Kessler and Wendy McKenna observe, cultural scripts of gender become embedded in dichotomous frames and, through those dualistic schemas, come to be connected to myriad other characteristics of the gender so framed. See

Suzanne J. Kessler and Wendy McKenna, *Gender: An Ethnomethodological Approach*, Chicago: University of Chicago Press, 1978, pp. 161–2.

9 See Sylvia J. Yanagisako and Jane F. Collier, "Toward a Unified Analysis of Kinship and Gender," in Jane F. Collier and Sylvia J. Yanagisako (eds), *Gender and Kinship: Essays Toward a Unified Analysis*, Stanford: Stanford University Press, 1987, pp. 16–29.

10 See Francette Pacteau, "The Impossible Referent: Representations of the Androgyne," in Victor Burgin, James Donald, and Cora Kaplan (eds), *Formations of Fantasy*, New York: Methuen, 1986, p. 80.

11 Images of androgyny in this chapter encompass images of hermaphrodites, transsexuals, transvestites, and forms of "gender blending" (in Holly Devor's phrase). A. J. L. Busst, Holly Devor, and Robert J. Stoller variously note the analytic difficulties in distinguishing among these terms. Indeed, such distinctions often seem arbitrary, inconsistent, contradictory, overlapping, and of little analytic utility when the focus of concern is cultural images of androgyny. See A. J. L. Busst, "The Image of the Androgyne in the Nineteenth Century," in Ian Fletcher (ed.), *Romantic Mythologies*, New York: Barnes and Noble, 1967, pp. 1–95; Holly Devor, *Gender Blending: Confronting the Limits of Duality*, Bloomington: Indiana University Press, 1989; and Robert J. Stoller, *Presentations of Gender*, New Haven: Yale University Press, 1985, p. 19.

12 Beyond institutionalized homosexuality and transvestism, anthropology has rarely explored the phenomena of androgyny. For general views of cross-cultural variation in androgynous imagery, see Hermann Baumann, *Das doppelte Geschlecht: Ethnologische Studien zur Bisexualität in Ritus und Mythos*, Berlin: Dietrich Reimer, 1955, pp. 129–249; Charles Callender and Lee M. Kochems, "Men and Not-Men: Male Gender-Mixing Statuses and Homosexuality," in Evelyn Blackwood (ed.), *The Many Faces of Homosexuality*, New York: Harrington Park Press, 1986, pp. 165–78; Mircea Eliade, *Mephistopheles and the Androgyne: Studies in Religious Myth and Symbol*, trans. J. M. Cohen, New York: Sheed and Ward, 1965, pp. 78–124; and Richard Green, "Mythological, Historical and Cross-Cultural Aspects of Transsexualism," in Richard Green and John Money (eds), *Transsexualism and Sex Reassignment*, Baltimore: Johns Hopkins University Press, 1969, pp. 13–22. Beyond ethnographic studies of androgynous beings and images in a number of sociocultural contexts, special attention has been devoted to *berdache* phenomena in aboriginal North America. See Evelyn Blackwood, "Sexuality and Gender in Certain Native American Tribes: The Case of Cross-Gender Females," in *Signs*, vol. 10, No. 1 (Autumn 1984), pp. 27–42; Sabine Lang, *Männer als Frauen – Frauen als Männer: Geschlechtsrollenwechsel bei den Indianern Nordamerikas*, Hamburg: Wayasabah, 1990; Will Roscoe, *The Zuni Man-Woman*, Albuquerque: University of New Mexico Press, 1991; Harriet Whitehead, "The Bow and the Burden Strap: A New Look at Institutionalized Homosexuality in Native North America," in Sherry B. Ortner and Harriet Whitehead (eds), *Sexual Meanings: The Cultural Construction of Gender and Sexuality*, Cambridge: Cambridge University Press, 1981, pp. 80–115; and Walter L. Williams, *The Spirit and the Flesh: Sexual Diversity in American Indian Culture*, Boston: Beacon Press, 1992.

13 See Jacques Derrida, "Différance," in his *Speech and Phenomena And Other Essays on Husserl's Theory of Signs*, trans. David B. Allison, Evanston: Northwestern University Press, 1973, p. 129.

14 See Thomas G. Rosenmeyer, "Tragedy and Religion: *The Bacchae*," in Erich Segal (ed.), *Euripides: A Collection of Critical Essays*, Englewood Cliffs: Prentice-Hall, 1968, p. 154. See also Charles Segal, "The Menace of Dionysus: Sex Roles and Reversals in Euripedes' *Bacchae*," in John Peradotto and J. P. Sullivan (eds),

Women in the Ancient World: The Arethusa Papers, Albany: State University of New York Press, 1984, pp. 195–212.

15 See A. J. L. Busst, "The Image of the Androgyne in the Nineteenth Century," in Ian Fletcher (ed.), *Romantic Mythologies*, New York: Barnes and Noble, 1967, pp. 1–95; Sara Friedrichsmeyer, *The Androgyne in Early German Romanticism*, New York: Peter Lang, 1983; J.-C.-L. Halley des Fontaines, *Contributions à l'études de l'androgynie: la notion d'androgynie dans quelques mythes et quelques rites*, Paris: Le François, 1938; Jean Libis, *Le Mythe de l'androgyne*, Paris: Berg International, 1980; and Jean Molino, "Le Mythe de l'androgyne," in *Aimer en France, 1760–1860*, Clermont-Ferrand: Actes du Colloque International de Clermont-Ferrand, 1980, pp. 401–11.

16 Indeed, Paul de Man interprets the figure of the *schöne Seele* as an embodiment of the romantic ideal of the "unity of appearance (sign) and idea (meaning)." See Paul de Man, "Crisis and Criticism," in his *Blindness and Insight: Essays in the Rhetoric of Contemporary Criticism*, Minneapolis: University of Minnesota Press, 1983, pp. 12–13.

17 See Joanne Blum, *Transcending Gender: The Male/Female Double in Women's Fiction*, Ann Arbor: UMI Research Press, 1988, and Kari Weil, *Androgyny and the Denial of Difference*, Charlottesville: University Press of Virginia, 1992, pp. 144–69.

18 See especially Carolyn G. Heilbrun, *Toward a Recognition of Androgyny*, New York: W. W. Norton, 1973.

19 See especially Sandra L. Bem, *The Lenses of Gender: Transforming the Debate on Sexual Inequality*, New Haven: Yale University Press, 1993. Her work has moved from an emphasis on an individual being both masculine and feminine in psychological orientation to a focus on the significance of a culture's concepts of masculinity and femininity for an enculturated individual.

20 Feminist concerns about the problems and limitations of notions of androgyny have largely attended to their subtle, veiled perpetuation and reinforcement of gender polarity, emphasis on feminized males and heterosexuality, focus on individual psychology or behavior and not on sociocultural realities, tendency toward vacuous or unrealizable abstractions, and preoccupation with Western images. See Mary Daly, *Gyn/Ecology: The Metaethics of Radical Feminism*, Boston: Beacon Press, 1990; Barbara C. Gelpi, "The Politics of Androgyny," in *Women's Studies*, vol. 2, No. 2 (1974), pp. 151–60; Daniel A. Harris, "Androgyny: The Sexist Myth in Disguise," in *Women's Studies*, vol. 2, No. 2 (1974), pp. 171–84; Bernice E. Lott, "A Feminist Critique of Androgyny: Toward the Elimination of Gender Attributions for Learned Behavior," in Clara Mayo and Nancy M. Hemley (eds), *Gender and Nonverbal Behavior*, New York: Springer-Verlag, 1981, pp. 171–80; Janice Raymond, "The Illusion of Androgyny," in *Quest*, vol. 2, No. 1 (Summer 1975), pp. 57–66; Cynthia Secor, "Androgyny: An Early Appraisal," in *Women's Studies*, vol. 2, No. 2 (1974), p. 164; and Catherine R. Stimpson, "The Androgyne and the Homosexual," in *Women's Studies*, vol. 2, No. 2 (1974), pp. 237–48. Indeed, Adrienne Rich suggests that the very lexical structure of the term androgyny "replicates the sexual [gender] dichotomy and the priority of *andros* (male) over *gyne* (female)." See Adrienne Rich, *Of Woman Born: Motherhood as Experience and Institution*, New York: W. W. Norton, 1976, pp. 76–7. Yet, earlier feminist enthusiasms for androgyny as a social ideal for diminishing gender polarity and enhancing gender equality persist in tempered form. See Nancy T. Bazin and Alma Freeman, "The Androgynous Vision," in *Women's Studies*, vol. 2, No. 2 (1974), pp. 185–215; Mary Daly, "The Qualitative Leap beyond Patriarchal Religion," in *Quest*, vol. 1, No. 4 (Spring 1975), pp. 20–40; and Mary A. Warren, "Is Androgyny the Answer to Sexual Stereotyping?,"

in Mary Vetterling-Braggin (ed.), *"Femininity," "Masculinity," and "Androgyny:"* *A Modern Philosophical Discussion*, Totowa: Rowman and Allanheld, 1982, pp. 170–86.

21 The momentary reflective distance that androgynous images may enable *vis-à-vis* normal and normative categories of gender often seems only a temporary disruption that is quickly absorbed or enveloped by or enfolded in the contours of dualistic difference. On occasion, however, the androgynous may be embodied or be ritualized, mythologized, or otherwise institutionalized in a manner that suspends that distanced vision in a more stable mode of signification, which may provoke a different and less fleeting kind of cultural contemplation. Even so, such androgynous imagery probably does not ever escape the cultural clutches of a more ordinary and ideologically ordained gendered world, which almost inevitably etches something of its dualistic structures of gender into the composition of such images.

22 Gowpnuuk is represented as possessing birth canals connected to sexual orifices and protuberances on forehead and buttocks and abdomen, rows of breasts and penises along the back, and an immense "penis-clitoris" (*maiyoob'mem fuun*) as a tail. The figure of Gowpnuuk, however, mostly remains shadowy and ambiguous.

23 The return of Afek's lastborn child is often associated with the advent of Europeans, who are sometimes believed to be androgynous.

24 Both Afek and Yomnok are vividly portrayed as androgynous in terms of bodily structures and processes, sexual capacities, spiritual constitutions, and ritual adornments.

25 On trance and possession, see Fitz John P. Poole, "Ritual Rank, the Self, and Ancestral Power: Liturgy and Substance in a Papua New Guinea Society," in Lamont Lindstrom (ed.), *Drugs in Western Pacific Societies: Relations of Substance*, Lanham: University Press of America, 1987, pp. 149–96.

26 On mythic and ritual interpretation, see Fitz John P. Poole, "Wisdom and Practice: The Mythic Making of Sacred History among the Bimin-Kuskusmin of Papua New Guinea," in Frank Reynolds and David Tracy (eds), *Discourse and Practice*, Albany: State University of New York Press, 1992, pp. 13–50.

27 By Bimin-Kuskusmin reckoning, the cassowary, a large, flightless bird with a bony crest on its head, is not a bird but a unique and sacred creature. In general appearance, behavior, and genitalia (a cloaca), it is thought to be complexly double-gendered. In turn, the egg-laying echidna, New Guinea's only monotreme, is believed to be a descendant of androgynous birds and a totemic sibling of the cassowary. The *yom'saaganiim* fruit bat is imagined to be a descendant of both cassowary and echidna.

28 The androgynous characteristics of the "sky world" (*abiir am*) are said to be analogous to those of the "ancestral underworld" (*kusem am*), with the center-place and its gendered divisions wedged between and in tension with them. It is that cosmological "tension" (*biing'uum saanuniim*) which is said to keep these realms apart and, also through ritual effort, to keep remnants of the androgynous in the center-place.

29 This wild boar, distinctive in its coloration, is sometimes said to be a feminized male that never breeds but scatters its semen and menstrual blood to fertilize only androgynous plants of ritual importance.

30 These different species of marsupials are totemically aligned as younger sister (the ever-menstruating *diriim*) and elder brother (the semen-filled *duboor*), and their incestuous mating, as in other representations of close, sacred incest, is thought to have strongly androgynous connotations.

31 This black centipede, which Afek wore live in her pierced nasal septum, is female

on its left side and male on its right side, and its powerful venom is a secretion of male semen and female fertile fluids that brings death to all non-androgynous beings but gives life to new androgynous centipedes.

32 These large larvae are believed to oscillate between being male or female as they consume female or male plants.

33 This enormous, androgynous python, a totemic descendent of the mythic *anaangan'temkyaak* pythons that once laid eggs of sacred cowrie shell in Afek's time, metamorphoses in the decay of death into young pythons, who feed upon its decomposing androgynous substances.

34 These ancestral taro and sweet potato, used only in special sacrifices and only when bound together, are an androgynous sacrificial food of ancestral spirits.

35 This pandanus is said to produce female and male nuts within single nut clusters.

36 Beliefs in the gender transformations of certain birds claim that the less elaborate plumage of females and immature males represents young male birds that will become transformed into adult female birds with more spectacular plumage (actually male birds).

37 These birds of paradise are believed to be special spirit messengers of Afek and Yomnok and to exhibit multicolored plumage or long head or tail feathers at maturity. Their distinctive arrangements of feathers are thought to replicate some of the ritual adornments of Afek and to mask their always transforming bodily characteristics of gender difference.

38 This bowerbird not only is androgynous itself, but also builds an elaborate nest which always includes remnants of female and male flora in which to enfold and nurture its androgynous young.

39 These night birds appear at dusk and disappear at dawn. As they cross the threshold from day to night and night to day, they undergo a double metamorphosis from being female or male during the day (the night of the ancestral underworld) to being androgynous during the night (the day of the ancestral underworld).

40 On the formation and transformation of substance and spirit, see Fitz John P. Poole, "Symbols of Substance: Bimin-Kuskusmin Models of Procreation, Death, and Personhood," in *Mankind*, vol. 14, No. 3 (April 1984), pp. 191–216.

41 Women and men, while essentially but not entirely agreeing on the gendered anatomical map, tend to attribute differing significance to differently gendered anatomical elements.

42 On a high incidence of male suicide, see Fitz John P. Poole, "Among the Boughs of the Hanging Tree: Male Suicide among the Bimin-Kuskusmin of Papua New Guinea," in Francis H. Hezel, Donald H. Rubinstein, and Geoffrey M. White (eds), *Culture, Youth and Suicide in the Pacific: Papers from an East-West Center Conference*, Honolulu: The Pacific Islands Studies Program of the Center for Asian and Pacific Studies of the University of Hawaii at Manoa and The Institute of Culture and Communication of the East–West Center, 1984, pp. 152–81.

43 On birth rites, see Fitz John P. Poole, "Couvade and Clinic in a New Guinea Society: Birth among the Bimin-Kuskusmin," in Marten W. deVries, Robert L. Berg, and Mac Lipkin, Jr. (eds), *The Use and Abuse of Medicine*, New York: Praeger Scientific, 1982, pp. 54–95.

44 On infancy and early childhood, see Fitz John P. Poole, "Coming into Social Being: Cultural Images of Infants in Bimin-Kuskusmin Folk Psychology," in Geoffrey M. White and John Kirkpatrick (eds), *Person, Self, and Experience: Exploring Pacific Ethnopsychologies*, Berkeley: University of California Press, 1985, pp. 183–242.

45 On early male initiation, see Fitz John P. Poole, "The Ritual Forging of Identity:

FITZ JOHN PORTER POOLE

Aspects of Person and Self in Bimin-Kuskusmin Male Initiation," in Gilbert H. Herdt (ed.), *Rituals of Manhood: Male Initiation in Papua New Guinea*, Berkeley: University of California Press, 1982, pp. 99–154.

46 On analogies between androgyny and netbags among the neighboring Telefolmin, see Maureen A. MacKenzie, "The Telefol String Bag: A Cultural Object with Androgynous Forms," in Barry Craig and David Hyndman (eds), *Children of Afek: Tradition and Change Among the Mountain-Ok of Central New Guinea*, Sydney: Oceania Publications, University of Sydney, 1990, pp. 88–108.

47 On the persona of female ritual elders, see Fitz John P. Poole, "Transforming 'Natural' Woman: Female Ritual Leaders and Gender Ideology among Bimin-Kuskusmin," in Sherry B. Ortner and Harriet Whitehead (eds), *Sexual Meanings: The Cultural Construction of Gender and Sexuality*, Cambridge: Cambridge University Press, 1981, pp. 116–65.

48 This phenomenon among Bimin-Kuskusmin, a small and highly inbred population, appears to be 5-Alpha Reductase Male Pseudohermaphroditism. For a portrait of 5-Alpha Reductase Male Pseudohermaphroditism, see Julianne Imperato-McGinley and Ralph E. Peterson, "Male Pseudohermaphroditism: The Complexities of Male Phenotypic Development," in *American Journal of Medicine*, vol. 61, No. 2 (August 1976), pp. 251–72. For an analogous phenomenon among the Sambia of New Guinea, see Gilbert H. Herdt and Robert J. Stoller, "Sakulambei – A Hermaphrodite's Secret: An Example of Clinical Ethnography," in *The Psychoanalytic Study of Society*, vol. 11 (1985), pp. 115–56.

49 Unknown to Bimin-Kuskusmin, the *yomnok'min aiyem* is sterile, although capable of sexual intercourse. By forbidding him to marry or have sexual intercourse, however, empirical evidence of sterility is culturally masked.

50 Extensive and intensive interviews with several *waneng aiyem ser* and *yomnok'min aiyem*, nonetheless, reveal the complex personal problems, ambivalences, isolation, and pain that being androgynous in a much gender-divided society and being elevated almost to the status of a ritual icon can bring.

51 On witchcraft, see Fitz John P. Poole, "*TAMAM*: Ideological and Sociological Configurations of 'Witchcraft' among Bimin-Kuskusmin," in *Social Analysis*, vol. 8 (November 1981), pp. 58–76.

52 On trickster figures, see Fitz John P. Poole, "Morality, Personhood, Tricksters, and Youths: Some Narrative Images of Ethics among Bimin-Kuskusmin," in Lewis L. Langness and Terence E. Hays (eds), *Anthropology in the High Valleys: Essays on the New Guinea Highlands in Honor of Kenneth E. Read*, Novato: Chandler and Sharp, 1987, pp. 283–366.

53 On cannibalism, see Fitz John P. Poole, "Cannibals, Tricksters, and Witches: Anthropophagic Images among Bimin-Kuskusmin," in Paula Brown and Donald Tuzin (eds), *The Ethnography of Cannibalism* (Washington, DC: Society for Psychological Anthropology, 1983), pp. 6–32.

218

INDEX